PRAISE FOR *THE MISSION WALKER*

"*The Mission Walker* is a marvelous book. Edie Littlefield Sundby writes of her battle against cancer with simple grace and enormous dignity. The journey she takes us on—her mission walk—is often arduous and at times harrowing, yet there's a spirit of uplift in even the most difficult passages. Sundby turns her mantra of 'To move is to be alive' into a moving meditation on the relationships between courage and faith, endurance and transcendence. I wish the author a long life, but even if she lives to a ripe old age, I think she's created a work that will be here after she is gone."

—Randall Sullivan
Creator/cohost, *The Miracle Detective*, Oprah Winfrey Network (OWN),
and writer/contributing editor at *Rolling Stone*

"Edie Littlefield Sundby's account of her amazing trek along the entirety of the California Mission Trail is not only captivating and inspiring but also one heck of an outdoors adventure. Anyone who doubts the capacity of the human spirit to triumph over incredible odds needs either to read this book or walk a few miles with Edie."

—Les Standiford
Author of twenty-one books, including the highly
acclaimed *Water to the Angels: William Mulholland,
His Monumental Aqueduct, & the Rise of Los Angeles*

"This powerful story of determination and faith will stay with you forever. I was so moved to be with Edie on each dusty step of her journey, sharing her cactus wounds and life-affirming moments. We can all learn from this moving and memorable tale of strength, resilience, and spirituality."

—Ken Budd
Writer and author of *The Voluntourist: A Six-Country Tale of Love,
Loss, Fatherhood, Fate, and Singing Bon Jovi in Bethlehem*

THE
MISSION
WALKER

THE
MISSION
WALKER

EDIE LITTLEFIELD SUNDBY

W PUBLISHING GROUP

AN IMPRINT OF THOMAS NELSON

Published in Nashville, Tennessee, by W Publishing, an imprint of Thomas Nelson.

Map created by Mike Powers at Maps.com.

Thomas Nelson titles may be purchased in bulk for educational, business, fund-raising, or sales promotional use. For information, please e-mail SpecialMarkets@ThomasNelson.com.

ISBN 978-0-7180-9350-1 (eBook)

Library of Congress Cataloging-in-Publication Data
Library of Congress Control Number: 2017939571

Printed in the United States of America
17 18 19 20 21   LSC   10 9 8 7 6 5 4 3 2

To my mother, Dora Emma Looney Littlefield (1910—1989)
I do know that saints exist, and I do know that you are one.
I do know that angels exist, and I do know that you are one.
I do know that God is love, and I do know that you are, too.

CONTENTS

PART 3: HOLY GROUND

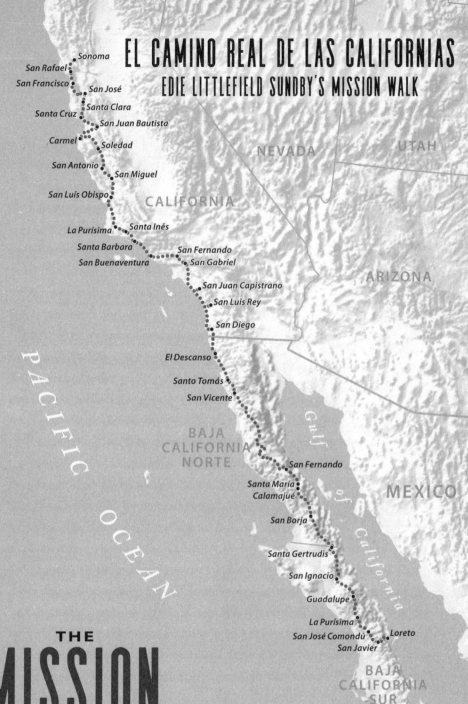

EL CAMINO REAL DE LAS CALIFORNIAS
EDIE LITTLEFIELD SUNDBY'S MISSION WALK

Sonoma
San Rafael
San Francisco
San José
Santa Clara
Santa Cruz
San Juan Bautista
Carmel
Soledad
San Antonio
San Miguel
San Luís Obispo
La Purísima
Santa Inés
Santa Barbara
San Fernando
San Buenaventura
San Gabriel
San Juan Capistrano
San Luis Rey
San Diego
El Descanso
Santo Tomás
San Vicente
San Fernando
Santa María
Calamajué
San Borja
Santa Gertrudis
San Ignacio
Guadalupe
La Purísima
San José Comondú
San Javier
Loreto

NEVADA
UTAH
CALIFORNIA
ARIZONA
PACIFIC OCEAN
BAJA CALIFORNIA NORTE
BAJA CALIFORNIA SUR
Gulf of California
MEXICO

THE
MISSION
WALKER

MAPS.com

THE
MISSION
WALKER

PROLOGUE

I didn't need a mirror to know how I looked.

I was nothing but dry skin clinging to bone. Closer to dust than to life.

I stood at the edge of the cliff and stared at the two-thousand-foot drop in front of me. Missionaries called the valley below El Paraíso. *Paradise*. While the steepness of the descent made my knees shake, it was the cactus that terrified me. There was no clear path down; the entire drop was covered in a thick jungle of Mexican cactus with needles ready to stab me, blind me, or maim me. Some needles were as thick and long as my little finger. Some were curved like fishhooks. Some flowered with other needles, a sunburst of claws waiting to snare me and rip my flesh.

I'd faced an abyss before. I had been told that I had three months to live. To gather my family, deal with the fact that I had widespread cancer, and prepare to die.

It was the scariest moment of my life. I stood there, on the precipice of death, and wondered, *What can I do? How can I live?*

Oh Lord, how much I wanted to live.

I had been miraculously pulled back from that abyss. But now, eight years later, I was not being pulled back from the abyss. A Mexican vaquero was pushing me forward.

The only way out was through.

I turned to Tomás.

"*¿Cómo?*" I asked. How?

He just nudged me forward. He wanted me to go first. Alone.

Dear Lord, have mercy on me.

I gazed at the stark beauty of the Baja desert. This was the dream that had gripped my heart. I had planned and prayed to finish what I started two years ago—walk the entire 1,600-mile El Camino Real mission trail. If I could do it, I would be the first person since Junípero Serra, the Franciscan priest who was the father of California, had forged his way almost 250 years ago.

The southern portion of El Camino Real winds through the Sierras and one of the hottest, driest deserts in the world. Father Serra was asthmatic and had a lame, cancerous leg. Many people told him he wouldn't make it.

I'd heard that feedback as well: "Edie, it is a miracle you are still alive. Why put it all at risk to walk a dusty, forgotten mission trail in Mexico? That's crazy!"

But that was precisely the reason I wanted to do it: nothing is more exhilarating than pursuing an improbable goal without regard to consequences.

We all die. Not all of us live.

If I've learned anything from facing death, it is that life is not meant to be survived. Life is the greatest adventure there is. And why stop your adventuring when you know the end is near? The truth is, we never know when the end will actually come. None of us will avoid it forever. What's the point in trying?

This story is not about avoiding death but living life.

I held tight to the reins, fearful of letting go. Queso was practically bucking in fright. He knew this was crazy just as well as I did.

Here we go, I thought, as I threw down the reins and plunged alone into the abyss.

PART 1

ABYSS

I trembled inside . . .
   my lips quivered with fear.
My legs gave way beneath me,
   and I shook in terror.
                —HABAKKUK 3:16 NLT

1

I was alone when I learned I was going to die.

The doctor who told me was a stranger. Until that moment, I had not been to a primary care doctor in more than twenty years.

But abdominal cramps had been plaguing me. They had come suddenly in the night three months earlier while my daughter Stefanie and I were in India. Through our local Episcopal church we learned of a Swedish woman who'd started teaching poor and orphaned children in her apartment outside Chennai, India. After a dozen years, the school had grown to two hundred children. She relied on volunteers to help and needed someone to teach English. Stefanie had taken a gap year to travel and work before starting college. So she ordered *Hooked on Phonics* and bought a small portable CD player, and we both volunteered for two months.

I thought the cramping and diarrhea were bowel issues relating to diet in a remote country, or possibly a parasite, and didn't think much more about it. And yet, on the long flight home, as we struggled to get comfortable in the cramped tourist-class seats, Stefanie asked to lay her head in my lap. The pressure of her head against my lower pelvis was so painful I had to ask her to sit up.

Once home, the cramping and diarrhea continued, but I considered it more of a nuisance than a serious problem. I was fifty-five years old; I had always been robustly healthy with boundless energy, and I was careful to eat nutritious, organic food. I exercised daily, doing yoga, lifting weights at the gym, or walking along the beaches and in the canyons around San Diego where we lived.

I was healthy. I was sure of it.

A few weeks after returning from India, my younger sister Juanita came to visit. We were planning to take a road trip to visit an elderly and ailing uncle, our mother's last living brother. On the six-hundred-mile road trip, my pain became unbearable. After the first day, I could hardly sit still, constantly adjusting my position while driving, trying to lengthen and expand my body for temporary relief from cramping and back pain. At night, I soaked in a hot bath and slept with legs elevated and knees bent to relieve the pressure in my lower pelvis.

Juanita looked at me in the morning and said, "Edie, this isn't normal. There is something seriously wrong."

I promised to visit a doctor as soon as we got back to San Diego.

I looked online and found one who took new patients, though his first appointment was three months away. I booked the first appointment available and gave the receptionist my symptoms.

His physician assistant, Jane Davidson, called me within an hour. *I must have said something to alarm her*, I thought when I heard her on the other end of the phone.

She asked me to come into the office. As I stood on the scale, I stared at the number in shock. I weighed 20 percent less than my normal weight. I had always been tall and slender, but now I was skinny and bone thin. We did blood tests and urine analysis. I went home hoping for more news. Jane called me in again the next day, this time for an abdominal ultrasound.

It seemed this investigation was far from over.

The ultrasound technician was interested in yoga and, as she moved the ultrasound wand over my abdomen, was talkative and curious, asking me about beginner classes and teachers. Suddenly, she stopped talking and became quiet and serious. After a few minutes of continued probing, she stopped the ultrasound without any explanation and left the room.

It seemed like a long time before she came back into the darkened room with the radiologist. They both sat down beside me and together continued probing my abdomen. They spoke in hushed whispers: "See that?" "Look closer at this." They finished about an hour later.

Before he left the room, the radiologist squeezed my shoulder. I asked the technician if everything was okay. She would say no more than, "There are a few things we would like your doctor to take a look at."

That night, Jane called me at home and asked if I could come to the clinic the next morning for a pelvic ultrasound. She had also scheduled a CT scan right after lunch.

We were going on day three of what I had thought would be a simple checkup.

I didn't sleep well that night, tossing and turning and going over everything I could remember about the abdominal ultrasound, and not liking where my fears were taking me. The house was quiet, with children off at college and working, and my husband, Dale, across the ocean in Ukraine, on a business trip for the company we had recently founded together. I was grateful my family wasn't here for this long waiting game. Much easier to laugh about the scare I had after this was all over.

The pelvic ultrasound was quick, a much more pleasant procedure than the CT scan that followed. I had to sit outside in the cold basement lobby and drink two large containers of contrast solution. It was two hours before the scan, and it took the entire time to drink the awful-tasting fluid. I almost gagged on each small sip. My bladder was bursting full, and I was not allowed to go to the restroom.

The next morning, my life changed forever.

Dr. Murad walked in and shook my hand. He looked confused to see me sitting there alone.

"Where is your family?" he asked gently.

"Two children are away at college, another has taken a year off before starting college and is working. My husband is in Ukraine with a software development team putting together a new business," I replied, searching his face, fearful of what might be behind his question. "Why?"

"You need to call them immediately and have them come home," he said, dodging my direct gaze and question.

I clenched my fists, unsure of what that meant.

"Why?" I asked again, my voice not so strong.

He closed the folder he held in his hands and leaned forward over his desk. His eyes met mine.

"I'm sorry, Edie, but you have cancer."

It felt as if my heart skipped a beat, but then picked up again as usual, my trusting source of life. I took a deep breath as I tried to let its steady beat calm my anxious spirit.

I asked the only question I knew to ask next.

"Where?"

He didn't answer and seemed to be pondering the question, searching for the right way to answer.

I pressed on. "How much?"

He pursed his lips and looked at me with professional, yet soft, directness. "It is hard to determine exactly how much cancer there is and where it is, but the ultrasound and CT scan suggest it is your gallbladder."

I knew hardly anything about cancer, just enough to ask the most important question. "Has it spread?"

"Yes."

I took another deep breath. Just three days before, I had been arrogantly healthy and joyously happy. Now, here I was, in an unfamiliar room with a stranger, my new doctor, looking through images and test results in a fat file folder with my name on it. How could this be happening? I felt strangely removed from the conversation, as if watching from afar.

Dr. Murad's initial reluctance vanished, and he began to speak candidly, evidently resigned to having to help me face this news alone.

"You have cancer, lots of it," he said, no longer mincing words. "It appears the source may be your gallbladder, but there are multiple tumors in your liver and several other organs. You have a very large seventeen-centimeter solid mass within the peritoneum."

I wasn't exactly sure where the peritoneum was, nor did I care. I asked, "How big is seventeen centimeters?"

"Almost seven inches." He looked straight at me. "Edie, this is serious. You need to call your family home immediately."

He continued speaking, but I didn't hear anything further. I had spread my hands seven inches apart, and realized the tumor was as long as my abdomen. I couldn't take my eyes off the distance between my hands or connect with what he was saying.

I did hear him say that I should hear back from an oncologist that afternoon about getting scheduled for a liver biopsy. My gallbladder was black with cancer; there was no doubt there. But the gallbladder is tucked underneath the liver and is hard to biopsy. So having the biopsy from the liver would answer some essential questions about where the cancer started and what stage it was.

I somehow got from the office to my car and got in to drive home. But I soon found myself pulling over to the side of the road under a shade tree, next to an old tarnished mission bell hanging from a rusted pole curved at the top. I rolled down the window. I felt dazed, as if someone had just punched me in the face. I needed to connect with reality, to feel the wind on my face, and hear the quiet, comforting sounds of nature.

I breathed in. I breathed out. God was always in the stillness between breaths. I needed to find him now.

"Lord, have mercy on me," I prayed, and felt my breath slowly deepen as my heart stopped its frantic pounding. The morning was sunny with a gentle breeze. It was peaceful under the tree, quiet, with the soft rustle of wind moving the leaves. A narrow beam of sunlight flickered through the branches above the mission bell and into the open car window, and its warmth relaxed my clenched jaw. How could I die and leave this? This morning, I had been looking forward to a long life, eventual retirement, travel, grandchildren, and more, and then in a span of an hour, it all seemed to be ripped away. I looked around me at the stunning creation. I tried to absorb its beauty into every sick cell in my being.

I knew this news was devastating, but I'd been a fighter my whole life. It was not time to lie down and die. It was time to gather forces. Surrender was not an option. I was not going out without a fight.

2

I was home from the appointment not ten minutes before I quickly dove into the rabbit hole of the Internet to learn exactly what I was faced with. I knew I needed to call Dale, my husband, but wanted to understand more, knowing the questions he would ask. I soon learned the gallbladder is a puny organ tucked under the liver and nestled close to the stomach, pancreas, colon, the hepatic artery, and the portal vein. Gallbladder cancer is a deadly and demonic form of the disease, spreading silently and viciously to other organs with few symptoms until cancer has taken control.

Gallbladder cancer preys on women; we are 75 percent of its victims, and 80 percent of us are diagnosed after cancer has spread beyond the gallbladder. My cancer was stage 4. There is no stage 5. My odds of surviving five years were less than 2 percent.[1]

The diagnosis was a death sentence.

I was in for the fight of my life, *for* my life. It would take a miracle to make it through this, an enormous amount of luck, and help from a battalion of angels—family, friends, doctors, strangers, and departed loved ones.

I had no time to waste. There would be no second chances.

Dale was groggy with sleep when I finally reached him in Ukraine, and the telephone connection was weak. He couldn't hear me. I wasn't surprised. I could barely speak above a whisper. "You need to come home," was all I could say. I didn't want to say the word *cancer*. It was evil and repugnant. I wanted to keep it buried and not give it shape or power by uttering its name.

Dale was wide-awake now, and his voice was loud and fearful. "Has there been an accident? The girls . . ." His voice cracked, and he was unable to complete the sentence.

"I have cancer."

There was silence on the other end, and then Dale's faint, whispered voice. "How bad is it?"

"Bad. Really bad," I replied, and I could say no more.

Dale started gearing up for the fight the minute he hung up the phone. It took him fifty hours to travel home to San Diego from Ukraine. Every minute he could get connected online he was researching gallbladder cancer and reading every published research article. I was too. We e-mailed back and forth almost the entire fifty hours. We decided to wait until he got home to call our children. We both needed time to digest what this meant and to determine what to do.

Alone for two long days waiting for Dale to get home, I found myself on my knees, praying for God's help to live with dignity and tranquility however short my life, for wisdom to face cancer factually and honestly, and for strength to deal with what was to come.

I took Mama's Bible down from the bookshelf and dusted it off. I grew up on a farm in Oklahoma, born in a decade when nature turned its fury on itself. The first years of my life were during some of the worst droughts in Oklahoma history. Though we were utterly, completely dependent on nature for our livelihood, Mama and Daddy knew better than to lose their faith or trust in God, or become bitter, or turn to drink. Daddy worked a little harder, and Mama used a little less. As a family, we accepted and adjusted. We prayed and patiently waited for a good year with spring rain and a bountiful harvest.

In both good times and bad, Daddy and Mama relied on God to provide.

They showed me how to trust in God, to be flexible, and to moderate expectations. They taught me to be happy with what I have, to guard against blame, and to refrain from feeling sorry for myself. Now, facing cancer, I would remember the strength of my mother and father, and go forth with faith in God, but do my part to make the miracle happen.

Mama's Bible was one that she had given to James, my brother Edmond's son, when he was ten. Mama had raised James and his older brother, John, since they were babies, and she had ordered a large-print Bible for each of them so they could read them when they were old men with failing eyesight. Tragically, they died in a motorcycle accident on the way to school when James was fourteen and John was fifteen.

Mama died of a broken heart less than five years later. She was holding James's Bible when she passed. Edmond died of a broken spirit five years after Mama.

Now I held the Bible in my hands, closed my eyes, and tried to breathe in Mama's presence. She had been such a guiding force in my life, a woman who had come from nothing, but dared to dream, and instilled in her seven children that passion as well. She was a woman of faith and courage, and I knew I needed her strength as I faced this journey.

I slowly and prayerfully read Ecclesiastes, absorbing its ageless wisdom that there is a purpose and a season for everything under heaven. Life is but a short season to be lived joyously, whether one breath or many.

On the same bookshelf as Mama's Bible was a worn and dog-eared book saved from my college days, the classic *Manual of Epictetus*, compiled from Stoic teachings in the second century. I took it down from the shelf and smiled at his persistent reminders that few things are within our control. Death is not one of them. How we choose to live life is.

As I read Ecclesiastes and *Epictetus*, I felt spiritually strong and mentally ready to deal with whatever was to come. Acceptance of death and cancer did not mean I intended to give up, just the opposite. I was prepared to fight cancer not out of fear of dying, but out of joy of living.

———

By the time Dale walked in the front door, we knew the top oncologists and research hospitals in the country. We also recognized that we had made two decisions years earlier that made our battle plan easier.

Two years before, we had purchased a catastrophic health insurance policy providing PPO coverage for our family. This meant I could go to any doctor in any state for treatment, and the policy paid for unlimited treatment regardless of cost after we paid the annual deductible. The PPO meant freedom to choose. In catastrophic illness, freedom or lack of it predetermines destiny.

Ten years earlier, I had purchased a life insurance policy with an accelerated death benefit that paid 50 percent of the policy if I were diagnosed with a terminal illness with a high probability of death in fewer than six months. Within three weeks of my diagnosis, I received a check from the insurance company. The money meant freedom to seek out the best medical treatment and fly across the country to see doctors. It also allowed me to consider options outside the United States, if needed, in places where cancer researchers, unencumbered by the FDA, were pushing the envelope on cancer treatment and surgery.

While the cancer diagnosis was mine alone, Dale and I would share the battle. We had been married thirty-two years, and we had been true comrades from the start, meeting in an IBM marketing class in Endicott, New York, and fighting for first place in class. I had been elected president of the class, but Dale edged me out for first place. That playful competitiveness developed into a fun, jovial friendship. We also discovered we had much in common. He'd spent the first five years of his life in rural North Dakota, his father a farmer and his mother a homemaker. His parents emphasized honesty, respect, hard work, and Christian values. We loved being together from the moment we met and were married three months later. Dale's beloved forty-six-year-old mother was dying of breast cancer, and his Lutheran minister married us in the hospital chapel so his mother could attend. She died a few weeks later.

As soon as Dale was home, I felt a sense of peace. While we wished this wasn't a battle we had to face, we were stronger because we had each other.

Our children arrived within hours of Dale's return, twins Whitney and Stefanie and my brother Edmond's daughter Sarah; her sister, Rebekah, was living with a cousin and attending high school in Minnesota. She was a few weeks away from graduation, and we decided to not spoil her senior year until we knew more. We'd helped raise Sarah and Rebekah after their father died when they were two and four, and we loved them like our own.

The moment we were all in one room together, everything shifted from controlled, rational thinking to pure, overwhelming emotion—which swung wildly from sharing joyous memories and laughing to clinging to one another and crying our hearts out. When we could cry no more, we resumed our preparation for battle, arming ourselves with information, and preparing ourselves emotionally for the worst possible news.

We knew a biopsy of the tumor was critical. We had an appointment with an oncologist the next day.

We dressed up for the appointment. "I want them to know I am healthy and capable of saving," I explained to my family as I fussed with my makeup and hair. Dale wore a suit, and the girls their Sunday best.

And as an exhausted, panicked, scared group of five, we were piled into a small, cramped examination room with a very young medical resident student, who started asking what we considered to be irrelevant and senseless questions. He seemed to be completely unfamiliar with my diagnosis.

Lack of sleep, exhaustion from travel, and panic had frayed our nerves to the breaking point. We all exploded at the same time, venting our frustration at the poor medical intern, who quickly left the room to fetch the oncologist.

The oncologist confirmed that we needed to schedule a biopsy right away, but we encountered another obstacle when we discovered that the earliest appointment we could get was three weeks away.

We looked at each other with wide-eyed disbelief. We were astonished. "I'm sorry," Whitney said, "but my mother appears to have widespread cancer. We don't have time to wait three weeks. We need to find out what we are dealing with now so we can develop a treatment plan."

The scheduler remained unmoved. "Three weeks is the earliest appointment. You are welcome to add your name to the cancellation list."

We couldn't get out of there fast enough.

Cancer was growing inside me faster than we were making progress to stop it. Dale and I were both on our phones before we left the parking lot.

We had a close friend whose brother was a doctor at the respected Sharp Memorial Hospital. By the time we were home, I had reached him, Dr. Thomas Sullivan, asking for help to schedule a liver biopsy.

We then turned to choosing the right doctor to be my oncologist. We knew choosing the right doctor was the difference between life and imminent death.

Within four hours, we felt confident we had found him. Dr. George Fisher, MD, PhD, head of gastrointestinal oncology at Stanford Cancer Center. He was one of the top oncologists in the country, but just as important, he was head of clinical trials at Stanford and engaged in pioneering dendritic cell immunotherapy research. A video posted on the Stanford website got our attention. A study of mice with stage 4 tumors showed near-miraculous results when they were first treated with chemotherapy and then injected with dendritic cells. Dendritic treatment might be the earthly miracle we were fervently praying and searching for, and Dr. Fisher my savior.

Before going to bed that night, we e-mailed my medical records and CT images to Dr. Fisher's office, and said a prayer that he would view them, understand my urgency, and find a time to meet with us.

Dr. Tom Sullivan called back early the next morning. He had reviewed my medical records and shared them with the radiology team at Sharp Hospital. A liver biopsy was scheduled the next day.

Before hanging up, Tom asked to speak to Dale alone. Later, I found out what Tom said: "Dale, I am really sorry. It doesn't look good. Edie's disease is too widespread. I'm not sure what can be done, but I will help any way I can."

I had not been in a hospital for nineteen years since the birth of my twins. Dale and I were surprised how busy the place was at such an early hour.

When I stepped on the scales to weigh in, we were frightened to see that I had lost thirteen pounds since I had first weighed in at Dr. Murad's office. Until I got sick, my weight had been in the same five-pound range for thirty-one years.

The needle biopsy procedure took less than an hour. While I was lying in the hospital recovery room, Dr. Sullivan and several doctors, including the radiologist who had done the biopsy, came in to see Dale and me. A pathologist had examined the liver tissue samples, and they already had a preliminary diagnosis.

"The liver tumors and the seven-inch tumor in your abdomen appear to be an adenocarcinoma that may have originated in or near the gallbladder. As it grew, it broke through the wall and spread to the abdominal cavity, the liver, and other organs," explained one of the doctors.

"Do you have a history of gallbladder disease in your family?" one asked.

In fact, it had plagued my family for generations. Mama's grandmother, Isadora Saunders Looney, had died in her early fifties. A doctor told the family it was her heart, but Mama said everyone knew it was "her darn old gallbladder." Great Grandma Looney was part Native American, and gallbladder cancer hits Native American women especially hard. My mother and four of my five sisters had also had their gallbladders removed.

I never had a single issue with my gallbladder before learning it was blackened from cancer and the cancer had spread throughout my body. If God wanted to smack me, he couldn't have chosen a better weapon.

As the doctors were leaving, Dale walked with them out to the hallway. It seemed a foregone conclusion of the initial screening team that I didn't stand a chance. Words such as *palliative* had slipped clinically and coldly off tongues. I could hear them talking in hushed tones.

Later, Dale confided in me there was no mistaking the shared opinion. It was, "Go home and prepare to die."

Doctors believe in facts. They call their profession evidence-based medicine, and it is normally a good thing. It dictates a standard of care for every cancer patient seen by a doctor, regardless of where the patient lives, or how much money she has, or the skill of the doctors available to treat her.

The doctors at Sharp believed they were doing the right thing when they counseled me to look into palliative care. They knew the median survival for advanced gallbladder cancer was two to four months. Oncologists are told (and many believe) early hospice referral discussions are important because we are dying, and very quickly.

But I wanted to fight. I knew the stats were grim, but they didn't know me.

That afternoon, Dale and I went to see the ninety-two-year-old pastor from our church, Reverend Lawrence Waddy. He prayed with us and gave me a worn, ivory-covered 1880 prayer book he carried in his breast pocket, that I might carry it with me and find the same comfort he had found. Father Waddy's parting words surprised yet thrilled my soul. In his determined, British voice, he exclaimed, "Fight like hell!"

Father Waddy was a ship chaplain in Churchill's navy during the Second World War. He knew about hell and fighting.

I prayed I might one day be like him, ninety-two years old, having lived a full life, a life of courage, faith, and commitment.

3

Since I was a child, I've always seen possibilities instead of probabilities. The statistics for a woman who grew up on a cotton farm in rural Oklahoma would say I *probably* would not get an advanced education, and I *probably* would not be a corporate executive or a cowboy in Mexico. But I refused to believe any of it. I was a child of the wind, and I'd always been a dreamer and stargazer and lived my life as a life of what-ifs.

Probabilities are just numbers, whereas possibilities are endless.

Any doctor will tell you that the probability of surviving late-stage gallbladder cancer is very, very remote. But the possibility exists that you can survive it. Someone defies the odds. Why not me?

I knew that in order to survive, I had to help my doctors believe they *could* save me.

I had done enough research to know that the ideal way to fight cancer is to cut it out. I was soon obsessed with the idea that someone might be willing to operate on me. Tom Sullivan arranged a consultation with Dr. Paul Goldfarb, a senior oncology surgeon affiliated with Sharp Memorial Hospital in San Diego.

Dr. Goldfarb was instantly likable, with a friendly smile and a sincere desire to help, even though he knew I would never be his patient. He didn't believe surgery was an option but encouraged my hope.

"If I were you, or your wife, what would you do?" I asked.

"I would do everything within my power to live," he didn't hesitate to answer. "I encourage you to go wherever you need to go, and see whomever you need to see."

He paused, then added, "Who knows?"

That's right, I thought. *Who knows?*

He stopped in the doorway before he exited the room. "Edie, after thirty years working with cancer patients, I can usually tell within half an hour who has a chance and who doesn't. If a patient says, 'I can't start chemo until after my daughter's wedding,' or 'I have a golf tournament coming up; let's do the surgery afterwards,' or 'Let me think about surgery awhile; I'm just not convinced yet,' or my favorite, 'I want to try raw vegetables,' I know they probably aren't going to make it. They really don't get it. Cancer doesn't wait for anything. It is death growing inside you. And it loves raw vegetables too."

I looked at him with hope in my eyes. I wanted to be miracle-minded. "So you think I've got a chance?"

He smiled. "Edie, I can tell you are a fighter. I pray you have a chance."

Dr. Goldfarb had advised getting a PET scan so we could assess in a different way from the CT what, exactly, we were dealing with. When I read the PET radiology report, I couldn't understand any of it; it was as if I were reading a foreign language. It described gallbladder cancer with tumors in the porta hepatis, retroperitoneal, iliac chain, inguinal, subclavian, presacral, distal sigmoid, liver, and portal vein. Stefanie quickly looked up the words and reported back to me with tears streaming down her face, her voice like that of a small child in pain. "Mom, you have cancer in your gallbladder, liver, abdomen, bile duct, hepatic artery, portal vein, colon, rectum, groin, and neck." Her last words were a faint, choked whisper.

I didn't hear a word she said. I was staring in horror and disbelief at my computer screen.

As we loaded the CD with the PET on my computer, a rotating three-dimensional picture of my transparent body from head to lower torso had popped up on the computer screen. It was amazing and terrifying at the same time. Tumors showed up as dark black or light gray spots. Some were small and some were large, very large. The seven-inch mass from my diaphragm to my liver looked like a series of dark, intersecting, irregular forms. It wasn't one large, solid tumor but many small tumors pressed tightly together.

When I moved the mouse over a dark or gray spot on the rotating body image, an image popped up on the screen. The image glowed red with a number showing how "hot" or active the cellular mass was. My hand controlling the mouse started to shake uncontrollably, and I let go and stared numbly at the rotating image. My cancer was no longer a shadowy nightmare, something evil and mysterious growing inside me.

I could now see the cancer clearly on my computer screen.

I could see it eating me up, one cell-sized bite at a time.

I was looking eye to eye with the most evil and demonic enemy I would ever face.

One of us had to die.

———

Early the next morning, I was up at dawn for my daily walk around La Jolla Cove, a restorative walk alongside sea cliffs and beaches that edge our small village. Most mornings, one of my daughters, or Dale, or a close friend, joined me—but that day I was alone. There was a dense marine layer with heavy fog, which was not unusual for March. It was hard to see even a few feet ahead.

As I neared a small beach tucked between sandstone cliffs, through the mist I saw a black-robed man sitting on a bench. He was facing toward the inlet sea, his eyes closed as in prayer, and he was holding a small, black book that looked like a Bible. His thin face was covered with a long, gray beard and a black, cylindrical, close-fitting hat covered his head. Around his neck was a large, ornate cross, and his black robe covered his legs. In the foggy mist, he looked like an apparition or a figure in a dream.

I hesitated, wanting to come closer, but I was a bit fearful. *Is this an angel of light?* my heart questioned.

He opened his eyes and turned his head. The instant our eyes met, I knew he was holy. As I approached, he stood up. His long, flowing robe rippled in the wind, and I was filled with a sense of wonder.

"I was just diagnosed with cancer," I stammered, "and the cancer is widespread. I have been told I am going to die."

He looked at me calmly. "May I pray for you?"

He placed both hands on my bowed head and said a short prayer aloud. Afterward, he took a small glass vial from his pocket, removed the lid, and sprinkled water on my forehead.

"You will be okay," he said. "May our Lord Jesus Christ be with you and bless and comfort you."

In a few seconds, it was over, but the tingling feeling of hope lingered in my heart for days.

That Monday morning, our family flew to Stanford, eager to get in front of Dr. George Fisher, the man we believed could save me. His assistant had said his first available appointment was in three weeks, but we came anyway, without an appointment, and were willing to wait all day to see him.

When Dr. Fisher walked into the examination room after his appointments for the day, he introduced himself, shook hands with Dale, gave the girls hugs, and then put his arm around my shoulder and gave me a hug.

He was fit and tall, in his early fifties, clean-shaven, with silver hair that touched his brow and gave him a friendly, boyish look. He was completely relaxed and unhurried. He spoke softly, made eye contact with each of us, and paused often to make sure we understood what he was saying. I knew immediately Dr. Fisher was my doctor. I could see in their eyes that my family felt it too. He was with us more than an hour, politely answering our questions.

He did a thorough exam, pressing hard in the area around my liver and gallbladder. When he found almond-sized tumors in my neck and clavicle, he joked for me not to keep touching them now that I knew they were there. He told us there were no clinical trial treatments for my rare cancer, and surgery was not an option with widespread metastatic cancer. The only option was aggressive systemic chemotherapy, which he planned to schedule immediately, along with a CT scan. He was very matter-of-fact and confident. I would have four cycles of chemo, three weeks apart, and at the end of three months we would do another CT scan to determine what the next steps were.

I couldn't believe it. We had a plan. The fight was on.

"How much time would Edie have left if she did nothing?" Dale asked Dr. Fisher.

Dr. Fisher took a deep breath. "Given the amount of disease, I would guess two to three months, but that is just a guess," he replied softly.

"And with the chemotherapy treatment you are suggesting?" I asked.

"Historically, with advanced gallbladder disease, the response rate to chemotherapy hasn't been good—fewer than 25 percent of patients respond. I recommend we go with an aggressive treatment program proven successful against a range of adenocarcinomas, although not much is known about its effectiveness with gallbladder cancer, since it is quite rare."

His eyes met mine, and I knew he could tell this wasn't what I wanted to hear.

"I'm sorry, Edie, but we won't know how the chemo is working until we do another CT scan, and I wouldn't advise doing another scan until you have completed all four treatments. So the earliest indication will be in about three months."

I felt my heart pounding as I took in what he was saying: if the treatments weren't working, we wouldn't know for three months. And then there might not be time left to try anything else.

4

When I was a child, I loved the wind. It blew hard all the time out on the Oklahoma plains. Our small, wood-frame farmhouse sat on a hill in its path, and the timbers would creak as the wind swept up from God knows where and gathered speed along the vast prairie, often forming tornado funnels. I spent my childhood days letting the wind blow me around, hair whipping across my face and stinging my eyes. I was free to chase and try to catch it, with nobody to tell me I couldn't or shouldn't.

I loved to dance in the wind. I would sneak quietly into the house, hoping my older sister wasn't in her room. I would put on her high-top gym shoes and run outside and stand in the middle of the dirt road in front of the house. The wind braced my tiny four-year-old body as I practiced standing on my tippy toes, preparing to become a ballerina. Hour after hour, I practiced my ballerina moves with the wind catching underneath my dress, blowing it above my head and almost ripping it off my body. The wind caused the branches of the cedar trees surrounding the farmhouse to clap together, applauding and cheering. "Thank you." I would smile and bow deeply at the waist, basking in the attention. That is, until my sister realized I was wearing her gym shoes and, unimpressed by my fame and talent, unceremoniously ripped them off my feet.

I came from a family of twelve children. Three years into the Great

Depression, Daddy lost his young wife to heart disease and his mother to cancer; they died two weeks apart. Another drought was raging across the Oklahoma prairie, turning it into what would be called the Dust Bowl, and Daddy was a widower with five children to provide for. Mama was the oldest of fifteen children, so when she married my father, nothing much changed, except she was baking for his five children (and soon the seven she added to the family) instead of fourteen siblings.

We descended from generations of farmers. There was a spiritual interconnectedness from generation to generation between soil and family. We lived close to nature and to God. Living on the land defined who I was, how I thought, and what I believed.

I was the next to youngest of Daddy's twelve children, and by the time I was born, they were both exhausted from hard work and children. They left me alone. I was free to live life without fuss or supervision.

My brother Edmond and my younger sister, Juanita, and I ran everywhere. We ran through the wheat field when Daddy wasn't around to stop us; we ran in the pasture, causing the spooked cows to stampede, and we ran to the cotton field to bring lunch to our father. We ran until we were exhausted and then fell into bed at sunset.

I was nine years old when Mama sent me alone on a bus more than one thousand miles away from home. In her junior year of high school, my oldest sister, Leann, had married a soldier, who moved her to a farm in North Dakota. She now had two children under the age of three and needed help with the house and wheat harvest.

As I boarded the Greyhound bus, Mama kissed my cheek, gave me a hug, and told me she loved me. She had never done that before, and it made me feel tingly and special. In Kansas City, I changed buses and had an eight-hour layover before the next bus to North Dakota. The bus driver had given me strict orders to stay in the bus station. It was too much of a temptation, and I left the Greyhound building and walked around the block, feeling powerfully independent.

That thousand-mile trip stirred within me a sense of adventure and self-empowerment that was to last my entire life.

The older I got, the bigger my dreams. I soon hoped to become a war correspondent and cover the Vietnam War, or a foreign correspondent with a large newspaper or newsmagazine. I applied to the University of Oklahoma to study journalism, but didn't know how I could afford it. My parents certainly hadn't saved enough money to send me, the second youngest of twelve, to college. I received two scholarships from the university for tuition and books, and then an opportunity came along that provided the answer: selling Bibles door-to-door for the Southwestern Company of Nashville, Tennessee.

Since the Civil War, the Southwestern Company had recruited young men to sell Bible reference materials door-to-door to earn money for college. They started recruiting women the year I signed up, and there were fewer than a dozen women hired that year. Pay was strictly commission-based. If I didn't sell any books I wouldn't make any money.

A neighbor, Alan Weedn, had sold Bibles for the past two years. When he came to our high school to recruit for the summer, I raised my hand instantly. But I was seventeen and underage and needed Mama's permission. Alan wanted Mama to be aware of what the job entailed and the risks involved. He came out to the farm and gave the sales pitch exactly as he had given it hundreds of times before to customers. It was a fifteen-minute memorized sales pitch for three Bible reference books—*Bible Encyclopedia*, *Bible History*, and *Bible Story*—beautifully bound in burgundy leather with gold lettering and sold as a set for $29.95. The commission was 50 percent, so the salesman made $15 for each set sold.

After Alan made his sales pitch, he asked Mama, "Mrs. Littlefield, if Edith were to talk to thirty people a day and give them the presentation you just heard, how many sets do you think she would sell a day?"

Mama replied, "Thirty."

Alan was stunned. Most parents said two or three or were doubtful their child would sell any. He had never met a parent with so much confidence in her child.

Mama was like that with all of us. She believed if we wanted something bad enough and worked hard enough, we could do just about anything. After all, at thirteen, the daughter of a tenant farmer living in a dirt-floor shack down on a riverbank, she had tramped streets to find jobs as a live-in hired girl, and as the oldest of fifteen children, had finished college during the Depression. She had done the impossible, and so could anyone who believed strongly enough and put heart and mind to it. "Where there is a will, God will provide a way," she told us.

Selling door-to-door was as hard as anything I've ever done.

We first attended five days of sales instruction in Nashville. We were encouraged to have the sales pitch memorized by the time we got there, and I did. We gave it over and over again, and practiced objections and closing techniques. The self-motivation techniques they taught were the most helpful practices, and I have used them ever since.

Every day, I would wake up and say loudly and spiritedly, "I feel healthy. I feel happy. I feel terrific." While getting dressed, I listened to the same recording over and over again by Earl Nightingale, *You Become What You Think About*. His words became molded into my seventeen-year-old brain.

I was given a sales territory in Jackson, Tennessee. I got up at 6:00 a.m. every day, rode an old secondhand bicycle, and knocked on the first door by 8:00 a.m. and the last door at 9:00 p.m. I tried to give the sales pitch to thirty people a day.

We paid our own living expenses, and I kept mine low, renting a decrepit one-room walk-up apartment for ten dollars a month. It was in the back of an old house lived in by a very nice young couple with small children. My apartment faced a dirt alley; it was so old the screen door was coming off the hinges and didn't latch properly. It was scary coming home after 10:00 p.m. to the dark, unlocked apartment. I trusted in the Lord to watch over me, and I knew Mama was praying too.

My first week of work, a detective from the Jackson police department stopped me on my bicycle. He was suspicious I was a runaway. He couldn't believe any mother would allow her seventeen-year-old daughter to be far from home in a strange town, selling books door-to-door. I gave him Mama's phone number, and he called her, asking her to make me come back home. Mama told him it was my decision and that I needed to earn money for college. She trusted me to know what was best for myself. She also had faith in the goodness and kindness of others.

From then on, I noticed a police car patrolling the neighborhoods where I was selling, and several patrol cars would be along the streets as I rode my bicycle back to the old apartment late at night. The detective had the whole Jackson, Tennessee, police force keeping an eye out for me.

Mama was right. There were good people all around.

I sold a lot of Bible books that summer—seven sets a day on average. They were all shipped to me at one time, and I rented a vacant house to store them. Book boxes were stacked floor to ceiling in two large rooms of the house. Because I didn't have a car, Mama drove out to Tennessee to help me deliver what I had sold. It took Mama and me two weeks, working sunup to sundown, to deliver them.

I left Tennessee with a check for more than $7,000 in my pocket. At seventeen, I had earned almost 20 percent more in three months than the average adult worker made a year. A week before college started, I bought a new car and had enough money for almost two years of college.

This experience shaped me profoundly.

I learned that in life a lot of doors were going to be slammed in my face, and to overcome rejection and not take it personally. *No* is part of life; you can't let it get you down.

The job taught me to not let failure dim my spirit, and to remain optimistic and cheerful.

I knew firsthand that with hard work—and despite people's disbelief—you really could do anything when you put your mind to it.

I knew that belief would help me in my cancer journey.

I had a burning desire to live and a true and honest will to fight. I knew my doctors would provide what weapons they could to arm me on the battlefield. I had faith that God would equip me with enough strength for the battle.

Yet I had no idea what was truly in store.

5

Although our research had given us hope for a surgical solution, we knew now that it wasn't an option.

When cancer is growing fast and in multiple organs, surgery is not an option, and neither is radiation—there are just too many tumors to cut out or burn out; in fact, surgery can spread the cancer and make it grow faster.

Systemic chemo is the only option. The chemo has to be toxic and strong in order to destroy cancer.

So tolerating chemo becomes the first and most important step in surviving cancer.

Chemo is a bitch—the only thing worse is cancer.

It is important to remember when you have little or no hair, blisters in your mouth, and scabs on your skin, when your feet are numb and you are throwing up and wearing rubber panties, that chemo will *almost* kill you, but cancer *will* kill you.

So, no matter how bad it gets, if you really want to live, you have to learn to deal with it.

On my first day of chemo, the oncology nurse and I picked out the most visible vein, a long blue vein in my left forearm. I was so thin from weight loss that the skin on my arms looked as if it were stretched over bone. The thin vein would be used that day to spew CT contrast solution into my chest and pelvis to take pictures of the spreading cancer; to extract six large vials of blood to check every blood marker before chemo; and to infuse almost six hours of toxic chemotherapy into my body.

As soon as the oxaliplatin began to course through my veins, my saliva glands reacted with sharp, pulsating pain. My mouth became very dry, as if my saliva glands had shut down and stopped working. When I blinked, my eyelids felt numb and sticky. The drug was attacking every moisture gland in my body, temporarily numbing and paralyzing. I tried to take a sip of room-temperature water, but it froze my throat and I could not swallow properly.

I read Psalms and Proverbs from Father Waddy's worn prayer book and clutched my family's hands for strength and comfort.

After six hours of oxaliplatin and Avastin infusion, I still was not finished with chemotherapy. One of the prescribed chemotherapies, Xeloda, was not infused directly into my veins; I took it orally in pill form. Before leaving Stanford Cancer Center, Dale picked up the two-week prescription. It came with a warning: potentially fatal toxic effects cannot be excluded.

I was to take six chemo pills a day, three in the morning and three at night, for fourteen days—a total of 42,000 milligrams.

Within days, the skin on my hands and the bottom of my feet darkened and started to peel, revealing blister-looking sores. Those innocent-looking peach pills were burning the skin right off my feet and hands, from the inside out.

I soon learned that before every chemo infusion, the nurse steps you on the scales and weighs you. The amount of chemo they can inject in your veins that day depends on your weight. Knowing that chemo was the difference between life and death, I meticulously recorded every milligram of chemo injected and my weight.

When my weight started to plummet, I picked up a pocketful of large smooth rocks from the beach near where I lived, each weighing a pound or more. When I went to the cancer center for chemotherapy, I wore my husband's extra-large jacket and put the rocks in the pockets, in plastic baggies to keep them from clicking together.

I told no one, not even my husband. My secret was safe until one chilly day he put on the jacket and discovered rocks in his pocket. He laughed—and understood.

I was determined to not die from cancer. Even if it meant putting rocks in my pocket to make up for weight lost, and never reducing the chemotherapy keeping my cancer under control.

That is how much I wanted to live.

———

My body became my soul mate, my dearest friend, and my battle buddy. I was not going to make it through chemo unless my body allowed me to. The physical body does not like to be hurt, but when it is hurt, it wants to be comforted. I learned quickly to console my body, to hug it before chemo, and afterward to caress tender arm veins bruised from needles. I treated my body like a hurt baby with no understanding why something was happening and no control over what it was going through.

But my body wasn't enough to get me through this. My body could withstand vicious physical assaults, but it could not control fear. I would need to learn to control my emotional mind and not let it interfere with my body.

The emotional mind can make the body sicker; it can paralyze the body with fear. The mind is full of falsehoods like, "I am dying, and there is nothing I can do about it." The emotional mind is quick to despair, and even quicker to deny. Dr. Goldfarb had warned me about denial, about patients who put off chemo or surgery, in denial of cancer's venomous nature. Denial plus delay equals death.

I could not allow my mind to despair.

The only thing powerful enough to control my emotional mind was spirit. Just like my instinct that day of diagnosis to stop the car, to feel the wind on my face, to breathe into the space between breaths to find God; I knew I had to continually do that to not let fear find safe harbor within.

Even more important, family and friends surrounded me in prayer. Their prayers caressed and comforted my soul, much as warm blankets caressed and comforted my body during chemo.

A few days after my first round of chemo, my close friend Carmel Gouveia and I attended a three-hour deep healing workshop. The first hour of the workshop was a series of calm and soothing yoga postures. There was pressure in my lower right abdomen from the large tumors, and I was in too much pain to do deep forward bends or abdominal twists. I stopped frequently to drink water. Water seemed to help ease the nausea that came in waves; so did moving through the asanas.

After the slow yoga movements, we stretched out on the cold, bare wood floor. For two hours, I lay there in deep relaxation, all the while praying, "Lord Jesus, have mercy on me."

I looked up through the open skylight draped in a thin flowing cloth at wisps of clouds floating by and sea birds gliding in slow motion on wings of wind. I again tried to absorb the beauty into every cell in my being. Intense longing for healing and yearning for grace swelled within me. And in an instant, both the answer and resolution to the central question of my soul simultaneously flooded my heart, in the form of a prayer: *"Through the grace of God and his medicine, I am healed."*

I knew I would need both: the gracious Spirit of God, along with the determined logic of the physicians managing my care. In my mind, I saw them working together, fighting for my survival. I saw a vision straight out of *Braveheart*: a line of Scottish Highland warriors in kilts with huge shields and long spears marching in brave unison and attacking and killing the cancer. They were advancing toward the cancer, striking and killing it with strong, accurate thrusts from their sharp spears.

The vision was so strong I could hear marching feet and see the cancer in me dying.

"Through the grace of God and his medicine, I am healed" became my constant prayer. The prayer awakened with me each day, coming on the wings of the morning. It followed in my heart through the day and was on my lips as I drifted to sleep at night.

After the second chemotherapy treatment, the intense abdominal cramping slowly began to subside, and there was also less pain in my pelvic area. My appetite remained healthy. I had learned to control the nausea and diarrhea, though sores and dry mouth were a constant issue.

I prayed that all these were signs the chemo was working. I would not allow any other belief into my mind.

———

I was determined to do whatever it took to kill the cancer.

After each chemo infusion, I had difficulty swallowing and was extremely sensitive to cold. I couldn't drink any liquid, even tap water, without first warming it up. I wore plastic gloves to reach into the refrigerator. The arm where chemo was infused felt like sharp needles pricking the skin, and I was unable to bear any clothing touching the entire forearm. When I tried to eat, the first release of saliva caused intense jaw pain. Even taking a warm sip of tea was enough to cause me to cry out in pain.

I felt a daily need to flush the toxic chemo from my body. I drank more than a gallon of water a day and walked an hour or more, usually in the early morning dawn. Walking was a spiritual experience, a time to pray and connect with joy. I had to do everything in my power to enable the chemotherapy to flow through quickly and not to linger, to focus its destructive forces on cancer cells, and then remove its poison from my body.

Shortly after I was diagnosed, someone brought over a copy of Lance Armstrong's book, *It's Not About the Bike: My Journey Back to Life*. I knew he had kicked cancer's butt and come back stronger than ever, so I was happy to gain his knowledge from his experience.

And when I put down his book, I understood something profoundly. *Edie, if you can move, you're not sick.*

I decided right then and there that no matter what cancer did to me, I would continue to move. Movement was what the physical body was designed to do; it was how it coped and functioned. Movement was vitality. It was life.

I would move. Always. No matter what. Until my last breath, I would move.

6

Dale successfully managed our programming team for a month from home, but the software development was at a critical stage and required his oversight and management. With trepidation, he boarded a plane for Ukraine, leaving nineteen-year-old Stefanie to watch over me.

I was so thankful to have Stefanie still with me. God moves in mysterious ways, and I knew Providence had smiled on me when Stefanie decided to take this year as a gap year. On really bad days, Stefanie would crawl in bed and wrap her arms around me to keep me warm and keep me from shaking. And my daughter's presence brought me inexplicable joy, something I knew my spirit needed in this fight.

Almost as soon as Dale boarded the plane, overpowering waves of nausea, vomiting, and diarrhea hit, and I could hardly move from bed. My stomach and abdomen were swollen, and it was hard to sit up. As the abdominal cramping grew worse, Stefanie rushed me to the emergency room.

The emergency room doctor stabilized my condition with IV infusions of hydration fluids and strong nausea and diarrhea medication. Administrative personnel came immediately with end-of-life care directives for me to sign, expressing concern about my current condition, my terminal cancer, and only a teenage daughter accompanying me.

I put the papers aside without signing. I knew if it became necessary Dale would be there to make the right decisions. It would be too much of a burden for Stefanie to make them, and I did not trust strangers to.

A million faces rushed at me, reviewing CT images and monitoring my vitals. "Ma'am," they said, with concerned professionalism, "you're either suffering from chemo toxicity or cancer-related obstruction." The doctors were pressing for a procedure called an upper endoscopy, in which a long, flexible tube with a tiny camera would be inserted through my mouth down my esophagus and into my stomach and upper small intestine.

I refused.

I had put my life and faith in the hands of one doctor, Dr. George Fisher at Stanford Cancer Center. If he ordered an endoscope, I would not hesitate. But I did not want an invasive procedure done at a hospital more than four hundred miles away. I was afraid that given my precarious medical condition, once an invasive procedure was started, the situation could spiral beyond my consent and control.

I asked the doctor to release me from the hospital so my daughter and I could fly immediately to Stanford.

I used negotiating skills honed over years as a corporate executive and from selling door-to-door. We made a bargain. If I were able to eat solid food, he would release me the next day. If I could not eat, or keep food down, or the cramping intensified, I would agree to the endoscopic procedure.

The next morning, I slowly ate scrambled eggs, praying and relaxing between each tiny bite. By the time I saw the doctor, it had been sixteen hours without vomiting and diarrhea. The doctor released me, and Stefanie raced me to the airport.

A friend, Pat Erzinger, had made beef broth from organic marrowbones simmered overnight in a kettle with vegetables, and on the way to the airport, Stefanie stopped at Pat's to pick it up. Pat was a devout Catholic, and in the paper sack with the broth was the crimson-beaded rosary she had held through the night while praying for me. I put Pat's rosary around my neck, and from that day forward, I carried it with me. I hung it from IV stands during chemotherapy and surgery and on hospital bedposts.

We arrived at Stanford Cancer Center late that afternoon. Soon, I was in an exam room with Dr. Fisher and another oncologist visiting from Yale, Dr. Andy Chen, as they examined the CT scans.

Dr. Fisher was visibly excited. Despite my acute pain and seemingly dire situation, this was the first time he was seeing my insides since he had first diagnosed me. After only two chemotherapy infusions, he saw a significant decrease in the size and number of cancer tumors.

"You are doing really, really well!" he exclaimed as he and Dr. Chen excitedly compared the new CT images to pre-chemo scans. This emergency had given us the chance to see that the chemo was doing its job. It gave me hope, and I managed to smile despite the intense abdominal pain. *This could work. I could live.*

After reviewing the blood test results and conferring with Dr. Chen, Dr. Fisher gave his diagnosis: "We believe you have enteritis, and it is causing abdominal pain and diarrhea. Enteritis could be caused by chemo toxicity or bacterial infection. Because your white blood cell count is high, we tend to believe it is an infection. Shrinking and dying tumors can leave small holes or tears where bowel debris gets trapped, which leads to bacterial infection. I am going to assume it is a bacterial infection and treat you with broad-spectrum oral antibiotics for the next seven days. Hopefully, that's it, and you can resume chemotherapy next week."

I stayed at Stanford that week, in a hotel bed, unable to move except to crawl to the restroom to purge my insides. Stefanie cleaned up after me and spoon-fed me baby food and rice cereal.

The baby food tasted awful, and so did the Pedialyte she kept forcing me to drink. With a laugh, Stefanie said, "Mom, I'm getting back at you for making me eat and drink this stuff when I was a baby."

I was losing two pounds a day, and my weight dropped to one hundred pounds. The strong antibiotics were killing bad bacteria but also wiping out what good bacteria remained. With loss of muscle mass and body fluids, only a bony skeleton remained. I looked and felt like death.

Whitney cut class and brought over sunflowers. The sunflowers and I would turn our faces to the sun, toward the light. Pat Erzinger's crimson rosary hung from the windowsill, reflecting the same light. Slowly, the cramping subsided, and my bowels stopped erupting.

By the seventh day, I was out of bed. With Whitney and Stefanie's help, I managed to walk to a local park, where we listened to gospel music. I felt joy and health slowly return. The next week, my body was recovered enough for the third chemotherapy infusion.

———

By the time of the fourth and final chemotherapy infusion, Dale was back from Ukraine, and he came with me. We met with Dr. Fisher, and he passed on the good news that my cancer blood markers had dropped.

"I am feeling good, and we know from the scans last month the tumors have shrunk. I want surgery," I told him.

Dr. Fisher smiled, knowing that I had been adamant about surgery from the beginning. "Edie, I'm sorry, but I am not sure surgery is a realistic goal," he said. "The realistic next step is to achieve disease stability."

But I could hardly hear him. My heart was unwilling to consider any possibility other than surgery, and my mind was even more stubborn and just as determined.

Yet we had also connected with a friend, Catherine Lazarides, who had experience with cancer surgery. She spoke with us honestly and in detail about the risks of gallbladder cancer surgery and why most oncology surgeons will not consider surgery for stage 4 gallbladder cancer.

"Unfortunately, when a large primary tumor is surgically removed, it almost seems to trigger metastasis," Catherine explained. "Research suggests there may be lots of micrometastasis held in check by not having a blood supply, and surgery may trigger blood vessel growth." She paused. "It's maddening, like so many aspects of cancer. Surgery to remove cancer may actually spread cancer."

I was thankful for her attempt to temper my expectations, but nothing could quell my excitement that I might have a chance to live.

Three weeks later, our family arrived at Stanford for the CT scan. My appointment with Dr. Fisher was in the afternoon, after he had viewed the CT images and discussed them with the radiologist. He came into the examination and handed us a copy of the preliminary report. He was beaming.

"There has been significant tumor response to the chemotherapy," Dr. Fisher said, smiling. He sat down at the computer to bring the images up on the screen. "Actually, Edie, the response is stunning."

I squinted at the scans, not really sure what I was looking at.

"How much of the cancer is gone?" I asked.

Dr. Fisher paused and turned his chair around to face us. Dale, my daughters, and I were wide-eyed with anticipation.

"Eighty percent of the cancer is gone," he said.

My daughters tearfully hugged each other, but I all I could say was, "Wow," as Dale and I held each other tightly. The relief was enormous. I felt as if a thousand-pound weight had just been lifted off my shoulders.

"Is that response unusual?" Dale asked, his eyes twinkling with happiness and fresh tears.

"In almost thirty years of oncology practice, I've hardly ever seen this." Dr. Fisher said with a smile. He was obviously a bit stunned too.

"That's the good news," he continued. "The bad news is there is 20 percent left, and the cancer is widespread. You still have a lot of cancer in your liver and pelvis."

Dale and I refused to hear bad news.

"How fast can surgery be scheduled?" we asked at the same time, and then laughed.

Dr. Fisher continued to be reluctant to discuss surgery and recommended mild chemotherapy.

But I couldn't accept that. I had to act now. "I trust Stanford and want the surgery done here, but I will go wherever I have to, even overseas." I pushed back.

"I would not want to see you do that." Dr. Fisher paused. "Let me talk to Jeff Norton. He is one of the best liver surgeons in the world and is pretty aggressive. If Jeff thinks he can remove all the cancer, he might agree to surgery. If someone as skilled as Jeff can't do it, then the risks are too high."

I knew Jeff Norton's name. He was the chief of surgical oncology at Stanford. "Surgery is the only treatment that can result in cure," he had written in a medical journal we read while waiting in the lobby.

Dr. Fisher called the next morning. He said four words that would change my life.

"Jeff will do it."

This was it. Finally, someone would operate on me and get this cancer out.

Those four simple words were the end of an intense journey that had begun sixteen weeks earlier when I was told I was filled with cancer. At the time, surgery seemed impossible, and my life was quickly coming to an end. The four simple words also signaled a beginning and a new path still filled with uncertainty but with hope of extended life.

To come so close to the edge of the abyss and be pulled back made life more intense and sweet. I saw everything through new eyes. Every day was a bonus day, every moment precious. My conscious mind turned inward to prayer: *Thank you, dear Lord.* I felt humbled and filled with gratitude, knowing that I had done nothing worthy of this gift.

7

In what Dr. Norton declared was a successful operation, he removed my gallbladder, about 60 percent of my liver, and several dozen surrounding lymph nodes.

Movement is wellness. Doctors know it too. Less than twenty-four hours after surgery, Dr. Norton wanted me out of bed and walking.

I hung Pat Erzinger's red rosary on the IV stand, and two nurses helped me out of bed. The pain was intense, but by moving very slowly and holding on to my two large IV stands, with a nurse holding on to a third IV stand and me, I was able to walk up and down the corridor. By the next day, I was walking unassisted several times around the corridor, eager to gain strength and get out of the hospital.

If I can move, I'm not sick.

On the seventh day, Dr. Norton released me from the hospital. That evening, Dale and I flew back to San Diego.

Radical liver surgery slices through the abdominal wall and three layers of muscle and nerves. Within hours of leaving the hospital, I discovered the smallest twisting movement could trigger the severed nerves and cause pain so intense I buckled underneath it and couldn't move. I could not open the lightest hinged door. I could not put on pants or tie shoes. To get out of bed, I needed Dale or the girls to support my upper back and lift me upright. Even the tiniest use of abdominal muscle produced pain so intense I cried aloud.

The one thing I could do was walk. I walked every day, slowly building up distance from the front sidewalk to around the block. Sarah was home from college for the summer and loved to walk with me, and soon our daily goal was to walk eight blocks to Baskin-Robbins and split a super-large Jamoca Almond Fudge Milkshake. By the time I returned to Stanford a month later, I was walking more than an hour a day.

It was time to meet with Dr. Fisher to discuss a going-forward plan. I expected a "get out of jail free" card of sorts, a stamp of "healthy" from Dr. Fisher, and a diploma that I had graduated from the college of cancer.

"Dr. Norton is confident he cut out all the cancer." I beamed at Dr. Fisher. "Am I now cancer free?" I asked excitedly. My body was weak and broken, but my voice was strong and confident.

I fully expected Dr. Fisher to be equally excited. He wasn't.

"Edie, I wish I could say that was true. But despite what Dr. Norton said, surgeons look at cancer a bit differently than oncologists. They look for visible cancer and surgically cut it out, and then they are done." Dr. Fisher spoke in his characteristically soft and unhurried manner.

"The bad news is that once a cancerous gallbladder is surgically removed, new metastases appear and grow quickly." There was an audible sigh in his voice. "We've made it to third base and hope to make home plate, but we are not there yet." He paused, knowing the next words he would say were not what I wanted to hear. "I strongly believe cancer cells remain in your body. We should continue aggressively treating them with oxaliplatin, Xeloda, and Avastin for four more cycles. Afterward, you will probably be on a milder chemo maintenance schedule, but we will determine that depending on how well the next three months go."

I looked at Dale. This was not what I had expected. I didn't know if my body or my spirit could withstand months more of strong, toxic chemotherapy.

"Do I start today?" I asked.

"Not yet. First, we will do a simple procedure to insert a central port line." Dr. Fisher explained that because chemo was going to be a part of my new normal, and my veins were completely destroyed from three months of oxaliplatin infusions, the port line would help them inject chemotherapy quicker and without the dance of needles that I had long dreaded.

But though this was good news, I still couldn't believe that I was back to having chemo every three weeks. I felt as if my victory touchdown had just been overturned, and I stood in the end zone confused and alone, having to start all over again.

———

I soon would find out that having a port installed transformed blood draws and chemotherapy infusion from high-anxiety events to calm, relaxed experiences. From that day forward, toxic oxaliplatin was infused as painlessly as hydration fluids. There was no longer stinging pain in my arm or a need for heat compresses. And best of all, chemotherapy was infused much quicker, meaning I could catch a flight home to San Diego sooner and return to life.

But cancer is always unpredictable. I developed a life-threatening infection after the port surgery. Then we discovered my liver wasn't functioning well enough to withstand chemotherapy.

Once I managed to bring my body to a place where I could tolerate the chemo again, I had to address how taxing the process was on my mental health. I had to retreat from the world and crawl into my mental and spiritual cave to conserve energy and remain strong.

The accumulation of destruction was taking its toll on my body. I refused to stop walking, even if just around the block. Walking was my connection with life. Regardless of what was happening inside, if I could get outside and walk, I felt better, and I didn't feel sick.

And in this way, I survived four more months of chemotherapy.

The three weeks between the last chemotherapy and CT scan was a time of prayer and acceptance. My body had had enough and was tired. My desire to hold on to life gradually lessened. If this was it, and it was my time to go, I knew I would be okay.

It was two weeks before Christmas when we met with Dr. Fisher after the CT scan, and I knew it was good news the minute he walked into the examination room and handed us a copy of the report. Our eyes lingered on the concluding paragraph: "The CT scan reveals no evidence of recurrent or progressive disease."

There it was, in black and white. No evidence of disease. I didn't want to take my eyes off of it, in case it was all a dream.

But I soon looked up at my angel, Dr. Fisher, who had so miraculously brought us to this place.

"Congratulations," he said. I jumped up to hug him as we all sighed with exhausted relief.

We sat back down to discuss exactly what this meant.

"Edie, we are thrilled at this result. Yet there is almost certainly residual disease. We should continue treatment, but back off the harsh chemo. You are showing signs of cumulative chemo toxicity, which isn't surprising considering how much oxaliplatin and Xeloda you've had. I think we are safe to stay with Avastin and discontinue Xeloda."

He paused.

"The only other thing I want you to do at this time is take eighty-one milligrams of aspirin a day. The data is convincing on how effective a daily dose of baby aspirin is to cut the recurrence of gastrointestinal cancers."

"That's it?" I asked, a bit incredulously. "Just a baby aspirin a day, and Avastin every three weeks?" It seemed too simple, almost bizarre, after what I had gone through the past nine months.

"That's it," Dr. Fisher said with his encouraging smile.

I had received the most profound Christmas gift—the gift of life.

The entire flight home, Dale and I kept looking at each other as if we had won the lottery. We talked at length about how very fortunate I was. I had no idea why I responded to chemotherapy when many cancer patients don't, or why my immune system was able to take such a beating.

I thought back to my childhood. During the first month of first grade, a very pretty little girl in my class who lived in town stepped on a nail in the playground. She started to scream in pain. When the playground teacher removed her punctured shoe, I gasped. The bottom of the little girl's foot was clean and pink.

I couldn't remember ever seeing my feet look that way. The bottoms of my feet were blackened and hardened from running barefoot for most of my life on dirt littered with cow manure, pig wallow, and chicken droppings.

Taking a bath on the farm was hard work. Mama had to carry water from the cistern on the front porch to the propane stove, heat the water, and then carry it out back to an old, worn porcelain bathtub on our screened-in porch. So we got a bath on Saturday night—to be clean before God on Sunday morning, Mama said—and the rest of the time we washed up by the kitchen sink.

After I started school, I wanted to be like the little girls with pink feet. From then on, I scrubbed my feet every night with Mama's soapy dishrag and wore shoes outside more often. At the time, I had been ashamed and anxious about my dirty feet. But now, I wondered if they could have been the difference between life and death. All that exposure to dirt had toughened my immune system.

People say that everything happens for a reason.

But even as I tried to figure out how I had been spared, I thanked God for the grace he had extended. I couldn't explain why he didn't save others far more worthy and far more holy.

Dr. Fisher told me at our first appointment nine months earlier that he had seen the most loving, healthy, and positive people succumb to this disease, and the most unhealthy, negative, and sometimes unpleasant people survive it. I think this was his way of telling me I wasn't responsible for the disease or the outcome. Praying, invoking the healing Spirit, eating the right food, taking the right supplements, thinking positive thoughts—each of these can help with healing, but if any of them were the one thing that was needed, all of us would do it, and none of us would ever die.

When we are hit with a catastrophe like cancer, it is hard—if not impossible—to understand why. Our rational minds demand answers. Why would a loving God do this?

But God is mystery. Life is mystery. And even with all our scientific knowledge, cancer is still 99 percent mystery.

I did not know why I had survived cancer. I did know that I had a life to be lived, and no time to waste. The sage in Ecclesiastes wisely suggests living well, keeping the commandments of God, and enjoying every bit of life we have the good fortune to spend. The sage is saying, "While alive, live!"

That's what I intended to do.

My situation had gone from dire and dramatic to procedural and watchful. To live, it was necessary to keep my cancer under control and prolong remission as long as possible. We were stalker and prey residing together.

Dr. Fisher prescribed Avastin infusions every three weeks. Medical scientists are not sure how it works, but they theorize that Avastin starves and kills cancer by cutting off its blood supply. It stops cancer tumors from creating new blood vessels, which limits the supply of nutrients and stops its growth.

Avastin held my cancer in remission for more than three and a half years. During that time, I received forty-nine continuous infusions with no evidence of Avastin's known harmful side effects, such as high blood pressure and internal bleeding.

Soon, I was doing so well I no longer needed a physical examination before each Avastin infusion. I had progressed from flying solo to flying on autopilot. Only time would tell how long I could maintain altitude and continue soaring.

Dr. Fisher was honest. The cancer would come back. It always does.

I became thirsty for information. Now that I was no longer in the throes of trying to fight-fight-fight, I wanted to find inspiration that I could keep at this and survive. At night, I scoured the Internet, looking for people who had walked—or were walking—the same lonesome valley as I was, looking for detailed personal stories of people with advanced late-stage metastatic cancer, especially gallbladder cancer, who had beaten the odds. It was hard to find what I was looking for—there aren't many stage 4 patients alive after five years.

Like a beacon searching for life in the universe, I searched. I wanted to know everything survivors were willing to share about their journey. How long they have been alive. What they do to survive. How they cope.

Searching the online universe night after night, I found only one person with stage 4 gallbladder cancer. He had posted on a cancer website and identified himself as WoodyB. I sent an e-mail, introducing myself. WoodyB never responded.

The Internet is a vast graveyard of data, ideas, and people, and allows travel back in time. People never die. Their words survive forever. I began an intense search to find WoodyB.

I discovered his name was Woody Beckman and he lived less than an hour from me. Woody had started a blog called *Gall Bladder Cancer Data*. He was a mathematician hoping to help others with the disease.

No one with stage 4 gallbladder cancer had come to Woody's site; there was no data. There was only one comment: "Woody was an incredible person—I communicated with him a lot as he tried to compile data on his own to help battle this terrible disease. He was still trying when he died. I never met him personally, but I grieve for him. He will be missed."

I grieved for Woody, too.

I couldn't find stage 4 cancer survivors on the Internet, but I found them at Stanford Cancer Center, and most were patients of Dr. Fisher and were serious walkers: Joan Johnston, ten years with colon cancer and the most heartwarming smile and cheerfulness, who hiked Zion and Bryce and played with grandchildren; Barbara Isgur, six years with stomach cancer, who carried a canvas bag made from the sail of her husband's beloved sailboat and who brought sachets of fresh lavender from her garden, and hiked up an Andes mountain with a broken pelvis; Steve Wang, six years with colon cancer and an infectious grin, who biked and skied and shared pictures of his lovely family; Mary Holz, a ten-year breast-cancer patient of Dr. Carlson, who amazed us with her health and beauty and who loved everyone; and Marko Glogovac and his beautiful wife, Patty, who held hands and read the Bible together. They were my heroes and my inspiration. I looked forward to seeing at least one of them every three weeks. The chemotherapy infusion rooms were bright, cheerful, and sunny, and on the west side of each room was a large picture window with a bench seat where we would sit together during chemotherapy and enjoy the afternoon sunshine and beautiful greenery of the world outside.

For nine months, facing death, I had dwelt in a state of almost total mindfulness. Cancer had been like a Zen master's slap on the face, a call to wake up. The alertness led to inner calm and a desire to eliminate all nonessentials. All visages of impatience, anger, and busyness melted from my body and soul. Illness was a cleansing experience. I discovered in that instant that life is too short for negative feelings, whether God has granted us years or months.

But as months slipped by, sunrise to sunset, the mindful intensity began to fade away. I had to learn new ways to ensure that I was focused on joy, on spirit, on living life, not just surviving.

Month after month, I said a prayer of gratitude after each Avastin infusion, and every time I walked out of the cancer center with good news, I knew how lucky I was. Instead of walking out defeated and preparing for death, I was given another gift of life.

How was I going to spend it?

8

Four years after radical liver surgery and aggressive chemotherapy had saved my life, and after forty-nine infusions of Avastin to hold the line against cancer, I got the news that Dr. Fisher had been expecting.

Cancer was back again, with a vengeance.

I sat numbly in Dr. Fisher's office as Dale huddled over the computer screen and Dr. Fisher quickly flipped through three-dimensional PET images of my body, rotating and displaying detailed close-ups as he moved the mouse. There were glowing red spots, indicating cancer, in both lungs and my liver. Margreet Fledderus, my nurse practitioner, stood in the back of the room, holding the radiology reports and silently taking notes.

Dr. Fisher was talking, but I had trouble hearing him above the rapid pounding of my heart.

"So I've got cancer in my liver and in my lungs," I finally said, trying to understand an overwhelming amount of information. My voice was hoarse, barely a whisper.

Dr. Fisher turned to face me, trying to find the right words.

I fought hard to remain calm.

He was honest.

"I'm sorry, Edie. The cancer in your liver surrounds the hepatic artery, portal vein, and bile duct—each are danger points. Together they make surgery almost impossible." He stopped, and there was a long pause.

I felt tightness in my chest, and panic. Dale held on to me, with his arm around my shoulder, to stop my shaking and keep me from collapsing into the chair.

When I didn't respond, Dr. Fisher continued. His voice became softer, and his words slower. "And with widespread cancer in your lungs, we couldn't operate even if we wanted to. Surgeons are extremely hesitant to do liver surgery when there is active cancer in another organ. The liver is a regenerative organ, and the same regenerative growth hormones can cause other cells, like cancer cells in your lungs, to grow too."

I sat silently, in a stupor, with a sick feeling in the pit of my stomach that cancer had once again gained the upper hand. And this time, it was determined to win.

"I've discussed your case in detail with the tumor board, and we believe the best treatment is radiation and chemotherapy. Would you like to meet with Albert Koong, our liver oncology radiologist, and Bobby Lee, our lung radiologist?"

I managed to blink my eyes in agreement, as Dale quietly said, "Yes, please."

My hands felt sticky with sweat, and I was shaky on my feet when I stood up to take the radiology reports from Margreet. She and Dr. Fisher gave us a hug, and then quietly left the room as Dale and I sat in stunned silence.

I felt overwhelmed and under siege.

I tried to just focus on what action we knew we were taking: radiation, more chemo, and then, hopefully, surgery.

But my heart knew the truth: another battle was under way.

Could I beat the odds again?

———

Four years earlier, when my cancer was diagnosed, Dale and I had carefully chosen Stanford, a university research hospital, confident that as my disease changed, they would have the expertise to deal with it. Now, with cancer exploding in my liver and lungs, their expertise was critical.

Dr. Fisher acted fast. He arranged for Dale and me to meet the next day with the lung and liver radiation teams. Dr. Albert Koong patiently answered our questions about radiation of the liver tumor.

"I am hopeful we can destroy your liver tumor as effectively with radiation as surgery would." Dr. Koong said. His cheery disposition and enthusiasm for radiation were reassuring.

"Stanford was one of the first cancer centers to test a new SBRT system called TrueBeam. We've had it eighteen months for clinical trials and gained a lot of experience with liver radiation. We've been able to do some pretty amazing things." He paused, his face lit up with belief in the technology his team had assembled. "The accuracy is truly close to the sharpness of a surgeon's scalpel."

Dr. Koong admitted my liver tumor was one of the most difficult tumors he had ever attempted to treat. To kill the tumor, he had to go "to the edge" of the hepatic artery and portal vein with maximum radiation intensity. Precision was critical. There was no room for error.

Three weeks later, Dr. Koong radiated the liver tumor for five days, and Dr. Bobby Lee radiated the two largest lung tumors.

It would be months before we knew if radiation was successful.

The first step was complete. But radiation does not halt cancer growth, and Dr. Fisher knew cancer was still alive and growing. Plus, there was cancer in my hilar and mediastinal lymph nodes, too close to my heart for radiation. Dr. Fisher recommended mild chemotherapy.

But my body was weaker this time. I'd been undergoing cancer treatment for four straight years. And this time, my body revolted.

Almost immediately, Xeloda caused rapid cell death, and the lining of my mouth became thin and inflamed. My fingers turned black, and my hands and feet became blistered with pus-filled sores and peeling skin.

Dr. Fisher became concerned. "If you have persistent or recurring problems, the dose of Xeloda may need to be lowered."

I told him I was handling it fine. It was too soon to think about lowering the dose of chemotherapy. Reduced chemo is the beginning of the end in late-stage cancer.

Despite the grim prognosis, toward the end of August, Dale and I headed for Alaska immediately after the third cancer treatment. My healing medicine was being close to God in the wilderness. My spirit was running on empty, and I longed to escape the constant and overwhelming presence of cancer.

My suitcase overflowed with oils and creams, protective gloves and socks, gel insoles, toe cushions, moleskin wraps, and blister bandages. We flew to Anchorage, rented the smallest campervan we could find, and headed north to Denali.

We spent two weeks in the Alaska wilderness, following gravel, hardpan, and brush roads over glacier streams into remote areas, and awakening to moose and deer outside the campervan and under blue skies with thousands of swans soaring overhead. We hiked miles to glaciers, old mining camps, and hunting lodges inhabited only by ghosts from bygone eras. We canoed rivers shared with moose. We stepped over fresh, steamy, red-berry grizzly bear scat, knowing bears could see us but we could not see them. It was an altered state of mind, a journey without a destination. I was completely lost in nature and didn't care what day of the week it was, that it was cold and rainy, that grizzly bears were close by, that my body was drowning in chemotherapy, or that my feet were blistered, raw flesh.

All too quickly, it was time to leave Alaska and return to Stanford. Dale and I walked back into Stanford Cancer Center, the Alaskan wilderness just a faint memory in our heads as we waltzed through the crowded halls of the hospital to go through yet another round of PET and CT scans. This time, Dr. Fisher came into the examination room looking visibly tired. Dale and I waited nervously as he pulled up scan images of my liver on the computer screen.

"There are tumors in both lungs but no significant growth. While this is concerning, my major area of concern continues to be the liver tumor. The area where we radiated the liver tumor is still PET positive, which may indicate radiation didn't kill all of it," he said.

"Did it kill enough that Stanford can operate?" I asked.

"I'm afraid I've checked with Jeff Norton and he still doesn't advise liver surgery," Dr. Fisher said.

He looked at the chemotherapy burns on my blistered hands and feet, signs of chemotherapy toxicity. "Starting today, I recommend we change the chemotherapy treatment schedule to minimize side effects. Instead of two weeks of Xeloda and one week off, I think we should do one week on and one week off. We will continue with Avastin since you tolerate it so well."

He swiveled his chair toward us. "Sound like a plan?"

I nodded.

———

Four months later, as Dale and I sat in the examination room, waiting for Dr. Fisher and the CT report, I had a sickening feeling in the pit of my stomach.

Earlier that morning, I had spent several hours in prayer, hoping for good news but emotionally preparing for bad news. I had found strength in the words of Moses: "Today you are going into battle against your enemies. Do not be fainthearted or afraid; do not panic or be terrified by them. For the LORD your God is the one who goes with you to fight for you against your enemies to give you victory."[1]

I was hoping and praying Dr. Fisher would tell me chemotherapy had subdued the cancer.

The moment he opened the door, I knew it was bad news.

He gave me a hug, sat down next to us, and handed Dale the report.

"Your disease is following a natural path of progression." Dr. Fisher's words were carefully chosen. His language was medical and factual. I became mindful of every word and every pause, and of his body language. When one hears a message of death, time slows, and every nuance becomes important and meaningful.

"The current treatment of Xeloda and Avastin is no longer holding your disease in check." Dr. Fisher's voice was soft to cushion the necessary words. "There are several options—"

I interrupted. "How bad is it?"

Dale had skimmed the CT report and cut in before Dr. Fisher could answer.

"If my calculations are correct, the lung tumor is twenty times larger than three months ago, and the hilar tumor next to your heart is six times larger. And there is a new tumor in the left lung, and three new spots in the liver." Dale's hand was steady, but his breathless voice was not.

Cancer waited until months of chemotherapy had weakened my body's resistance. Chemotherapy managed to cut off the tail of the snake—but it had left the head.

I looked at the notebook I held in my hands. That morning, I had scribbled, *If at all possible, try not to emotionally respond to what is happening,* and in all capital letters: *LET THE FACTS SLOWLY PRESENT THEMSELVES, AND THEN DEAL WITH JUST THE FACTS.* I sat there underlining the words, slowing my breath, relaxing my jaw and shoulders, and trying not to panic.

Dr. Fisher was discussing treatment options. "I recommend we add oxaliplatin and continue Xeloda and Avastin. That combination worked four years ago and should work again. I'd like to try that first. We've also had success with irinotecan and Avastin. It's a bit milder. We can try that next."

"What about lung surgery?" I asked, knowing it was a stupid question. No surgeon would operate with aggressively growing cancer.

Dr. Fisher didn't answer.

"There are a few wild card possibilities, immunological therapy clinical trials, but in my opinion, chemotherapy is the preferred option at this point." He finished before responding to my question about surgery.

"Surgery is unlikely, especially with growing tumors. But if you want, I will refer you to Joseph Shrager, our head of lung surgery." Dr. Fisher knew it was important to keep hope alive.

That night, after Dale had gone to sleep, I cried and cried. We would have to up the dose again, and, thus, my body would be going through the hell of toxic, systemic chemotherapy. To do so, it needed hope and reassurance. I wanted to imagine that after this next round of chemo, I might be able to do surgery. To cut out whatever remained. And finally feel cured.

I knew surgery was a pipe dream—impossible. However, before I started the oxaliplatin, I wanted to meet Dr. Shrager about lung surgery and get a second opinion from Dr. Steven Curley, a renowned liver surgeon at MD Anderson Cancer Center in Houston. Stanford knew I was getting a second opinion on liver surgery from MD Anderson and was very supportive.

I would look like a ghost after months of aggressive chemotherapy, and I wanted Dr. Shrager and Dr. Curley to see me in a healthier state.

Plus, if chemotherapy was successful at shrinking the cancer, I would have a very short window—less than a month—to schedule surgery. I knew that being an established patient versus a new patient could be the difference between life and death.

Later that week, I met with Dr. Shrager, looked him in the eye, and told him how much I wanted to live, that I was determined to fight, and I needed his help. I knew it looked hopeless. Cancer had attacked my liver twice in four years before spreading to my lungs, and even though I had been on chemotherapy the past eight months, cancer was exploding. Dr. Shrager later admitted, "When I saw Edie, my thought was that she was going to spread disease everywhere."[2] Nevertheless, Dr. Shrager kept my hope alive by agreeing to perform lung surgery *if* the tumors shrank and *if* Dr. Curley was able to remove the liver tumor.

After meeting with Dr. Shrager, Dale and I flew to Houston to meet with Dr. Curley for a second opinion on the liver tumor. He confirmed what we already knew: liver surgery was not an option with widespread cancer in my lungs.

Dr. Curley encouraged me to continue chemotherapy. He tried to be optimistic about the liver tumor. "Surgery is challenging, but not impossible. We will need two more PET/CT scans for a final assessment of chemo and radiation. Typically, scans are done three months apart, so that's six months from now. I'd like to see you then."

I was back where I started five years ago: aggressive chemotherapy would successfully halt the spreading cancer in my lungs, or I would die.

I had to do everything I could to give myself a chance to live. To beat this one more time.

The fight with cancer is fought on the physical battlefield. However, like many life struggles, it is won or lost on the spiritual battlefield.

During aggressive chemotherapy, my body and mind fight each other. Spirit referees.

My body screams it is nauseous and going to throw up and cannot eat. I must ignore my body and eat. "Eat!" my spirit commands. My mind scolds my body; if it doesn't eat, it will get weak and can't withstand the chemotherapy, and the cancer wins.

My body collapses under the constant chemo assault and begs to stay in bed. I must arouse my body and move. "Get up and walk!" my spirit demands. My mind nudges my body out of bed to circulate the chemo and flush it out completely. If not, chemo starts to do really nasty things to the body.

The Bible encourages us to use every piece of God's armor to resist the enemy whenever he attacks. Prayer is the most powerful of all God's armor. My family's and friends' prayers power my spirit and will and enable my body to resist.

My school classmates in rural Oklahoma organized prayer circles and prayed together. Our rural community was as close as family; the ties that bind go back generations.

We never walk alone when we walk with God. When times get really tough, God empowers our angel network to watch over and protect us.

My angel network prayed, and I prayed.

We prayed to God to strengthen my body to tolerate the chemotherapy.

We prayed to God to empower the chemotherapy to do its job and attack and kill and shrink the cancer in my lungs and liver.

We prayed that God would give surgeons at Stanford and MD Anderson the confidence and faith to perform high-risk surgery to cut out any remaining tumors.

I felt the prayers. Walking in the canyons, listening to Elvis sing gospel music, I felt healing grace wash through my body and cleanse the tumors from my liver and lungs.

I became a walking prayer; each in-breath became "grace in," and each out-breath became "cancer out." A thousand steps became a thousand prayers.

9

Six months later, I returned to MD Anderson for the follow-up appointment with Dr. Curley, to discuss liver surgery.

It had been eighteen months since cancer attacked my lungs and was back in my liver. I had made it through intense radiation and thirteen months of continuous chemotherapy. My singed, burnt hair was thinning and falling out, my brain was foggy, and my gait was becoming unsteady. My toes and fingers had turned black, and the soles of my feet had peeled so many times there was hardly any skin left

Chemotherapy had done all it could do. Was it enough? Had it killed enough of the lung cancer and halted the progression in my liver? Was it possible to cut the rest of the cancer out? If so, I would have a shot at living. If not, I would soon be overtaken by cancer.

MD Anderson Cancer Center is renowned for its diagnostic capabilities, and Dr. Curley was determined to get the clearest images possible of my liver and lungs with an MRI, a PET, and a liver-enhanced CT scan.

All three radiology reports indicated the lung tumors had shrunk significantly, but I still had a liver mass that "likely represents cancer rather than scarring."

I looked at Dr. Curley. He tried to explain.

"There is still a large mass showing up in your liver. It could be scarring from your liver surgery four years ago or from radiation last year. Or it could be more cancer." He paused. "The radiologists think it is cancer. But I have to disagree. The way I read it, the density of the mass is more consistent with scar tissue than liver cancer."

"But what does that mean? Can Edie do surgery? How do we know for sure?" Dale asked, a million questions running through our minds.

"I believe radiation and chemotherapy has killed the liver cancer." He pointed to the scan image on his computer screen. "What we are seeing here, and what the radiologists believe is cancer, I believe is really scar tissue."

Dr. Curley explained the difficulty of knowing for certain whether the liver mass was cancer or scar tissue. Needle biopsy was hit-or-miss and unreliable. PET scans deliver false positives on scar tissue and inflammation. Liver surgery was too high-risk and not an option.

"The only way to know for certain whether it is liver cancer is to stop chemotherapy, and wait and see. If there is growth, it is cancer. If not, it is scar tissue," he said.

"But if I stop chemo, the lung cancer could explode," I said, nervously looking at Dr. Curley, making sure I understood what he was suggesting.

"Yes, that is true. So try and have lung surgery as soon as possible," he said, adding, "We can do it here at MD Anderson if you want."

I returned to Stanford, humbly aware that Dr. Curley's belief the liver mass was scar tissue saved my life. Because cancer was no longer threatening my liver, lung surgery was possible.

In five years of cancer treatment, I had come to realize oncology medicine was a science *and* an art, especially when interpreting PET and CT scans after radiation or surgery. Medical professionals evaluating an image scan are not unlike art professionals evaluating a painting. Radiologists, oncologists, and surgeons can see the same image but interpret it differently.

Cancer treatment is often a tortuous decision for patient and doctor. Like Alice in Wonderland, one must choose a door to walk through, not knowing where it will lead.

After evaluating the MD Anderson scans, the Stanford oncology team concurred with Dr. Curley that the liver mass was likely scar tissue and not cancer, and they recommended immediate lung surgery.

Dr. Shrager scheduled the surgery for two weeks later.

"There is a fifty-fifty chance I may have to remove your entire right lung," Dr. Shrager cautioned when we met to discuss the surgery. "If so, there is a 5 percent chance you won't survive the surgery, and you will be lucky to walk a flat mile."

I had no hesitation, no doubt. "The risk for me is *not* going for it."

I knew that even with one lung I'd find a way to walk. A flat mile was better than nothing.

The day before leaving for Stanford and lung surgery, Dale and I took one last sunrise walk together in our favorite canyon above Torrey Pines beach in San Diego. Later in the day, I drove back alone at sunset and slowly walked the rim of the canyon, stopping frequently to pray.

I gave thanks for my family, friends, and doctors—and especially for Dale and my children, my angels without wings.

Afterward, at the canyon entrance, I sat in my car, listening to gospel music and watching the sun slowly sink below the ocean horizon. My view was partially blocked by an old mission bell at the side of the parking lot. It hung from a pole in a ditch filled with weeds, teetering to one side. A strong wind might topple it.

I wondered who put it there, and why. My mind fluttered off in a different direction, and I thought no more of it.

The seed was floating in the wind.

Lung surgery can require a lengthy recovery, so Dale and I moved into a patient apartment provided by the Hewlett Foundation across from Stanford Hospital.

The day before surgery, I laced up my hiking boots and walked three miles up rolling hills to the Dish, a radio telescope, and a favorite Stanford hiking trail. It was a beautiful late summer day, and from the top of the hill I could see from San Jose to San Francisco.

I filled my lungs slowly, and expanded them to maximum capacity. This was the last day I would have two lungs. I was going to miss my right lung. This was a special moment, a farewell to a beloved and treasured friend that had taken me to the tops of mountains and underneath the sea.

Dale snapped a photo to send to Dr. Shrager. "Lung today, gone tomorrow," he wrote with typical corny humor.

We arrived at the hospital before dawn. After I was transferred onto a gurney, hooked up to IVs, and prepped for surgery, Dale and Stefanie called Whitney, who was working on a project in Chicago and flying in after surgery. The four of us connected with my best friend, Jan Boelen Sinn in Oklahoma City, and prayed together.

The surgery took six hours.

I awoke hours later, groggy and in pain. Stefanie and Dale were all smiles.

Stefanie hugged me with excitement. "Dr. Shrager didn't take your whole lung, just the upper lobe and part of the middle and lower lobes. He wanted to leave as much as possible so you could walk!"

The next day, Dale read me the surgical report. "Do you understand how much skill was required for Dr. Shrager and the Stanford surgical team to preserve your lung capacity and get to all the cancer? They had to meticulously remove the upper lobe and hilar and mediastinal lymph nodes near your heart, and wedge-cut the middle and lower lobes."

Dale continued, "He could have done the easy thing and removed your entire right lung. It would have taken a fraction of the time. Shrager left enough for you to walk the canyon or wherever you want."

My heart filled with gratitude for Dr. Shrager, an incredible doctor and human being.

My hospital roommate was a woman named Sally Canfield Coupe, from Paradise, California. She, too, had gallbladder cancer, and her left lung had been removed. She was eighty years old, married to a real cowboy born in a log cabin in the Sierra Nevada, and as full of fun and life as a twenty-year-old. Her joy was infectious.

To remove the lung, my right chest was cut open from under my right breast to eight inches around my back. Ribs were pulled apart and nerves damaged. A shoulder muscle was removed and used to cover the bronchial stump of the missing upper lung.

It hurt to breathe, and I needed high doses of pain medication.

Sally and I were instructed to use a spirometer for deep-breathing exercises, and afterward vigorously cough up secretions from our chests. Even a shallow breath felt like a knife stab, and I was unable to cough. Sally coughed like a sailor and kept at me until I was able to cough. "You can do it, kid," she would yell from the other side of the privacy curtain that separated us.

Sally was like a drill sergeant in boot camp. Every day we walked the corridors together, pulling our IV stands with attached catheters. I couldn't keep up with her.

After three days in the hospital, Sally was ready to discharge early and go home, and so was I. I walked out of the hospital and, inspired by Sally, refused a wheelchair. It was half a mile to the patient apartment, and Dale and Whitney walked with me. Outside, life was intense and vivid in a way I had never experienced before. My senses tingled with excitement. I breathed in every color, sound, and smell as if each were my first. I felt transcendent. I wanted to walk forever.

I had a personal goal: to walk the Dish ten days after surgery.

I spent most of the first week in bed, healing and recovering. Twice a day, I laced up my hiking boots, took pain medication, and walked; each day a little farther, each day a little faster. Breathing was painful, but the joy of walking lifted me spiritually.

I had a lot of time to read. I had developed a real interest in the mission bells and wanted to find out as much as possible about them. I remembered the mission bell near where I'd parked for a moment the day I heard I had cancer. I remembered the mission bell that quietly witnessed my prayer of gratitude after my last canyon hike before the surgery. Why were they there? Who placed them?

Whitney brought over two well-worn books from the local library, *In and Out of the Old Missions of California*[1] and *California El Camino Real Mission and Landmarks.*[2] I learned that by the early 1900s, the twenty-one Spanish missions the Franciscan missionaries had built from 1769 to 1823 were falling apart out of neglect. The old El Camino Real—the California Mission Trail from San Diego to Sonoma that connected them—was all but obliterated. A librarian from Los Angeles, Miss Tessa L. Kelso, along with two unstoppable women from Pasadena, Mrs. Harrye Forbes and Miss Anna Pitcher, and dozens of other determined men and women, made it their life's work to save the missions and El Camino Real mission trail.

In 1904, an association was formed, the El Camino Real Association of California, to promote the old mission trail and restore the missions. Two women's groups, Native Daughters of the Golden West and California Federation of Women's Clubs, organized hundreds of volunteers to help. The idea was to install mission bells, like those that rang in the towers of the twenty-one missions up and down the California coast, along El Camino Real as a testimony to the trail and the missionaries who came before.

Forbes designed a ninety-pound mission bell, eighteen inches wide, which was hung from an eleven-foot rod in the shape of a shepherd's crook (or Franciscan walking stick). Her bell was chosen to mark El Camino Real.

The Quaker-born Forbes preferred to be called Mrs. Armitage Suton Carion Forbes, but everyone called her the "Bell Lady." She established the California Bell Company in 1906 to manufacture the bells and was often in the foundry making them herself. She chose iron instead of bronze to represent the iron will of Father Junípero Serra, the eighteenth-century missionary who traveled more than twenty-four thousand miles in his lifetime, mostly by foot, and founded ten missions along El Camino Real de las Californias, from Baja California (now a part of Mexico) to San Francisco, California. Forbes inscribed each bell "1769," the year Father Serra founded the first mission in San Diego and the beginning of El Camino Real mission trail in California. Her mission bells were wildly popular from the beginning, and El Camino Real soon became a California Historical Landmark. Volunteers, civic and religious organizations, and philanthropists lovingly restored the old missions to their former glory. Most became vibrant parish churches, and their bell towers with their ancient mission bells once again rang loudly and awakened joy.

I had been hiking on parts of the old El Camino Real mission trail for years in San Diego, yet had never realized it.

I had hiked this trail the day I learned I was dying of cancer, more than five years ago.

That day, I began to walk to stay alive and to *feel* alive.

And I'd been walking the old mission trail through the canyon ever since.

———

On the tenth day after lung surgery, Dale and I drove to the Dish, located off Junípero Serra Boulevard. I had never thought much of the name of the street, but now that the mission bells had touched my heart, just seeing Father Serra's name thrilled me.

The first part of the Dish walk is a steep hill. I had trouble breathing and felt as if I were suffocating. Each breath caused stabbing pains across my chest. My left lung could not keep up, and the mutilated right lobe wedges struggled to fill with air.

Though it took me much longer than usual, by the time I reached the top of the hill, an amazing physical transformation had occurred. For the first time since surgery, I was able to breathe deeply, and my pain went away completely. It was easy to finish the three-mile walk, and I finished just twenty minutes slower than before surgery.

Walking forced air into the lung and quickly restored my lung capacity. I knew I would need to keep walking and expanding my lungs to maintain a normal life.

Six weeks after lung surgery, Dale and I met with Dr. Fisher. I was nervous about the liver mass. Other than extensive nerve pain from my ribs being pulled apart during surgery, I felt physically fit and psychologically prepared for more chemotherapy. I was anxious to kill every cancer cell, seen and unseen.

"No more chemo," Dr. Fisher proclaimed, giving me a congratulatory hug. "There is no evidence of active disease in your remaining lung or liver.

Dr. Koong and I believe Dr. Curley was right that the liver mass is scar tissue from radiation and surgery. Edie, you don't need to have chemo. It's no longer necessary."

I looked at this man who had saved my life. For five painful and scary years, he had given me hope and treated me like a patient who could live, rather than someone who was doomed to die. And he was saying the words I had been praying for him to say ever since the day I first met him.

I felt the same intense, wild joy as I did while dancing in the prairie wind as a child. It was hard to keep my feet on the ground.

"George, does this mean Edie is cured?" Dale asked the question I was afraid to ask.

"Edie can hope this remission becomes a cure, because a cure really is nothing more than a remission that lasts forever." Dr. Fisher said with a faint smile. He had fought cancer in too many patients to declare victory. "We will continue to have CT scans every three months and keep a close eye on it."

"What does that mean?" I asked.

"My expectation is that we'll see this cancer again at some point—and then we'll deal with it as best we can." This was an honest answer.

Dale and I hardly knew what to do with this news. We had cried so many tears for so long, we had no more to shed. But we looked at each other and both exhaled. It felt as if we had been holding our breath for five years, and we could finally breathe normally again. We knew the battle wasn't necessarily over, but we had been given a reprieve. We would take it.

On the five-hundred-mile drive home to San Diego, we drove Highway 101, and I noticed hundreds of mission bells along the highway. I started looking for them, and each time I saw one, I tingled with excitement and anticipation.

I yearned to stand in the tall grass and hug each mission bell, and feel the wind of my childhood whip across my face and sting my eyes. I wanted the wind to blow me like a tumbleweed from mission to mission and to dance with the wind at night under God's starlit sky.

We'll see this cancer again. Dr. Fisher's words were a call to action. I had little time to waste. Whatever I yearned to do, or dreamed of doing, I must *do*, and do quickly.

Nancy Perry Graham, an IBM friend from years ago, was now editor of a national magazine and wanted to do a story about my cancer journey and lung surgery. The writer, Meg Grant, asked what I planned to do now that I was freed after five years from cancer treatments every three weeks.

I mentioned the wild, crazy dream stirring in my heart.

"I know it sounds absurd and ridiculous, but I have this crazy obsession to follow the mission bells and walk the old California Mission Trail. I am so grateful and thankful to be alive. I want to light candles and thank God for his wonderful gift." I half hoped she would discourage the notion.

"How long is it?" She asked.

This was the part that gave me pause. But I answered her honestly.

"Eight hundred miles."

She laughed, knowing by now that I was the kind of person who would be crazy enough to want to walk eight hundred miles after having just had lung surgery.

"Well, Edie, if you do it, I will walk part of the way with you," Meg promised. "I was married at Mission Carmel, and the missions mean a lot to me, too."

With those words, a plan began to take shape. I was going to do this. It wouldn't be easy, but I was going to walk that mission trail as a walk of gratitude. To God. To my family and friends and legions of angels who helped along the way. To the doctors who helped heal me. To my body, which had withstood so much.

If I can move, I'm not sick.

Could my broken and frail body do this? Only God knew.

I would walk one step at a time, one day at a time, and God would decide how long and how far.

PART 2

FOLLOW THE BELLS

Always go forward and never look back.
—FATHER JUNÍPERO SERRA

10

It was absurd and ridiculous to think I could walk eight hundred miles a few months after lung surgery. The longest I had ever walked was four miles. But I *believed* I could do it, and we don't know what we are capable of doing until we do it.

I soon discovered someone had walked the old mission trail just a year earlier, and afterwards had put together a hiker's guide, what he called a "self-published labor of love." Ron Briery, a high school music teacher, grew up on the mission trail in Arroyo Grande, California, and it was still calling to him. He walked the entire trail in less than two months. When he returned home, he sat at his kitchen table and pieced together his *Hiker's Guide to California's 21 Spanish Missions Along El Camino Real.*[1]

When I ordered a copy of the book from Ron, I mentioned that I dreamed of walking the entire distance from San Diego to Sonoma in one long walk. He encouraged me to go for it.

"Edie, you would be only the sixth person to do it. I've spent years looking for people who have walked the entire eight hundred miles to all the missions in one trek. I know of four others besides me: Father Richard Roos, a Jesuit priest; Stephanie Dodaro, a young lady from San Francisco; Beppe Sala, an Italian who walked with me; and Kurt Buckley, a former army officer."

I began sharing my dream with friends and family. A close friend, Ron

Graham, gave me the confidence that I really could do it. Ron grew up poor, but he became one of the world's most acclaimed mathematicians. He also became a professional acrobat, a world-class juggler, and a trampolinist who taught himself to speak fluent Chinese, play championship-level Ping-Pong, bowl perfect games, throw a boomerang, and play the piano.

Ron Graham never asked why I wanted to do such a weird, crazy thing. He knew why and thought it was great.

Ron loved to walk and often walked fifteen or more miles a day. He suggested we complete a seven-mile test walk, and though I was very tired at the end and grateful to be finished, he believed I was strong enough to walk the whole distance—which increased my confidence exponentially. Ron was well versed in statistical probabilities, and his life was a testament to possibilities. If Ron believed I could do it, I knew I could.

Ron and his wife, Fan Chung, also a renowned mathematician, offered to loan me their campervan, QRandom, for two months. The van—which bore QRANDOM on its license plate—was named after an obscure mathematical theory positing that many things that appear to be random really aren't. Instead of chaos, there is connectedness, a higher order.

Perhaps my quest wasn't really random after all.

The plan soon became that Dale would drive QRandom to my stopping point along the trail so I had someplace to sleep each night. I would set out each morning and hike according to Ron Briery's guide. I knew it would be challenging. Some days required hiking more than twenty miles. Ron Briery was a healthy man when he undertook this challenge, not a woman who had battled cancer for five years, was missing half her liver, and barely had a right lung. But I comforted myself with the thought that Dale would be waiting each evening in that campervan to encourage me and have food and water at the ready.

While the idea to walk was still taking form, tragedy struck. My friend Steve Wang lost his heroic battle with colon cancer. Steve had been with me steadfastly as we sat together during chemotherapy for four years. I had fought alongside other patients of Dr. Fisher as well—Marko, Barbara, Joan, and Mary, a breast-cancer patient of another doctor. When Steve died, just Mary and I were left.

Losing Steve was heartbreaking.

Steve was a man of deep Christian faith and prayer, and the bravest person I had ever met—the kind of person you want fighting beside you in the trenches. When we met in the infusion center and discovered we were both patients of Dr. Fisher and on the same aggressive oxaliplatin and Xeloda chemotherapy regimen, we made plans to compare notes and help each other during the toughest times. "Together we can make it through this," we assured each other. We had trust in God's grace and tender mercy to sustain our spirits, and in Dr. Fisher to help us fight. For months, we scheduled our oxaliplatin chemotherapy infusions for the same day so we could support each other.

As we sat there side by side, laughing and talking as the chemo slid through our veins, a nurse once came over after hearing we'd both survived five years of continuous cancer treatment. "How do you do it?" she asked. "How have you survived five years of this?"

Neither of us answered.

Steve and I knew cancer cells were survivors, not us. Cancer cells rapidly become resistant to whatever chemotherapy is thrown at them, and surgery is like taking an ax to a forest of a billion seedlings, with each hack releasing more seeds onto the ground. A single remaining cancer seed is all that is needed for recurrence and progression.

The truth was Steve and I felt more like hostages than survivors.

He skied, ran, and lived exuberantly while going through cancer hell. He was young and had teenage children, a beautiful wife, and a successful career.

Steve had fought a fierce battle, and now he was gone.

I tried to contain my tears at his memorial service, but my heart was breaking. A fellow warrior who had become a dear friend had finally succumbed. His wife, Lisa, tried to comfort me with the truth: "He's not suffering anymore, Edie; he's at peace."

I couldn't erase Steve's death from my heart and mind. He had fought so hard for life, and he deserved to live. *Why didn't he? Why am I alive? Why am I so lucky?* Some questions have no answers. We ask them anyway, over and over and over. My walk now had a new, unexpected purpose: perhaps I would be able to emotionally scatter the ashes of the many friends and loved ones who hadn't made it to this day.

I felt an obligation to live, *really live*, life—the life denied so many I had come to know and love at the cancer center.

———

I was making last-minute preparations when Ron Briery called. "Edie, my wife, Sandy, and I are attending a meeting in Santa Barbara and have decided to walk from San Diego to Santa Barbara. Would you be interested in walking with us?"

I couldn't believe it. The chance to walk the first three hundred miles with the very man who had charted the path before? Of course I wanted to do it with them. But they were leaving in a week. I had planned to leave in a month. Would I be able to get everything ready in time?

In addition, a business emergency arose that meant Dale could no longer leave. I needed to find someone to drive QRandom so I had a place to stay each night.

I called my best friend, Jan Boelen Sinn, in Oklahoma to update her on my plans and this new wrinkle. But in the course of the phone call, Jan had an idea. Her close friend Deb Dawley was in between jobs and might be able to drive the campervan. My heart fluttered with the thought that here was a solution. I promised to pay her. And before I knew it, Deb Dawley was flying out to California to help me with my dream.

I was now ready to follow the mission bells. I didn't know where they would lead or how far I could walk. I didn't care. I would be happy with an hour or a day, with a few steps or a mile. Whatever God allowed.

———

February 20, 2013, was a cold, wet morning. At eight o'clock, Dale, Ron Graham, Meg Grant, Deb Dawley, and I stood at Mission San Diego with Ron and Sandy Briery. Meg had followed through on her promise. She would walk the first twenty miles with me, and then rejoin for another ten days after Ron and Sandy ended their journey in Santa Barbara.

I had alerted friends and family. I told people they were welcome to join me for any part of the trip, that I would welcome the encouragement and the companionship. But really, this was a very personal walk, a walk of thanksgiving, to celebrate living, and to thank God for his bountiful blessings and tender mercies.

"You have only one life," Mama always said. "Don't waste it."

I had reached out to the missions along the way, and the priest at Mission San Diego, Monsignor Richard Duncanson, prepared a special blessing. As I bowed my head, feeling the light touch of his hand on my shoulder and hearing his melodious voice lifted in prayer, my heart soared. I felt more alive than I had in five years.

Thank you, God, was the cry of my heart.

Afterward, I paused for a moment under the five bells hanging aloft in the forty-six-foot-high bell tower. Directly above me was the enormous and majestic Mater Dolorosa (Our Lady of Sorrows), a 1,200-pound bell recast in 1894 from fragments of other bells that had been used and broken in bygone days. When Harrye Forbes had arrived at the mission in 1913 to install her first mission-bell guidepost, the massive Mater Dolorosa was "picturesquely posed upon a pile of crumbling adobe that was once the tall, graceful tower of the mission." Forbes said its clang was "like a mother of sorrow wailing over a crushed and broken child."[2] It took years of love and hard work to restore Mission San Diego to its previous glory.

As I walked out of Mission San Diego and headed north on El Camino Real mission trail, the bells were ringing, and none rang louder or more joyously than Mater Dolorosa.

———

The old El Camino Real is a former footpath, mule trail, and wagon road that zigzags from coast to inland valleys. In 1905, George Wharton James described it poetically: "The El Camino Real was never much of a road from the road-maker's standpoint, but to the historian, the romancer, the artist, it is one of the most fascinating highways in the world."[3] Even then, it was no longer a remote road far from civilization, in nature and peace and quiet as Junípero Serra would have walked it. It was paved in 1902, and California expanded rapidly along the mission trail. The first three hundred miles from Mission San Diego to Mission Santa Barbara is mostly concrete—sidewalks, bike lanes, and highways.

The fear of death by cancer was replaced on that first day by fear of death by vehicle. As a walker, I was the least important person on the road. Large trucks were number one, followed by cars, motorcycles, bicycles, horses, and last, walkers. At all times, I was attentive to traffic danger. The heightened awareness, rather than taking away from the pleasure of walking, actually enhanced it. I was walking in the now, in the moment, all my senses alert and awake.

A severe weather warning was in effect the first few days of our walk; there were scattered rain showers and a cold wind blowing from the ocean. I learned that outside stuff, like weather, is almost unnoticeable. It was pouring rain and I hardly noticed it. The first hundred miles were an inward journey, not an outward one.

The first day, Ron Graham and Dale stopped walking at noon to return to work, and Ron and Sandy Briery and Meg and I continued walking to Pacific Beach's Campland on the Bay. There, as promised, we found QRandom and Deb Dawley, a welcome smile at the end of a long first day. Meg and I stayed in the campervan while Ron and Sandy pitched the tent they carried in the backpacks they had strapped to their backs.

I was in awe of their ability to hike those distances with that pack on their backs. I carried nothing but essentials—like a can of bear spray and a tooth-brush with the handle sawed off—stuffed in a Cabela's multi-pocket fishing vest and a small lumbar fanny pack with water.

Meg and I awoke groggy before sunrise from a loud knock on the door: Dale and Whitney had brought us breakfast. We ate a quick bite before head-ing out, catching up with Ron and Sandy within half an hour. This would be a tough day on the mission trail—eighteen miles. Meg stopped her walk in Del Mar to take the train back to Los Angeles, and I continued walking alone. I was sad to see Meg go but so thankful she had both encouraged me to go for this and also followed through on her promise to walk with me.

The first week was a challenge to my body. Feet are tender and blister easily, and by day three, my toenails started turning black and coming loose. I wore guaranteed-blister-free double-layer socks and stopped every three hours to smother my feet in Vaseline. At noon, Ron Briery stopped and wrapped duct tape around each toe and both feet. By the seventh day, my feet were wrapped in duct tape too.

Sandy had had hip replacement surgery fourteen months earlier, but now she walked tall and confident—and fast. Sandy was my inspiration. She convinced me that if she could do it, I could too.

"Don't worry, Edie," she said one day when I was out of breath, my back ached, my hips creaked, and my feet dragged. "Just keep on walking, and you will feel better in no time. You are retraining your body to move."

She was right. I slowly walked all the hurts, pains, and stiffness out of my body. I learned to pay attention to even the smallest detail, and retrain my awareness to pick up my feet, align my head and shoulders, relax my arms, and tighten my stomach. I became owl-eyed. To avoid roadside hazards and move out of the way of whatever came hurtling toward me, it was important to look ahead, down, and around all at the same time.

El Camino Real north of San Diego followed the Pacific Coast Highway and historic Highway 101, the mother road of California. This old, narrow, winding coastal highway had retained its original charm, and vintage 1920s road signs marked the route.

Mission bells were every mile. Each bell filled my heart with indescribable joy.

It took four days to walk from Mission San Diego to the second mission, Mission San Luis Rey. The walk was along the coast, through the picturesque beach towns of Del Mar, Solana Beach, Cardiff-by-the-Sea, Encinitas, Carlsbad, and Oceanside, and along miles of uninhabited beaches. It was as beautiful a walk as existed on the planet.

Dale, Whitney, Stefanie, and Ron Graham drove up from San Diego to walk the last six miles to Mission San Luis Rey. Our group of seven arrived at the mission at noon, the bells ringing as if to welcome us. One of my oldest and dearest friends, Diana Holm, was there to greet us in a leg cast with crutches.

As we walked into the mission, I marveled at its beauty. In the noonday sun, it looked like a medieval fortress, and I paused for a few minutes to reminisce of days past when hardened men told of stopping their horses to gaze for a few minutes at its glittering white façade. It looked like a castle from afar.

I was physically exhausted but spiritually exhilarated. It was Saturday, and the mission, a thriving parish church, was filled with people. We didn't stay long, just long enough to light a candle, say a prayer, and head to a nearby Mexican restaurant for a celebration lunch before the six-mile walk back to QRandom.

11

This walk was not for the faint of heart.

As I woke up on day five, I was facing the longest walk on the mission trail: twenty-five miles. This would be a test of will, and it would take my broken body to its edge.

During World War II, the former Rancho Santa Margarita (originally part of Mission San Luis Rey, and later, a Mexican land grant) became Camp Pendleton, and 122,798 acres were transformed into the largest Marine Corps base in the country. Camp Pendleton is off-limits to walkers, but six months earlier, Kurt Buckley, a former military officer, had sought Ron Briery's help to walk the entire mission trail from north to south, and Kurt was eager to walk through the base with us. He called ahead for permission, and after a long wait at the entry gate, the marines let us through. We were not allowed to stop or eat, and would be escorted off the base if we left the road for any reason.

It was stifling hot, without a breeze. Somehow we managed to keep walking hours without a break, and made it through the ten miles on-base. After exiting Camp Pendleton, we still had four hours to walk to our campground, mostly along old Highway 101. The deteriorating highway hadn't been used for sixty years and was now a bike path that hugged the wild California coastline.

The twenty-five-mile walk left me famished and aching, but that was nothing compared to what I faced the sixth day, when my walk almost came to an abrupt and painful end.

We had been walking for several hours, and Ron and Sandy were far ahead of me. I was walking alone on a tight, narrow road with no shoulder and in the distance saw a group of cyclists coming toward me at top speed. Did they see me? Would they stop? I had found that bicyclists are more aggressive toward walkers than the drivers of cars and trucks. Ron Briery had warned me, "I've had a hard time deciding how to share the path with cyclists. Be careful! Some of them slow down, and some of them don't."

They saw me but did not slow down, and a guardrail blocked me from stepping into the ditch on the side of the road. In a panic, I tried to jump the guardrail, but instead tripped in a deep pothole. Luckily, I got out of the way of the cyclists, but my left ankle was screaming in pain. I had twisted it, and was still miles away from camp. I knew there was nothing I could do except lace my hiking boots tighter and keep walking.

Cancer had taught me that when you think you can't go on, you can.

I painfully limped three miles along the San Juan Creek Trail, a quiet, almost-empty creek bed to Mission San Juan Capistrano and completed the day's walk.

I hobbled in and sat my exhausted body in one of the wooden pews in the only original mission church in California still standing in which Junípero Serra celebrated the sacraments. I sat reverently under the ancient arched roof built of locally quarried stone and tried to breathe in Father Serra's spirit and be comforted that he had done this walk before me, also on a wounded left foot.

When Father Serra left Loreto, Mexico, for San Diego, his left leg was inflamed and his foot was badly swollen and infected, with oozing sores of raw, exposed flesh. He was in severe pain and could not stand on his feet; it took two men to help him onto a mule. His inflamed leg looked cancerous,[1] and it was feared the frail missionary would die in the scorching hot Mexican desert long before reaching San Diego. At one point, Father Serra was in too much pain to ride and had to be dragged on a stretcher behind a mule.

Compared to Father Serra's foot and leg, my injury was bothersome but insignificant. When I got to the QRandom, I soaked my bruised foot in ice and took two thousand milligrams of ibuprofen to reduce swelling. My ankle was swollen the next three hundred miles, but I walked anyway. After five and a half years of chemotherapy, radiation, and surgery, a sprained ankle was no big deal.

———

Ron and Sandy Briery were experienced pilgrims. They had walked Spain's Camino de Santiago many times before. Yet the California mission trail was like no other in the world. It was a wild and undefined walk, exuberantly rugged, unpredictable, scary, boring, beautiful, unpleasant, and exhilarating. We meandered through concrete and asphalt, freeways, huge cities, backcountry, wilderness, steep mountains, railroad tracks, creeks, and suburban sprawl. There was daily confusion—intersecting paths, trails that ended, streets that changed names, and roads on maps that no longer existed.

Like California, El Camino Real was crazy weird but also insanely beautiful.

Mapmakers in the early twentieth century described El Camino Real as a Broadway of Beauty, for the missionaries chose fertile valleys and breathtaking ocean vistas as locations for their missions, and the trail, therefore, meandered between the valley and ocean, from one spot of great beauty to another.

The untrodden wilderness is alluring and romantic, but also dangerous. Often, Ron, Sandy, and I walked miles apart. On remote stretches of beach and deserted roadways, I occasionally came upon old, beat-up vans with no side windows. Everyone knows that serial killers and kidnappers live in old, beat-up vans with no side windows. I didn't want to disappear without a trace. I walked faster, and sometimes carried on loud conversations with nonexistent companions. Once, when passing such a van, I heard a loud click as the doors locked from inside. The poor guy living in the van was scared and must have thought I was demented.

If Ron said he was going to leave at seven o'clock in the morning, he left, with or without me. It was my responsibility to be ready. I never missed a morning, and Ron's habit of timeliness became my habit. Discipline is important on a long walk and in life. You have to get up and get going.

Ron was also a stickler for honesty. If he walked 15.9 miles, he never fudged and said he walked 16. "Edie, walkers cheat ourselves when we aren't honest," he said. "I know some will buy my hiker's guide and say they walked the whole mission trail, but will fudge half of it. That's how they live life."

What Ron didn't say is what I felt in my heart. *If you miss even a fraction of a mile, it might be where you learn the greatest lesson of your life, or where you see the most magnificent beauty, or encounter a life-changing event.*

The mission trail was too wonderful to miss a thing. I was determined, God willing, to walk every inch of it.

———

After walking six days and eighty miles, our feet began to feel the test. The only time we paid any attention to our feet was the beginning of the day. If a toenail was hanging by a shred of skin, we either cut it loose or wrapped it in protective duct tape and kept walking. We paid little notice of body aches and pains. We kept walking, and, gradually, pain went away.

Our focus was entirely on the road and paying attention not to trip on a curb or turn an ankle. Trucks, cars, and cyclists sped by, and each was a potential threat. For hours we walked near the beach and ocean, and the scenery was spectacular. Later, we walked along picturesque streets abounding in whimsical stores and exotic places to eat. We hurriedly walked on; walkers have no time to shop or sip lattes, and if we stop, our feet swell and cripple us.

When I stopped, it was only for a brief moment to close my eyes and breathe deeply into my rasping lungs or feel the sun on my face. As my eyes turned in, my heart turned out.

It was a four-day walk from Mission San Juan Capistrano to Mission San Gabriel through sprawling Los Angeles. When we turned east from Newport, El Camino Real followed Harbor Boulevard past Disneyland. A friend from Newport, Joy Penner, walked with us. The old mission trail through Costa Mesa, Anaheim, and Whittier lies beneath 250 years of progress: the thirty-mile walk was all cars, concrete, and large buildings. There was a wildness to progress too.

The concrete jungle was as dangerous as a real jungle. We crossed overpasses above three major freeways (Interstate 405, Highway 22, and Interstate 5), weaving back and forth a dozen times. Traffic zoomed past and was a dizzy blur. We walked facing traffic and waited for just the right instant to run across busy turn lanes. A misstep or a fall would end our lives or maim us.

We stopped once a day, briefly, for lunch. We were sweaty and smelled. After hours of walking on city concrete, my feet started to swell in my hiking boots, a warning sign of blisters. Before ordering food, I removed my double-liner-guaranteed-blister-free socks and air-dried the lambswool liners in my hiking boots. Before putting shoes and socks back on, I rubbed petroleum jelly into my feet and toes. My feet were sore, but I had few blisters.

We were mistaken for homeless. People in cars at stoplights offered us money. In fast-food cafés we sat away from other diners, usually outside in a corner.

I was slow crossing a busy intersection in Anaheim, and someone yelled at me, "Get a job!"

Frankly, I would rather be yelled at than looked at with pity.

Late afternoon I walked into a convenience store for cold water. The manager met me at the front door, blocking the entrance. "Do you have money?" he asked. I was taken aback until it dawned on me that he thought I was homeless.

"Yes," I said a bit too eagerly. I took five dollars from a zippered pocket in my twenty-two-pocket fishing vest to show him I could pay for the water.

Cool air blew from the ceiling and felt good against my hot, sweaty face. I turned to face the ceiling air and saw my distorted, pathetic image in the rounded security mirror hanging from the corner wall above the refrigerated water. I looked deranged and, yes, homeless. In that instant, I felt it, too, and was filled with conflicting emotions of pride for being who I was, and self-contempt for being smelly and dirty and who *he* thought I was.

I noticed the dirt under my fingernails and my sweaty hands gripping the five-dollar bill; the money was wet and soiled.

I didn't say a word. I gave him the five-dollar bill.

"Let me get it for you," he replied, taking the soiled money carefully between two fingers. A few minutes later he returned with a cold bottle of water and change.

I thanked him and politely left.

He'd obviously had a bad experience with the homeless and was distrustful and suspicious. It clouded his judgment. He saw me as homeless and undesirable, instead of a person with dirty fingernails and sweaty hands.

He did me a great favor. When *we* become *they*, an inner transformation occurs. There is no longer separateness. I understood what it felt like to be scorned and homeless. But being homeless does not diminish a person, nor does it take away her human dignity. Neither do dirty fingernails and sweaty hands.

Only other people can do that. We must not allow them to.

Mama would never allow it. She taught us to never pay attention to what others think. "How you are outside is not as important as inside," she assured Edmond and me after a smart aleck on the school bus made fun of his farmer-style overalls and my old-fashioned hand-me-down shoes.

It was my first week of first grade riding the school bus, and with the five-year drought Daddy hardly had money for cotton and wheat seed, much less for school clothes. Edmond, a second grader, was wearing worn but clean overalls. I wore an old, scuffed pair of shoes, the laces tattered, with too little left to tie properly.

When the taunting started, Edmond pushed me protectively behind him on the bus seat. "Look outside the window, Edith," he ordered as he stood up to face the big bully, and started swearing, fists flying. Swearing was something Edmond was good at and did often. Fighting was too. Other kids, even big kids, didn't mess much with him. He could be like a junkyard dog let unleashed.

The bully ran to the back of the bus and never taunted us again.

At Christmas, Mama somehow scraped together enough egg money to buy Edmond a pair of denim jeans like the kids in town wore, and a new pair of shoes for me. Mama was like that, acutely aware, but never probing. She always found a way when something was important and never made a fuss about it.

I had little energy the last fifteen miles from Whittier to Mission San Gabriel. It was the tenth, and hottest, day of the walk, and there was no cooling breeze.

El Camino Real meanders through the Whittier Greenway Trail, built over the old rails of the Pacific Electric red cars that operated from 1903 to 1938, carrying rail passengers to local cities and beaches. It was a striking reminder of the hundred-mile Los Angeles metro rail system in place in the early 1900s that was dismantled in favor of carbon-fueled automobiles and freeways that are clogged arteries of traffic and congestion.

Places are born and they die, but spirit remains. Animal trails became human footpaths that became El Camino Real that became the Pacific Electric train line that became the Whittier Greenway Trail. El Camino Real was to California what the Via Appia was to Rome and the Great North Road to England.

The old mission trail sprouted new life with each passing generation. It was a trail for natives and explorers set on conquest; a road traveled by sinners and saints in the name of religion; a route traversed by miners seeking riches; a path of westward expansion and progress; a migrant highway of hope and happiness; and today, in the twenty-first century, it is a golden freeway of technology geniuses upending the world order.

I walked in rhythm to the gospel of movement and became a star rover journeying through a long chain of existences.

I felt overwhelmed with gratitude for having the opportunity to walk here, and become part of it, and breathe its spirit.

After leaving Whittier, the Friday afternoon walk along the San Gabriel River Parkway was spiritually intoxicating with the snow-capped San Gabriel Mountains in the distance and the sounds of nature caressing our senses. The terrain was rugged, and the trail was deserted. It was hard to believe we were walking in Los Angeles, home to four million people.

The dirt path under my feet probably looked much the same the day Los Angeles was christened in 1769, when the Franciscan missionary Juan Crespí celebrated mass next to a beautiful river he named Nuestra Señora de los Ángeles de la Porciúncula[2] (now the Los Angeles River) after the tiny country church of Our Lady of the Angels near Assisi, Italy, where St. Francis prayed.

Few places along the California coast don't have some connection to the missions or carry Spanish names derived from the calendar of saints.

We were dehydrated and exhausted by the time we arrived at Mission San Gabriel late Friday afternoon. The grounds were quiet, and the museum unmanned. I was surprised to be left alone to browse books dating to 1489.

I quietly lit a candle in the darkened church in gratitude and thanksgiving for the safe journey and this joyous life. I thought of the countless other pilgrims who had found shelter and solace in this beautiful old Moorish-inspired mission named after Gabriel, the most famous angel in the Bible.

"Make yourself familiar with the angels and behold them frequently in spirit; for without being seen, they are present with you," advised St. Francis de Sales more than four centuries ago.[3]

Angels came often in the night in my dreams. The night I discovered cancer was exploding again in my liver and lungs, Edmond came to me in a dream. He was older, with thinning gray hair, his body frail and worn with age. He was sitting in a chair with light behind him. I had to squint to see his face. To reach him I had to climb up stairs. At the top of the stairs the steps were missing. There was a mesh rope bridge with frayed ends, which I grabbed and climbed. I managed to get to the top floor, where Edmond was seated. He was speaking. I could see his lips move but could not hear his voice. I looked to my left and saw a dirt road and started walking.

I suddenly woke up. The clock read 1:11 a.m.

I felt at peace. Deep in my soul I knew what Edmond was telling me in the dream: that he was there with me every breath and every step of this frightening journey through cancer. And so were a host of other angels, living and dead, new and old, known and unknown.

Now, on the walk, sleep was a challenge. I slept almost upright in QRandom, propped up on a wedge, with pillows stacked on top. My lung sometimes made gurgling sounds. It was fluid. During the day when I walked, it drained. At night when I slept, it accumulated in my chest. Sleeping upright helped it drain. Or so I told myself. I did know that it was painful to sleep flat. There was too much pressure on the still-fresh lung incision, and sleeping flat irritated damaged nerves in my chest and ribs.

Yet when I slept upright, my swollen ankle ballooned and was so big that in the morning I had a hard time lacing my hiking boots. But as soon as I started walking, my swollen ankle deflated and my lungs inflated.

If I can move, I'm not sick.

12

It would take us two days to walk to the next mission, Mission San Fernando, through the legendary Los Angeles suburbs of Pasadena, Burbank, and Hollywood.

A walk through Hollywood and Burbank sounds like a romantic walk through movie land, but El Camino Real followed railroad tracks, and the neighborhoods were neither glamorous nor romantic. Where we walked, there were no people, and businesses and homes were hidden behind spiked iron fences and iron bars on the windows.

Walkers judge neighborhoods differently. Sights, sounds, and smells are as important as manicured lawns and big houses.

In Pacoima, an impoverished Latino community four miles from the mission, there were broken sidewalks but also dirt paths, which made my feet blissfully thankful. Many homes were abandoned and yards filled with trash. I hardly noticed them. What I did notice were the small houses with open windows and exotic cooking smells filling the air, which lifted my spirit.

The streets were filled with people and music. A street artist, Levi Ponce, was painting a huge mural of a beautiful Latina lady on the side of a crumbling wall. Men sat in plastic chairs in front of a Laundromat and liquor store, watching him paint and listening to music. I stopped to admire the mural and spent a few minutes talking to Levi. "Pacoima is considered the black eye of

San Fernando Valley, but this is my neighborhood and I want to fill it with beauty," he exclaimed as he dipped his brush in red paint and painted over gang graffiti.

The backdrop of his mural was the interior of a church with arched windows. In one window Levi had painted a mission bell.

I was walking in one of the highest-crime neighborhoods in Los Angeles, under a gang injunction by the police.

I walked quickly and attentively, but was not afraid. Walkers are more likely to be killed or maimed by the peloton of a bicycle gang than a tattooed street gang.

While I expected to miss the quiet wilderness, there was something invigorating about walking through cities bustling with life. There was beauty here, too, in the way we as a people have come together to build communities. It looked so different from the days of Junípero Serra, but when we come together to help each other, the spirit of the padres is here.

I soon came upon Mission San Fernando. The mission is a thriving religious center serving the greater Los Angeles area, with daily services in English and Spanish. It was midafternoon by the time I arrived—too late to attend Sunday services, but the historic church bells rang as I sat in the chapel, sending chills down my spine. An organist in the upper choir loft was practicing for a later service, and I closed my eyes and felt the healing sound of the hymn penetrate deep within.

I became a child again, sitting with my family on a wooden church pew in the small rural Baptist church in Oklahoma. The congregation quietly stood to sing the closing hymn, "I Need Thee Every Hour." Every head was bowed and bodies gently swayed back and forth with the music. It was not just a song. It was not just words. It was a prayer. The prayer lingered for days afterwards. Our family went about our chores humming the words, our hearts affirming our need for God. My mother cooked the evening meal, and I heard the soft sound of her voice: *"Temptations lose their power when Thou art nigh. I need Thee every hour, in joy or pain; come quickly and abide, or life is in vain."*

The organist stopped her practicing. My consciousness returned to this time and this place, and I heard the mission bells ring six times.

Long after the final vibration, I sat softly humming, softly singing, with tears and smiles flowing from the sweet joy of memory. *"I need Thee, oh, I need Thee; every hour I need Thee; oh, bless me now, my Savior, I come to Thee."*[1]

I had walked two hundred miles in twelve days without a break, and the next day was to be a twenty-mile walk over the Santa Susana Mountains. I hadn't walked in the mountains yet. On flat ground, my feet started to swell and ache after fourteen miles, and it was easy to stumble and fall. After sixteen miles, my bones would start to ache, especially my neck and shoulders.

But I knew, just like everything in life, if I just kept going, I would find a way. Spirit would soar, and grace would rush in.

———

I stood looking at the trail before me. It looked as if it were straight up. We were nine miles from the outskirts of Los Angeles in Old Santa Susana Pass. The pass was originally a wagon road between the missions and so steep and dangerous it was called Devil's Slide. In 1859, when the old mission road became a stagecoach road, mules and horses were blindfolded to keep them from panicking. Passengers were asked to get out of the stagecoach and walk, while the driver coaxed the blindfolded animals down the pass, using chains to slow their descent.

We were walking up the narrow road that replaced Devil's Slide. It was over ninety degrees and steaming hot.

I walked slowly and deliberately, wishing I had a chain to pull me.

For two hundred miles I had ignored lung and surgical pain. Now, it was impossible to avoid. My heart was racing too fast; my lungs couldn't keep up and supply oxygen fast enough. I gasped for air and felt as if I were going to pass out.

I stopped, unable to go on.

I remembered selling Bibles door-to-door at the age of seventeen, riding my bicycle alone in Jackson, Tennessee. After a dozen doors were slammed in my face, I kept knocking. How did I do it? I pulled an old affirmation from the recesses of my brain.

I can. I will. I'm going to.

I kept walking, to the rhythm in my head. *I can. I will. I'm going to.*

It took three hours to reach the top. The sight below was my reward—a panoramic view of Los Angeles. The City of Angels sparkled in the afternoon sun.

My breath was strong and steady. My lungs no longer hurt. But my feet were killing me.

Ron and Sandy had gone on ahead while I struggled up the road, and the three of us stood at the top of Devil's Slide, surveying the beauty and history that surrounded us. Mountains and valleys straight out of a Hollywood Western, literally—many famous Westerns had been filmed here during the 1940s and '50s. There was evil too. Charles Manson and his family had lived here in a secluded ranch when they murdered Sharon Tate.

Ron and Sandy were remarkable walking companions. Ron's knowledge of the old El Camino Real mission trail gave me confidence whether navigating city streets or mountain passes. Sandy spoke softly and was mild-mannered and even-tempered but was the strongest, grittiest walking companion imaginable. I longed to walk the entire trail with them, but I knew in a few days we would be parting company in Santa Barbara. I was already feeling sad and apprehensive.

We were soon out of the mountains and walking through miles of strawberry fields. Large trucks loaded with fruit thundered past, stirring up dirt and blowing us to the side of the road. Twice we passed over Highway 101, walking single file and making a wild dash across, to avoid cars whizzing by as they exited and entered the freeway.

The next day was another grueling nineteen-mile walk, and I woke up wondering if my exhausted body were capable of two long walks back-to-back. As with most things, the anxiety and dread were much worse than the actual doing. But we made it to Mission San Buenaventura. Six down, fifteen to go.

I heard the sound of church bells and knew the mission was near.

I tried to pick up the pace. My breath came out in heavy spurts. But, oh, how grateful I was for my poor lungs—that they were allowing me to do this journey.

When we arrived, Father Tom Elewaut was waiting outside to welcome us, and the tower bells were still ringing. The bells echoed through all of Ventura. I could still feel their soulful vibrations as I sat in the chapel and rested my weary body. The church was originally built with stone, lime, and clay from nearby *cañada*s and hills, now leveled and filled with homes. Rough-hewn ceiling timbers came from as far away as the Santa Ana forest near where Disneyland now stands.

El Camino Real mission trail was a daily reminder of the impermanence and fleetingness of life.

———

Friday morning I stood on the side of a busy freeway—cars, trucks, and motor-cycles cruising by at speeds of up to seventy miles per hour.

This was totally and completely crazy.

And maybe a bit stupid.

The walk from Ventura to Santa Barbara was as scary as anything I've done in my life. We were forced to walk on a California freeway in Friday rush-hour traffic. It wreaked havoc with my sprained ankle, and fear made my breathing shallow. Exhaust fumes burned my lungs.

The freeway was between beach bluffs and railroad tracks, and we had no choice but to walk the freeway. There was no shoulder, and the ditch was filled with weeds, broken bottles, hubcaps, and a thousand other items thrown from cars and blown out of truck beds.

Ron, Sandy, and I walked single file, hugging the right side of the four-lane highway, half in and out of the ditch. Large trucks almost blew us off the side of the road, coming so close we could almost feel door mirrors brush against our shoulders. There was no place for the big rigs to go, and they couldn't move over even if they wanted to.

Pickups with open backs, low sides, and filled with tools, trash, furniture, and myriad items were even scarier than eighteen-wheelers. If a nail flies off a truck going seventy miles an hour and hits you in the head, there is enough force to drive it through your brain or blind you.

Up ahead was road construction, and traffic came to a screeching halt before flowing through. If there were a pileup, we would be struck.

This was sheer insanity. I had fought too hard to save my life to foolishly end it on the side of a California freeway.

I could continue walking on the freeway and risk being killed. I could stop walking and call for help. Or I could walk on the railroad tracks.

Sometimes, as with cancer, all your choices seem doomed.

I chose to walk on the railroad tracks, and Sandy came with me.

A high fence separated the freeway from the railroad tracks, and we walked along the fence, knee-high in weeds, until we were able to slip under the fence near a small culvert.

There was less than five feet of walking space on the side of the tracks, and the tracks were elevated atop a gravelly slope. Sharp rock cut through our shoes, and sliding gravel threatened to re-sprain my ankle.

So we tried walking on the tracks, on the wood railroad ties spaced two feet apart.

Both Sandy and I were nervous. You are never supposed to walk on railroad tracks. Everyone knows this. But somehow we thought this was safer than walking on the freeway. We assumed that we would hear an approaching train and be given plenty of warning to jump off.

I was shocked to learn an approaching train is almost silent. There is no ground tremor or locomotive sound.

We were calmly walking around a curve in the hillside when we looked up and saw a train approaching at ninety miles per hour. Panic set in, and we scrambled down the embankment in time to feel it rush past above us.

We stared at each other, shaking. That was way too close.

Another train passed a half hour later. The conductor blared his horn, and it was so loud I temporarily lost my hearing.

We were afraid the conductor might hit the emergency brake, and we didn't want to be responsible for rail carnage. I was also afraid we might be arrested and fined for trespassing. Every few yards there was a sign forbidding entry to the rail tracks.

"This is insane," Sandy finally said. "Let's go back to the freeway."

A third train passed by the time we came to a place we could exit under the fence.

I had just climbed underneath the fence when a black truck pulled up in front of the small culvert. I was sure it was the police or railroad security. How was I going to explain our foolishness? It wasn't. It was two friends from church, Tom and Cori Grunow, who drove three hundred miles from San Diego to walk with me to Mission Santa Barbara. They had been following along, as many of my friends had, on Facebook and using Apple's Find Friends to track my exact location.

Tom was a passionate surfer and thrilled to walk the cliffs above Rincon Beach, one of the most famous surfing beaches in California. Surfing addicts call Rincon the Queen of the Coast, and the area is world-famous for large swelling waves and long rides.

I felt giddy after the emotional stress of the freeway and railroad tracks and the excitement of having two friends to walk with.

This is wild, beautiful California, and I am walking it!

I had walked three hundred miles in eighteen days. *It's not 300 miles, it's 271 miles,* my little voice inside heard Ron keeping me honest.

When we walked into Mission Santa Barbara, my spirit soared above painful feet, swollen ankles, and scarred lungs.

I had vowed to not let this second chance at life pass me by, no matter what.

———

Mission Santa Barbara, Queen of the Missions, stood majestically atop a gentle sloping hill in an amphitheater formed by the Santa Ynez Mountains. It was the tenth mission founded by Franciscan missionaries, and its name comes from the legend of Saint Barbara, a girl tortured and then beheaded by her own father for following the Christian faith. Afterward, her father, Dioscorus, was struck by lightning; consequently, the protection of Santa Barbara is often sought by sailors against the fury of lightning during storms at sea.

Father Charles Talley, the parish pastor, and associate pastor Father Larry

Gosselin greeted us with prayer, bear hugs, and offerings of food, tea, and a place to rest—the same Franciscan welcome to weary travelers since Mission Santa Barbara was built in 1786. The two priests were dressed in simple attire, called the habit of Francis, a hooded, ankle-length brown robe in the form of a cross with a white cord at the waist tied in three knots that symbolize the three gospel vows of the Franciscan life: poverty, chastity, and obedience.

Sandy and Ron Briery left to check in to a hotel, and Father Charles and Father Larry gave us a private tour, past No Entry signs and into hallowed chapels and chambers of the historic old mission. For more than a century, the grounds were a Franciscan sanctuary, and no woman, save a reigning queen or wife of the president of the United States, was allowed to enter the mission buildings surrounding the garden with its Italian cypress and hundreds of varieties of semitropical flowers and fountain of goldfish. Tom, Cori, and I finished the visit with a healing blessing in the main church by Father Charles, with anointment with olive oil from ancient trees on the grounds.

Dale was joining me the next day for the seven-day walk from Santa Barbara to Mission San Luis Obispo, and this was the end of the road for Ron and Sandy Briery. It was time to say farewell. I felt like a young bird, apprehensive and scared, but ready to fly the nest.

And then Deb Dawley announced she had learned of a job opportunity in Houston and was scheduling an interview. She could no longer drive QRandom. I was devastated to learn I might lose Deb and Ron and Sandy, all at the same time.

Deb had become a friend and soul sister, cheerfully arising at the crack of dawn for a big breakfast, helping load Ron and Sandy's backpacks in QRandom, and driving ahead to the end of each day's walk to look for unique and fun places to park QRandom for the night. She loved meeting people and spreading goodwill and cheer.

When I walked alone, I could always count on Deb using GPS to keep an eye on where I was walking. And when I arrived at QRandom, exhausted after the day's walk, she was there to greet me with a huge smile and heartfelt congratulations.

How could I continue the walk without Deb? I had a week to figure it out.

13

Dale arrived in Santa Barbara with a surprise—*Whitney!* Whitney had taken three days off work to walk with Dale and me. Their arrival helped fill the void of Ron and Sandy Briery's departure and ease the shock of soon losing Deb too.

I needed a day of rest—my first in nearly three hundred miles—and Dale and Whitney spent the time mulling over what route to take next.

The forty-eight-mile walk from Mission Santa Barbara to Mission Santa Inés crossed the rugged Santa Ynez Mountains. Missionaries had followed three different trails over the mountains, none good.

One trail, called Arroyo Burro, was an old Chumash Indian footpath through the wilderness. It was a three-day walk requiring full camp gear, food, and water. I could carry, at most, six pounds, and even that little amount of weight was painful, as sensitive nerves in my abdomen and shoulder, damaged in liver and lung surgeries, became irritated. Dale and Whitney weren't keen on carrying three days of camping supplies for three people, and quickly nixed the idea.

A second mission trail through Refugio Pass would require a three-day walk along ten miles of beach, careful planning, and luck. The ability to complete the beach leg of the walk would depend on tides and weather. Whitney also discovered that the beach north of Santa Barbara was home to an endangered bird, the western snowy plover, and the beach would be closed wherever and whenever it was spotted nesting in beach scrapes. Even if we were successful maneuvering around changing tides and nesting birds, after walking the beach, we would still have a steep twenty-mile climb over the mountain.

Ron's hiker's guide followed a third route—a two-day walk through the San Marcos Pass. It was the most direct, but also the most terrifying: an exhausting and steep two-day walk up twisty Old Wells Fargo Stagecoach Road on a deadly stretch of pavement described by the local newspaper as littered with "gratuitous gore." The thirty-two-mile paved road was mostly a two-lane no-passing zone without a shoulder, following tight and blind switchbacks cut into the mountain. Rocks tumbled down as cars sped by day and night.

This was the route Dale and Whitney decided we should walk.

The first nineteen-mile day, Dale and I walked in sheer terror, leaning toward the mountain to keep from being hit by speeding cars. Dale and I looked at each other, wondering if we should have left Whitney at home.

Whitney, infused with the immortality of youth, was unfazed and seemed to relish the excitement. Halfway there, I glanced back and was aghast to see Whitney walking in the traffic lane, expecting cars to slow, or move over.

The next morning, we wouldn't let Whitney walk with us, which was okay because by then Whitney had become bored with walking.

Dale and I set out walking at sunrise, and the San Marcos Pass was even more dangerous than the day before, with drivers blinded by the morning sun. We had walked no farther than a quarter mile when Dale stopped suddenly and picked up a blue bicycle flag beside the road. "A gift from God, to aid in our protection," I said with a smile. With his bright yellow shirt, the newly found blue flag waving above our heads, and blinking headlamps, we felt a bit safer. We chuckled over the difference in our attitude and Whitney's and how, as we grow older, our sense of the value of life deepens. By midafternoon, Whitney had decided not walking was more boring than walking, and rejoined us to walk ten miles to Mission Santa Inés. We received a hearty reception and a healing prayer from Franciscan pastor Gerald Barron. I was still shaking from the frightening two-day walk, and I lit a candle in gratitude for our arriving safely at the mission.

The mission was named after Saint Agnes (Santa Inés), one of the best-known early Roman martyrs, beheaded in AD 304 when she was just twelve years old. Legend has it that when the son of a Roman governor sought her as his wife, she refused, stating that she was already betrothed because she had dedicated her life and heart to Jesus. It is said the Romans forced her to become a temple prostitute for the Roman pagan religion before her beheading.

I lit a second candle for Saint Agnes. The pain she must have gone through as she clung to her faith. I wondered if my faith would be as strong or if I would be as courageous.

———

The next morning, Whitney had to return to work and caught a train to San Francisco, but Dale walked with me another four days—long enough to lose three toenails and develop painful blisters on both feet, despite wrapping his toes and feet in duct tape. We walked hours alongside monotonous straight highways and carried food, because there were no towns where we could stop and eat. We passed miles of vineyards and longed to stop to rest in the shade, but they were set back away from the road, and our feet were unwilling to walk even a quarter mile farther than necessary.

We didn't stop for eighteen miles, until we reached Mission La Purísima Concepción, named in honor of Mary, mother of Jesus. The mission was painstakingly restored by the National Park Service and the Civilian Conservations Corps in the 1930s and was dedicated as a California Historic State Park. It is not an active parish church.

The park ranger gave Dale and me a tour and led us up the rickety old stairs to the bell tower to ring the mission bell. It was a thrill to pull the thick ropes of the giant iron bell and hear the sound vibrate in the quiet country air. With each ring, I felt energy and warmth radiating through me, and I was struck by its healing power. Bells weigh up to two thousand pounds and are the largest musical instrument; it is well known that music can invoke emotional and physical responses that relax, stimulate, and assist in healing. Perhaps that is why bell ringers live long and productive lives.

Another good-bye awaited me at Mission San Luis Obispo. Work duties called, so Dale caught the Amtrak train back to San Diego. He vowed to be back by the time I reached Carmel, and walk the final two hundred miles with me. I was sad to see Dale go, but we were both relieved when Deb Dawley's job interview in Houston was scheduled in three weeks, and she agreed to drive QRandom until he returned.

I took a day off in San Luis Obispo. My sprained ankle hadn't had a chance to heal, and I wanted to soak my swollen foot in ice, buy food, and clean QRandom. I didn't like days off; they reconnected me with the mundane, and I wanted to stay connected with God.

However, the day of rest allowed me to spend a few quiet hours at the mission, and I sat lazily in the warm sun out front near a fountain with grizzly bear sculptures, a reminder that Father Junípero Serra had founded Mission San Luis Obispo two miles from the Valley of the Bears, where hordes of man-eating grizzly bears terrorized the Chumash natives. The Spanish gained the goodwill of the locals by killing a large number of the enormous beasts and sharing the meat. There have been no grizzlies in California since 1924, but there are many black bears, and I shuddered the next day when I saw caution signs to watch out for bears and cubs.

I was nearly at the halfway point. I had walked twenty-six days and 382 miles. Meg Grant arrived that evening to walk with me to the next three missions—San Miguel, San Antonio, and Soledad—which were the most wild and remote. Her friend JoBeth McDaniel came along to drive their small, lime-green conversion van, which had a miniature kitchen sink, gas cooker, and refrigerator in the trunk, and a pop-up container on top for sleeping. It promised to be quite an adventure, and I could hardly wait to get going. But I also needed to take a moment to savor how far I had come.

I had learned that with a journey of this magnitude, you can't look too far ahead, or you'd just get overwhelmed by how much is left to do. Instead, you focus on the now. Each step is always in the present, the next step is always in the future, and no one knows when there will be no more steps and the journey ends.

To walk purposely was to experience wide-eyed wonder, the magical kind that we left behind in childhood. Peace washed through me, stilling my mind. "Perhaps this is nirvana," I often thought to myself.

What I had experienced on the mission trail was what travelers experienced two centuries ago—life as it once was. There was silence and a slowness in walking. But sometimes, even walking, I felt I was moving too fast.

I tuned out the nonessentials, all the busyness that distracts us from the one thing that matters: our connection to God, to spirit, to the source of life. Instead, I flowed with nature's more primal rhythm, one oblivious to hurry and rush.

I didn't want to miss anything. The essence of life is undiluted experience. In the sounds around me—the warbling of bird song, the rustle of wind—I heard the voice of God. When wildflowers closed their beauty for the night and opened to the rising sun, I saw God. God was everywhere and in everything.

Walking had become intoxicating and hypnotic, filling me with an ever-present sense of well-being. The cadence of walking became my entire world, and I felt as if I were vibrating. There were brief moments when I became one with nature, with soul, with God, and I understood that I was a child of God, imperfect and ignorant, yearning for wholeness.

Walking connected me with God and made me feel whole.

On a long walk, people walk alone, together. After several hours and many miles, a person walks in silence. The walk becomes deeply personal and each person a solitary walker. On long stretches of flat, seemingly endless roads when there was nothing to break the monotony, Meg would put on earphones and listen to music, but I was cautious and preferred to listen to traffic, ready to move out of harm's way in a split second. I filled monotony with short, sooth-ing repetitive prayers, like "God, Love" and "Jesus, Mercy." I paid attention to breathing, a conscious, mindful synchronizing of breath, word, and step.

I had become accustomed to walking alone. I never let down my guard, and I paid extreme attention to my surroundings. The mission walk was a walk of faith, and I was in God's hands. I accepted risk but was determined to not be foolish.

It was a four-day walk from San Luis Obispo to Mission San Miguel, and Meg and I arrived on the first day of spring. The interior of Mission San Miguel was a burst of color. The walls were painted by indigenous Salinan artisans, under the direction of a master builder from Monterey, and frescoed in vivid blues, greens, and gold crowned by red-brown horizontal bands atop a burnt brick floor. The color was still vibrant and fresh after two hundred years.

The mission trail, too, was a canvas of spring color. Wildflowers in every hue of the rainbow lined the road, but yellow seemed to dominate. Franciscan missionaries scattered mustard seeds as they walked, from a sack with a small hole in the bottom slung over their back. They purposively created a kind of map for those who came after them, and yellow flowering branches of wild mustard grew everywhere. This was deeply symbolic, of course: Jesus com-pared faith to a mustard seed, which is a small seed that grows a plant so large that birds nest in its branches.

There is something about spring that causes one to seek renewal and transformation. Each day on the mission trail I felt reborn.

This morning, I had looked heavenward, and a morning hawk soared overhead. I felt its heart beat within my heart, and in our one heart I felt the presence of God that connects all living things. The out breath of the animal world sustains the plant world; and the out breath of the plant world sustains the animal world. God breathes life into both.

Now Meg was up ahead, and as I walked I noticed two crows following me. They followed me for hours. They circled above me, disappeared awhile, then flew from behind and squawked loudly, to call attention to themselves. They flew ahead and sat on fence posts, waiting for me to catch up. They laughed at me. They played with me. They cheered me. I wanted them to stay, but they flew away. I missed them.

Mission San Antonio was a four-day walk from Mission San Miguel, and I arrived at sunset on the thirty-fourth day. I felt humble in the presence of its beauty. The mission was nestled against the impenetrable Santa Lucia Mountains, which rose to the west and eventually plummeted in coastal cliffs. It was the most remote of the twenty-one missions and the least disturbed. It was quiet, romantic, and felt abandoned.

I listened for the ringing of bells at sunset, as had been the custom. The bells were silent, and the grounds appeared empty. It was all mine, and as I inhaled its air, I felt I was entering an altered state of being.

In the summer of 1771, Junípero Serra traveled south from Monterey over rocky summits and thick chaparral to establish his third mission here in the Valley of the Oaks. Then, as now, it was a place of unparalleled beauty and solitude. There was no one in sight. Undaunted, Father Serra hung a large bronze bell on an oak tree and rang it vigorously, calling out for all who heard it to "come and receive the faith of Jesus Christ." A lone, solitary Salinan approached out of curiosity and listened to the dedication mass. Father Serra showered him with gifts and affection, and was confident this "first fruit of the wilderness"[1] would tell others and bring them to the mission. He was right. Later in the day, many members of the tribe arrived, bringing gifts of pine nuts and acorns. They stayed and energetically helped the missionaries build a church and dwellings. The mission prospered and grew, just as Father Serra had envisioned. The mission became famous for its fine horses, and the Salinans renowned as expert vaqueros.

Mission San Antonio seemed vacant when Meg and I arrived. The entry door facing the road was locked. We stood under the bell tower, wondering what to do. In the center niche of the old bell tower hung the first mission bell made in California. It was two feet in diameter and weighed five hundred pounds. It hung silently above me, waiting to serve.

On the door was a quote, in Spanish and English, from Father Serra: "*Siempre adelante, nunca retroceder*. Always look forward, and never look back." I smiled. Walking was a physical reminder of this wisdom. If you look back while walking, you trip and fall.

We knocked again and a lovely woman with soft, angelic eyes and silver-gray hair unlocked the door from the inside. "You can come with me or go around back through the courtyard. We lock the front door at four o'clock, but the back door is always open." Meg followed her inside.

I lingered in front, under the bells. To the east, perched atop the hill overlooking the mission, was the Hacienda, William Randolph Hearst's private hunting lodge designed by Julia Morgan, the principal architect of Hearst Castle. With its gold dome it looked like a blinding ball of fire lit by the setting sun, as intense as Moses' burning bush.

A full moon rose in the east as the sun set in the west, bathing the mission in light. As the day slowly faded into night, I walked the grounds, mindful of the notorious population of rattlesnakes that resided in the tall grass, and I looked for mountain lion and bobcat tracks in soft dirt under towering oak trees in back.

The mission had thirty bare, monastic rooms with a communal shower and restroom. The rooms were empty; Meg, JoBeth, Deb, and I would be the only guests.

The chapel was left unlocked at night, its priceless treasures unguarded behind a heavy wood door that hung on eighteenth-century hinges made of iron forged at the mission. I pried open the door, and recorded Gregorian chants softly descended from the rear balcony; a small light flickered to life near the altar. Lighted candles faded quietly along the back wall.

I sat in silence and became prayer.

Holiness hovered in the air, and when I listened with my heart, I heard the faint echo of a choir. Juan Bautista Sancho, the Franciscan missionary who lived here twenty-six years and is buried at the foot of the altar, composed sacred music and assembled a Salinan orchestra and choir who were among the finest musicians in nineteenth-century California.

The monastery was arranged in a quadrangle around the mission garden. I sat mesmerized by its beauty. It was getting late, and I had a brutal nineteen-mile walk the next day, but I couldn't leave.

I lingered in the garden on a bench next to the ancient fountain majestically lit by the light of the full moon. Creatures of the night arose from the quiet of San Antonio Valley to worship the moon, and the air was alive with the sound of crickets, night birds, hoot owls, and the mission's two feral cats, Rosario and Spirit, romping in the Italian cypress trees next to the fountain.

Centuries of Franciscan priests have left behind a holy world of serenity and peace. I sat with eyes closed, breathing the holiness.

Lord, make me an instrument of Your peace. Where there is hatred, let me sow love; where there is injury, pardon; where there is doubt, faith; where there is despair, hope; where there is darkness, light; where there is sadness, joy.

O, Divine Master, grant that I may not so much seek to be consoled as to console; to be understood as to understand; to be loved as to love; For it is in giving that we receive; it is in pardoning that we are pardoned; it is in dying that we are born again to eternal life.[2]

That night, I knew I would never be the same again, and my soul would be forever restless. For the remainder of my life, I would be consumed with an insatiable desire to walk and follow the bells of St. Francis.

My body succumbed to deep sleep.

I dreamt and saw my lungs clearing and opening.

I dreamt and saw my cells releasing six years of toxins and my blood becoming pure.

I dreamt and saw new, healthy cells replacing damaged cells all through my body.

I dreamt and saw soothing moonlight mend my broken body and cleanse my spirit.

I awoke fresh and whole.

14

The mission trail became deeply personal.

For more than a hundred miles through the Central and Salinas Valleys, I walked through land overflowing with milk and honey, beside fields of red strawberries, green vegetables, and purple grapes. The harvesters reminded me of my own family members who traveled west to look for work.

This was where Uncle Wilburn was killed working in the fields, where Grandpa Littlefield picked grapes to make enough money to return home after his dream of striking it rich ended badly, and where Edmond worked on oil rigs when the oil bust hit Oklahoma.

For generations, Okies were inspired by hard times to roam and ramble. The prairie wind blew them like tumbleweeds from one place to the next. Man is by birth an itinerant traveler, and life allows no more than a fleeting amount of time in any one place. El Camino Real was just another hot, old, dusty road to a Dust Bowl Okie, and "so long, it's been good to know yuh, and I gotta be moving on."

The mission trail was a daily reminder that it's not how fast we walk—it's how far; it's not how long a relationship is—it's how deep.

After Mission Soledad (Our Lady of Solitude), Meg and JoBeth returned to Los Angeles, and I walked alone to Mission San Carlos Borroméo del Río Carmelo, named after the sixteenth-century archbishop of Milan. The mission is known simply and affectionately as Mission Carmel. Dale had hoped to meet me there, but problems at work delayed him a few more days. I didn't mind. Deb had one week left to drive QRandom before her job interview in Houston. I enjoyed walking alone, and I knew I could count on Deb to use GPS to keep track of me on wilderness trails.

I arrived at Mission Carmel on Easter Sunday, the fortieth day of my walk. The timing was coincidental and unplanned—at least by me. After a few morning sprinkles, the sky cleared, and the day was radiant and hot. By the time I reached the mission, my shirt was drenched in sweat, and when I took a seat in the cool stone interior, the sweat running down my back made a wet imprint on the wood pew.

Mission Carmel is the crown jewel of the missions, and where Junípero Serra died and is buried.

Father Serra passed away so quietly that all thought he was sleeping. The tiny room at the mission where he died was filled to overflowing with wildflowers of every color, gathered by Esselen tribal members who spent the night-watch hours after his death in prayerful lamentation, singing with extreme tenderness and affection the "Rosary for the Soul of the Deceased."[1] His dear friend Fray Francisco Palóu laid him to eternal rest in a plain redwood coffin at the foot of the altar he loved so dearly, beside another cherished friend, Father Juan Crespí, who had died two years earlier. Nineteen years later, Father Fermín Lasuén joined them, uniting in death the lifelong friends who preached the gospel together from Mallorca to Mexico City to Loreto to Carmel.

As I arose from the pew and stood near the altar where Fathers Serra, Crespí, and Lasuén lie side by side, the mission bells rang out their joyous Easter hymn of praise.

I closed my eyes and turned inward. The music of mission bells is not in the chimes, but in the silence between. *Be still, and know that I am God.*[2] It is in the space between breaths where I find him and where I now heard the bells of Mission Carmel.

Finally, after six hundred miles, my feet stopped hurting. I know it sounds like hyperbole, but life became transcendent and intensely vivid and even the most ordinary was infused with wonder and awe.

The final two hundred miles was a slow remembering of how tragic and sad and profound and wonderful life is.

The mission trail from Salinas Valley to Mission San Juan Bautista was filled with roadside memorials. Each memorial marked the spot where someone had died in an accident, suddenly and unexpectedly.

Mama's younger brother, Wilburn, died here, a thousand miles away from family, but there was no memorial for him.

When the Depression hit in early 1930 and a drought turned Oklahoma into a dust bowl, Grandpa Looney lost his farm. To survive, everyone in the family worked in the cotton fields, starting in April, and ending when the last boll had been picked, usually early November. Year by year, the drought became worse. The dark rain clouds ceased to come, and the cotton fields, like everything else in Oklahoma, dried up and blew away in huge clouds of dust.

After Yvonne, the baby of the family, died of untreated whooping cough because they had no money to pay a doctor, Wilburn—the fourth child and second son—realized he had to leave Oklahoma and find work to help the family. When Grandma refused to let him take the rails or hitchhike, he fixed a broken motorcycle and took off for California on a hot July morning. Wilburn soon found work here in the Salinas Valley and further down the dusty dirt road in the San Joaquin Valley. He took what work he could find and was grateful to have money left over to send home.

Two months later, after a long day of working in the fields, Wilburn was killed when a large farm truck struck his motorcycle. His mangled body was sent back to Oklahoma for burial. A cloud of gloom hung over Mama's family, devastated by the loss of two children in less than four months.

Soon after the accident, Grandma Looney received a letter from Fresno, California, informing her of the death benefits payable by the insurance carrier of the company whose truck had struck and killed Wilburn.

Grandma Looney refused to talk about the letter, and it lay unanswered on the table for months. After a while, the insurance company sent a representative to the Looney house. Grandma Looney listened in silence as he pleaded with her to sign the paper and take the money. Grandma Looney quietly but fiercely asserted they would not take a penny of blood money.

The insurance representative looked around the dirt floor shack at the hungry children and the gaunt, long faces of the parents. Never had insurance money been refused by anyone. He pleaded with Grandma Looney to take the money for the sake of the family.

"No," she whispered resolutely, slowly shaking her head, "I will never accept money for the death of my son." He pleaded with her to reconsider. She refused.

As the door closed behind him, Grandma Looney took the letter and placed it on the burning fire logs. The barefoot children watched the letter burn until the last ember vanished.

As I passed humble wood crosses in ditches and farm fields, on the side of railroad tracks, and on fences, trees, and telephone posts, I said a prayer for Uncle Wilburn and each precious life that ended suddenly and tragically on the side of the road.

The road through Salinas Valley was long and tedious. A spot underneath my big toe felt hot, a sure sign a blister was forming. I sat on a rock and removed my socks to dry my feet with a small paper towel I kept in my pocket, and applied petroleum jelly.

And then I saw the small "teardrops" scattered in the dirt below where I sat. They were the small, droplet-shaped seeds of a wild grass, called Job's tears, named after the Old Testament prophet who endured great suffering.

The grass filled the shallow ditch in front of me. I stared in silent reverence at the thin green stalks blowing in the wind. Almost hidden in the tall grass was a small wood cross. A faded yellow plastic rose was next to the cross.

It was another roadside memorial. Someone had planted Job's tears next to a cross, and wind had scattered the seeds.

I was hot and tired, thirsty and exhausted, and my body hurt.

I was walking to forget. For five hundred miles I had walked quickly, hoping to leave myself and my fears behind—but my fears were still with me. Job's tears opened the vault where they were buried.

The seeds ripped open old wounds and unleashed years of emotion. Waves of grief and sorrow swelled up inside me and poured out, assaulting my thin body. I heaved and shook with anguish, and tears cleansed the raw, open wounds.

I cried for Mama and Daddy, and Grandpa and Grandma Looney, and Uncle Wilburn, and Grandpa and Grandma Littlefield, and my brother Edmond, and all the souls who begged God for relief and mercy as they lay dying.

I cried for Steve Wang, and Marko, and Barbara, and Joan, and Sally, and Mary, and the hundreds of patients who had sat beside me at cancer clinics and hospitals—who begged God to let them live.

I cried for my friends and family who lived honest and simple lives, and begged God to give them strength and courage.

I cried for Job and Saint Agnes and missionaries and persecuted people of faith who begged God to protect them from evil.

I cried for me. For the thousand dark days and sleepless nights when grace and gospel music kept me alive, and I pleaded, on bended knee, *Lord, help me, please. I'm begging you.* I cried until the paper towel I dried my sweaty feet on was soaked to shreds with tears.

And then I could cry no more. I felt a sense of release, of lightness. As if something I had been carrying for six hundred miles had now been shed. I didn't need to carry it anymore.

I put a handful of Job's tears seeds in my pocket and continued walking. Afterward, whenever I passed a roadside memorial, I paused to say a prayer and drop a seed or two.

You cannot avoid hardship in this life. It had been instilled in me in those drought years of childhood, as I'd watched Edmond struggle to overcome alcoholism, as I'd watched Daddy work so hard in the cotton field for so little and Mama make a life for herself and her children. We can't take away hardship. But we can stop and remember. We can acknowledge pain. We can pray for grace.

And, ultimately, healing.

—————

Walking up old San Juan Road north of Salinas, I heard someone call my name. The voice was clear and distinct. I stopped and looked around. "Yes," I answered. No one was there. The only sound was a quiet wisp of wind. *Thou knowest not the way of the spirit, as you do not know what is the way of the wind.*[3]

I never heard the voice again. I still listen for it.

I arrived at Mission San Juan Bautista two hours later.

An original, unpaved section of El Camino Real borders the mission, and I took off my hiking boots and walked barefoot in the dirt to feel its holiness.

Since the beginning of its history, this King's Highway is where missionaries and thousands of other souls have sung aloud, sunk upon their knees in prayer, and wept in anguish.[4]

As my bare feet stirred up their dust, I tingled with their aliveness.

I knew I was walking on holy ground.

The next day, Dale arrived to drive QRandom, and I said a very grateful good-bye to Deb Dawley. From then on, I walked alone, and each day, Dale parked QRandom and rode his bicycle to where I was walking and explored nearby roads and trails as I walked.

The next nine days took me through more strawberry fields and vineyards and over precipitous mountain trails. This section of the walk took me to four missions: Mission Santa Cruz, Mission Santa Clara, Mission San José, and Mission San Francisco.

Of all twenty-one missions, Mission Santa Cruz was the only disappointment. It was built next to Branciforte, a colony of ex-convicts and thieves banished from Mexico that later became the town of Santa Cruz. The mission suffered from disasters caused by both nature and men; it was abandoned in the early 1800s and destroyed by an earthquake in 1857. Today, there is no mission, only a small replica church and adobe dwelling with limited hours of operation, run by the California State Parks. I walked along busy city streets for three hours and asked a dozen people if I was on the right road. None were even aware there was a mission. Most didn't know what a mission was. I felt sad. When a mission becomes a museum and tourist relic and no longer functions as the spiritual heart of a community, something very precious is lost.

In contrast, Mission Santa Clara, a three-day walk from Santa Cruz, was alive and vibrant. The old mission moved five times, victim to floods, fires, and earthquakes, before its final resting place as the heart-center of Santa Clara University. Thousands of students pass the mission on the way to class, filling the air with laughter and vitality. The bell tower holds three ancient bells that still ring jubilantly over campus and town.

The three-day walk from Mission San José in Fremont to Mission San Francisco took me across San Francisco Bay. As I walked the five-mile Dumbarton Bridge across the bay, Dale gleefully raced his bicycle back and forth four times. I laughed at my husband, as giddy and adventurous as a ten-year-old boy. This was why I had married him. Joy was always present, adventure something to be sought. How thankful I was to have him by my side all these years.

———

I had a few Job's tears seeds left in my pocket that I had been saving for Palo Alto.

My friend Steve Wang and his teenage daughter, Jacqueline, were buried there, a few blocks from El Camino Real.

I missed Steve. Since his death, I had not been back to our favorite spot in front of the large floor-to-ceiling window at Stanford Cancer Center. The Job's tears were for Steve and Jacqueline—and Steve Jobs, who was buried in an unmarked grave in the same cemetery. Although I did not know Steve Jobs, I mourned for him too.

Steve Wang had seen him occasionally at Stanford Cancer Center. "Edie, we need to hang in there; there's got to be a breakthrough soon. Some of the smartest guys in the world are working on this, and a guy as rich as Steve Jobs can afford to spend billions on a cure," Steve would say, and we'd both smile and shake our heads with fervent anticipation.

Steve Jobs was a bright shining light to those of us living with stage 4 cancer. He was our superhero, a master of the physical universe—rich, creative, and uncompromising. Surely, we thought, with his wealth and sheer intelligence, he could outsmart cancer, even find a cure. We were betting on him to defeat cancer and save us. "Being the richest man in the cemetery doesn't matter to me," he said in a 1993 interview. "Going to bed at night saying we've done something wonderful, that's what matters to me."[5]

He loved to walk and was famous in Palo Alto for his long walks. It was the first thing he did with his sister when they were reunited as adults.

I wondered if walking kept his inner flame alive, too, the way it does mine.

Steve Jobs's final moments, as recounted by his sister, Mona Simpson, at his memorial service, had helped me reconcile the end of *me*. She wrote, "Steve's final words were: "OH WOW. OH WOW. OH WOW.""[6]

We can't know what he meant, but the words thrilled me. What did Steve see? I wanted to see too—but not yet.

Not yet. I wanted to live OH WOW, OH WOW, OH WOW *now*, and not wait until death.

I scattered the remaining Job's tears next to mission bells along El Camino Real in Palo Alto, pausing for a prayer of gratitude, and kept walking.

That evening, I fell asleep, feeling that I, too, had done something wonderful.

I arrived midafternoon at Mission San Francisco, known from the beginning as Mission Dolores, after the swampy lagoon in front that was later filled in and graded. Two new friends, Ruth West and Lin Galea, walked with me. Dale greeted us with cheers and applause in front of the mission, along with two lifelong friends, Arch and Jeannie McGill, and a group of tourists recruited by Jeannie.

After a quick tour of the mission, I had another hilly four miles to walk to

Lombard Street to a motel near Golden Gate Bridge, ready for an early morning departure when I would cross the bridge to Mission San Rafael.

Walking through Los Angeles, and now through San Francisco, I saw large numbers of people living in cars. They were modern-day Joads, parked in carefully selected residential areas and quiet streets. I felt compassion, but did not pity them; pity is often dismissive and diminishing. Maybe this was their choice; this is what they wanted. Their car was their home, and at least they had one. Many don't. Edmond often didn't. Grandpa Littlefield didn't. Most Dust Bowl Okies didn't. They hitchhiked mostly, or rode the rails, and stopped just long enough to make enough money to move on, leaving only a dusty footprint.

There are as many ways to live life as there are roads to walk. On the mission trail, we see them all.

———

The two-day walk to Mission San Rafael was divinely beautiful; from the marina and presidio of San Francisco, across the Golden Gate Bridge to Sausalito and Scotts Valley, and then along the Larkspur Path, up steep Wolfe Grade Road to the mission.

Mission San Rafael was founded as a sunny health resort, a hospital for Ohlone Indians sickened by foggy, damp, and windy San Francisco. There is nothing left of the original mission, not a stone or an adobe brick. A new chapel has been built in its place. I stopped to feel the sunny warmth on my face and to breathe the fresh morning air. Twenty miles to go. It was hard to believe I was nearing the end of El Camino Real mission trail.

———

If you ask Sandy Briery the most terrifying part of the eight-hundred-mile mission trail walk, she doesn't hesitate: "Crossing the Petaluma River Bridge on Highway 37 outside Sonoma."

The bridge was half a mile long, with only an eighteen-inch ledge to walk on and only a thigh-high concrete guardrail to protect a walker from falling off the bridge into the swirling water below. Cars and trucks whiz past, and there are frequent accidents.

If it scared Sandy, I knew the bridge must be bad, and I worried about it for days. To calm my fears, Dale walked the bridge the day before and felt it was safe. "Just don't look down," he advised, "and don't worry about trucks blowing you over the low guardrail; there's water several hundred feet below if you fall." I think that was supposed to make me feel better.

So I braced myself with deep breaths, calming thoughts, and prayer before I began. I forced myself to look straight ahead and not down at the river hundreds of feet below. The tips of my fingers skimmed the low railing, and I was acutely mindful to not fall. I breathed slowly and whispered the Jesus prayer. Afterward, I felt great personal satisfaction from facing and overcoming my fear. "Cross that bridge when you come to it" is a reminder not to worry, and surely comes from fear of crossing dangerous rivers.

After the Petaluma River Bridge, I walked several hours on Highway 37, past Pedestrians Prohibited signs. A highway patrolman stopped and cautioned me to be careful. I stepped over several rattlesnake carcasses and was more terrified of the tall grass at the side of the road than of traffic.

I arrived that evening at Cline Cellars, where Dale and Arch and Jeannie were waiting with a glass of champagne. Tomorrow would be my last day walking, just six miles to Mission San Francisco Solano in Sonoma.

When Dale and I woke up that morning, the parking lot next to QRandom was filled with friends who came to walk with me to the last mission. There was Ron Graham, who had loaned me QRandom; Ron Briery; two new friends, Steven Woody and Marucia Britto; and several strangers who'd heard about the walk and decided to join us. It felt like a fitting way to end this journey. In celebration, in community, in gratitude.

After just two hours, and 6.4 miles, I was there.

It had taken fifty-five days of walking, three rest days, and 796.5 miles, to reach Mission San Francisco Solano, the last of the twenty-one Spanish missions in California.

I had averaged fifteen miles a day.

As we approached the mission, Arch and Jeannie waved and cheered. The State Park manager had tied twenty-one white balloons above one of Harrye Forbes's small iron mission bells. An original three-hundred-pound mission bell hung in front of the mission, and before going inside I joyfully rang it twenty-one times.

Inside the mission, a special surprise was waiting. I couldn't believe my eyes when I saw Sally Canfield Coupe, my roommate at Stanford Hospital, where, seven months before, we'd both had surgery to remove cancer from our lungs. We collapsed in each other's arms, laughing and crying, too overcome with emotion to speak. Just for a moment, we shared the most utter, complete joy that comes from simply being alive and filled with grace. And we both knew why I walked all those miles and never wanted to stop.

The day I started walking the mission trail I didn't know how far or how long I would be able to walk. It was a walk of faith, taken one step at a time. It had connected me with God and grace, healed my body, empowered me emotionally, and cleansed my spirit. I was born anew.

I felt truly alive walking El Camino Real mission trail, and even though I was physically exhausted, I didn't want to stop. When I stopped, I felt the same rocking sensation people feel when they have been on a boat for a long time. My body was still walking even when I was standing still.

15

When I walked into Sonoma, I passed a large, weathered mission bell inscribed "Loreto 1697." The bell was a reminder that the California El Camino Real mission trail started in Loreto, Mexico, and the first mission was built there in 1697, seventy years before missionaries set foot in San Diego.

Looking up at the Loreto bell, I noticed several hawks soaring above me and riding the wind before turning south and out of sight. I longed to follow them, and I felt the stirrings in my heart for another wild and crazy adventure.

I knew right then that if God allowed me the time, I was going to Loreto. I was going to walk the mission trail where it started.

No one had walked the entire sixteen-hundred-mile El Camino Real mission trail from Mexico to California in 250 years, not since Junípero Serra.

I had already walked half of it. I yearned to walk all of it.

The long walk from San Diego to Sonoma was emotionally and physically cleansing and spiritually transforming.

It was also more.

Every long walk is a walk away from something, and I was walking away from cancer. I was motivated by fear. I walked to rid myself of the terror of cancer and to overcome the fear of it coming back. For more than five years, I had lived with a constant, pressing awareness of death. I had become a hostage. I had tiptoed around cancer, fearful of arousing it, fearful of its rage.

I knew the best way to live with fear was to keep moving. Once I started to walk, I was not afraid anymore; all was well. I felt that if I stopped walking, the cancer would come back.

I didn't stop walking.

Cancer came back anyway.

———

Exactly two years after the start of the mission walk, I saw it smiling back at me on a CT scan.

This time, it was in my remaining left lung, and the tumor was deep. Surgery would require removing a wedge of healthy lung tissue, and Stanford Cancer Center opted for high-intensity radiation instead. A month later, I had parathyroid surgery and a biopsy of a tumor in my throat.

Once again, cancer was a wake-up call—and a call to action. I was determined to not let cancer squash my dream.

Harry Crosby, a historian/photographer who grew up in the San Diego area, had come closer than anyone to retracing Serra's epic 1769 journey from Loreto, Mexico, to San Diego. Harry's dozen or so hand-drawn maps from multiple mule-pack trips in the mid-twentieth century were the only detailed maps that existed of the old eight-hundred-mile Baja El Camino Real mission trail.

For months, I pored over Harry's maps, comparing them to old trail maps and locations mentioned in historical reports and journals.

Eighty percent of Lower California was rugged sierras and a land so cruel that horses and even surefooted mules were known to plunge off sheer steep slopes, and where bones of parched, thirsty men melted into desert sand.

Could I make this more than a pipe dream? Could I really do it?

I read everything I could find about the mission trail in Mexico: missionary journals written three hundred years ago; diaries of gold rush prospectors who journeyed up the Mexico peninsula on the old El Camino Real to California; and three centuries of scientists, naturalists, and adventurers who had written of the treacherous deserts and mountains from Mexico to California.

I slowly began to develop confidence and belief that I could do what no one else had done. The desire felt almost primal, to beat not only cancer but also the elements I knew I would face; the improbability of somehow navigating this ancient trail was empowering.

I could do it.

I would do it.

I was ready.

I was ready to be free of worry.

I was ready to be free of fear.

I was ready to be free of cancer.

I was ready to be free of self.

I was ready for the grandest adventure of my life. I was ready to walk eight hundred miles through one of the driest deserts in the world and through the spine of the Sierras. I was not about to let cancer stop me.

And I had to do it now.

PART 3

HOLY GROUND

*"Take off your sandals, for the place where
you are standing is holy ground."*
—EXODUS 3:5 NIV

16

With no time to spare, I leapt into action. I met with Harry Crosby, who was in his early nineties, at his home in San Diego to review his maps. Afterward, I asked if he had any advice. "Never go into the Sierras of Mexico without a man bred in the Sierras," he said. "You've got to find vaqueros to come with you. They are the only ones who know those mountains and the trails. They will guide you and do their best to protect you along the way."

Vaqueros were men of legend, descended from conquistador and Indian, from cow herder and muleteer, from goat rancher and farmer, living in remote desert and mountain ranchos, their lives unchanged since the time of the missionaries. And their lives were still connected by the old El Camino Real mission trail.

Cowboys of the West owe everything to Mexican vaqueros. Spanish explorers, soldiers, and missionaries brought the first cattle and horses to America; they brought cowboy hats, leather vests and jackets, and cowboy boots with spurs. They brought know-how to make saddles, saddlebags, and canteens, to braid ropes and bridles, and to forge horseshoes. They brought the love of God and nature, and the good news of Jesus Christ. They also brought sad country songs and love ballads.

I googled "Loreto" and "mules" and "vaquero" and "cowboy" and found Trudi Angell. *What a serendipitous name and good omen*, I thought.

I e-mailed Trudi and discovered she was an American with dual citizenship who spent summers in California and the rest of the year in Loreto, arranging kayak and mule-pack trips for tourists. Trudi said she could loan one of her vaqueros for a week and rent me two mules for the first couple of weeks. She could make no promises or commitments beyond that.

I was undaunted. The call of the Old Mission Trail was louder than fear, and it drowned out common sense. There were vaqueros who knew the old trail. I knew in my heart that I would find them—or they would find me.

I was ready to start planning.

My life had been lived in three-month increments in between CT scans ever since I was diagnosed with cancer more than eight years ago. I had a CT scan scheduled in late September, and while I was anxious to book my flight to Mexico, I was reluctant to finalize plans until I was certain there were no new tumors.

As we stared at this new CT scan, we saw a larger mass in my left lung than before radiation. The Stanford imaging radiologist was concerned it was tumor growth, but both Dr. Fisher and my lung radiology oncologist, Dr. Maximilian Diehn, felt it was not cancer but inflammation and scar tissue from the high-intensity radiation six months earlier. Another scan was scheduled for the end of December. If it continued to grow, we would know it was cancer.

I wasn't going to wait around for three months wondering which doctor was right.

A day after my CT scan, Trudi Angell confirmed that her vaquero, Chema Arce, was available for six days, and could be ready with a saddle mule and pack mule to leave October 25—Founder's Day—in Loreto.

I had less than a month to get everything ready, and then two months to walk from Loreto to the California border—more than eight hundred miles—and arrive back home before my next scan at Stanford Cancer Center. Hopefully, before Christmas.

I immediately booked a nonrefundable flight from Tijuana to Loreto and bought a tent. I hadn't been camping in years. The salesman at REI assured me the tent was the lightest made, it had LED lights inside, and took less than three minutes to set up. I took it home and spent an hour untangling all the pieces and setting it up on my living room floor.

In the garage, I found an inflatable mattress, pillow, and small Jetboil that Dale had used on a 2,500-mile bicycle trip the summer before. I needed a camera that could withstand sweaty mule backs, cactus spurs, and being dropped on granite boulders and desert sand. Harry Crosby suggested I ask his friend Bill Evarts, a renowned desert photographer. Bill was full of practical advice and professional know-how and pointed me toward a pocket-size Olympus. After a few hours searching photography and comparison sites, I decided on an Olympus Tough camera—shockproof, waterproof, sandproof, and idiotproof.

I was so busy that a week slipped by before I remembered I had forgotten the most important thing to pack—emergency medicine!

I have a lot of unusual digestion and breathing issues. My liver, bile duct, gallbladder, and colon have been compromised by cancer, chemotherapy, and radiation, and hacked away by surgery. My throat was still sore and scratchy from the last surgery. And then there was my mostly missing right lung and possible large tumor mass growing in my left lung.

Not exactly the picture of health.

Yet I knew whom to call about emergency medicine. Someone who would know exactly what I needed and who would not tell me I was nuts to even consider such a crazy walk—Dr. Fisher's physician assistant, Annie Johnson. She had saved my life on more than one occasion when I was in an emergency room and Dr. Fisher could not be reached. Annie was a farm girl from Nebraska who dealt with life and death every day in the cancer center. She was fearless.

Annie had studied osteopathic medicine and wilderness survival medicine. She responded immediately and e-mailed a wilderness medicine list entitled "Dr. Donner Survival Kit—Physician Expedition Kit," along with a note: "We can choose the best ones and set you out on the walking trail with the most comprehensive but lightest survival kit for any medical need you might experience."

An hour later, she called with her specific recommendations and placed an order at the local pharmacy.

When I picked up the emergency medicine from the pharmacy, there were so many pills and bottles and containers that the carrying case they required was larger than my tent. I had already forgotten what Annie had told me about each one. She got back on the phone and patiently explained what to take for venomous snake and scorpion bites; for acute allergic reactions; for infections such as malaria, pneumonia, or Lyme disease; for broken bones and pain; for toothache and flu. There were multiple prescriptions for diarrhea, depending on the severity and whether it was from parasites, bad water, or bacterial infection. I was up until midnight labeling each container in Spanish and in English, and making a list of what to take given the calamity.

The next day, I was on the phone with my best friend, Jan Boelen Sinn. "Why are you doing this?" she asked.

I paused to think. Sure, I could be at home, living a leisurely half-awake life: sleeping late and never seeing the sunrise; occasionally glimpsing sunsets through paned glass windows; watching actors live fake, scripted dramatic lives on television; whiling away the hours sharing with friends on social media; shopping and stuffing my pantry, closet, and life with more unnecessary stuff; and participating in political buffoonery.

I had worked too hard to save my life to waste it.

"The only time I feel truly alive is when I'm outside walking with God along the old mission trail," I answered simply.

———

A week before I was set to depart, Trudi and Harry encouraged me to reach out to a mutual friend, Eve Ewing, for advice. Sixty years ago, Eve had ridden mules from Rancho San José Meling, high in the Sierras, down the coast of the Baja Mexico peninsula.

I could tell Eve was a straight shooter, and she reminded me of Sally Canfield Coupe.

"I'm not sure it's possible to walk or ride a mule through the Sierras," she warned. "No one has been on the old El Camino Real since before God was a baby."

I laughed. This woman was a kindred spirit.

"There's nothing but boot-destroying, ankle-twisting lava rock. I rode pretty much along the coast, and even there I wore through three pairs of shoes, and I only got off my mule to pee, adjust the saddle, or sleep!

"If you're a Southwest ranch gal, that will help." Eve looked at me quizzically.

She didn't wait for me to answer, and I was glad. I didn't want to tell her I was a down-in-the-dirt Okie, raised on a cotton farm; that I grew up dreaming of being a cowboy, and the only horse I'd ever been on in my life was Daddy's ancient plow horse, Old Nellie.

I smiled at that memory. Old Nellie's back was so broad that seven of us could ride on top of her together. We would ride around the pasture, spooking the cows and chickens, pretending to be wild cowboys. Never mind that we were barefoot and bareheaded, and didn't have a saddle or a bridle. The ones in front hung on to Old Nellie's mane, and the rest of us hung on to them. If one started to fall, we all fell, landing in a pile in the soft dirt or warm cow manure, laughing so hard we wet our pants and got a good scolding from Mama.

Except for a very short and very bad experience on an old mare in the Rockies, I hadn't been on a horse since Old Nellie died. And I had never seen a mule.

"It is said God protects fools and children," Eve continued in the same breath, smiling. "I hope you are both."

The flight to Loreto left Tijuana in the afternoon, and I was still cramming stuff into gear bags when the Mexican driver arrived to take me across the border to the airport.

I looked out of place in the departure lounge. The women, all American tourists, wore sandals, brightly colored sundresses, and sun hats, and were ready for the beach. I wore a wool felt cowboy hat with the chin cord cinched tight under my neck; desert boots made for the British Army; a long-sleeved, slightly wrinkled, western-style cotton shirt; desert sand–colored Cabela's nylon cargo pants; and my tattered twenty-two-pocket fishing vest, bulging with walking essentials and *pesos*.

I sat in a window seat, hoping for a view of the Sierras and desert, but the plane flew mostly along the coast. Most tourists coming to Baja (Lower) California aren't aware anything exists there but beautiful beaches and a few paved highways traversing the peninsula.

As we approached Loreto, the plane hovered above the huge Sierra de la Giganta, Mountain of the Giantess, a massive mountain barrier three hundred miles long. The missionaries named it *Giganta* because it looked like a sleeping giantess stretched out over the land. Down below her was what one missionary described as "a miserable, wretched land . . . nothing but a thorny heap of stones, a pathless, waterless rock . . . where time seems to stand still."[1]

I stared out the window at the giantess and shivered, knowing in two days I would be down there in her bosom amid huge slabs of steep rock and cactus, alone with a vaquero, a pack mule, and a saddle mule.

I was undeterred. Whatever might come, I would not turn back. The old mission trail was my Mecca, my Jerusalem, and my Canterbury.

The farm girl was going back to the country. I was going to be a cowboy.

———

I arrived in Loreto on October 24, a day before my vaquero, José "Chema" María Arce, was set to arrive. Chema lived hundreds of miles from Loreto, on a roadless ranch high in Sierra de San Francisco, and had a nine-hour bus ride to Loreto.

Trudi met me at the hotel early the next morning to ensure I was adequately prepared. Trudi was a no-nonsense woman with a genuinely friendly smile and long gray hair pulled back in a ponytail. She lived on a ranch on the outskirts of Loreto, where she kept a supply of mules and gear for adventuresome tourists who came her way. Trudi had brought two mules, Dulce and Ratón, down from the mountain pasture where they had been eating and resting over the long, hot summer months, so I could meet them. They would be two of my companions on this first part of my journey.

Ratón and Dulce were grazing in Trudi's backyard, and she was excited for me to see them, but first she wanted to see what a gringa tenderfoot had packed for a two-month trip alone, with vaquero and pack mule in the wild of the Sierras, in a land of scarce water.

I laid everything out on the bed in my hotel room: large classic wristwatch, wool felt cowboy hat and sports hat; nylon rattlesnake gaiters; two pairs of pants, three long-sleeved cotton shirts; one pair of military desert boots; three pairs of socks; one pair of silk long johns for pajamas and base layer; nylon jacket with zippered pockets; a down vest; three pairs of panties; Frogg Toggs rain poncho; microfiber towel; two Buff headscarves; my twenty-two–pocket fishing vest with essentials (passport and ID, hairbrush, toothbrush, shampoo, toothpaste, mouthwash, floss, hand sanitizer, sunscreen, Vaseline, Lubriderm, pocket light, bottle opener, money clip, eye drops, pocket-size New Testament, Moleskine pocket journal, pen, tissues, whistle, pepper spray, red Chanel lipstick, perfume); Dale's sleeping bag, inflatable mattress, pillow, ground cover, sixteen-ounce Jetboil and pan with utensils; small bottle of Dawn detergent; ultralight tent and ground cover, Olympus Tough pocket camera with two batteries, iPhone, satellite emergency phone with three batteries; two small USB rechargeable battery packs; pocket-size Spanish dictionary; four ten-liter dromedary water bags; Camelback UV light purifier and two water bottles; three butane lighters, pocket hatchet/hammer, collapsible camp chair, collapsible trekking pole; ninety Wet Ones antibacterial wipes, and sixty Pampers baby wipes; three large stuff bags and four small ones; forty assorted dehydrated packaged meals; Cashel pommel bag and saddle cushion; map case; two large medicine carrying cases; and four zippered money bags stuffed with *pesos*.

Altogether it weighed forty pounds and fit in two medium-sized REI canvas gear bags; one contained the water bags and packaged meals; the other, everything else.

Trudi looked over my gear, mentally ticking off items. "You've done just about the best job I've ever seen," she said as I beamed, happy as a first grader. I had learned a lot about walking long distances.

She added, "You will need an enamel cowboy cup for campfire coffee, and a machete, maybe two."

Trudi suggested I pack just what was needed from Loreto to Comondú, and she promised to bring the rest of my gear when she came to pick up Chema in a week. I was relieved. I had been nervous about carrying so much cash. I left all my money except enough for the week's expenses with Trudi in the locked gear bag.

I figured one gear bag would be enough. After all, when Junípero Serra left Mission Loreto in 1769 on his three-month journey to San Diego, he took only a loaf of bread and a piece of cheese.

Before I left, the couple who ran the hotel gave me a large polyester men's shirt that almost hung to my knees, after Trudi warned that cactus would shred cotton fibers. Nylon was more thorn resistant, she said.

Chema and I planned to depart Mission Loreto on Sunday, Founder's Day, after sunrise mass and a traditional blessing of the mules by the parish priest. Founder's Day celebrated the establishment of Mission Loreto Conchó on October 25, 1697. On that day, 318 years ago, Jesuit missionary Juan María Salvatierra placed a painting of his beloved patron saint, the Virgin of Our Lady of Loreto, in a small chapel with a wooden cross he had built a few days earlier, and founded the first mission in Lower California.

There was nothing here when the fifty-year-old Italian-born missionary arrived with a few sailors and soldiers, after twenty-two years of missionary work on the mainland in Guadalajara. Water was scarce or nonexistent. Every form of plant or tree life bristled with thorns. There was no food. The desert people barely survived on roots, seeds, and a worm about the size of a man's little finger. There was scant shade, and the naked Monqui Indians slept on bare ground under stars. They had never seen horses, mules, or cows. Their language consisted of fewer than four dozen words.

Salvatierra was a man of optimism and action and set out to tame this wild land, feed the Monqui, and share the word of Jesus Christ. For the next seventy years, the missionaries often starved and considered abandoning the godforsaken dust hole. It was impossible to grow food, so corn was donated by missionaries on the mainland and brought over the treacherous waters of the Gulf of California in rickety, leaking boats, often arriving spoiled.

The missionaries hung on and barely survived. Salvatierra cooked, built, ministered, learned the language, played the guitar, and danced with the Monqui. He was so loved that twenty years later, when he was slowly dying and taken back to Guadalajara, tribal elders gathered along the road to kiss his hand, ask for a blessing, and carry him. This great apostle of Lower California was buried in a Guadalajara church, near the altar of our Lady of Loreto he erected decades earlier as a young man. Surely, in the rafters, angels sang his praise.

Chema and I had to get started very early. We knew the desert heat would quickly sear the sand in immense Arroyo de las Parras, the only way out of Loreto, and the beginning of the old El Camino Real mission trail through Mexico to California.

But Trudi wanted us to wait until the ten o'clock mass. "The children will get a thrill from seeing the mules," she pleaded. I gave in, despite misgivings about leaving so late, with temperatures nearing one hundred degrees and a long walk of twenty-five miles to the next mission, Mission San Javier.

I was to meet Trudi and Chema before mass at the back of the old three-hundred-year-old stone church. I didn't speak much Spanish; Trudi would cue me when to go to the altar for the blessing. The church was filled with families, and children ran gaily up and down the aisles. I could hardly hear the mass. Everyone was dressed in Sunday best except for me. The children stared at me, a foolish-looking American woman sitting alone wearing a wool cowboy hat, military-style desert boots, and a fishing vest.

Mass was almost over when I finally spotted Trudi and Chema sitting in the front of the church close to Salvatierra's altar of Our Lady of Loreto. I sheepishly made my way down the side aisle to join them. Although I didn't understand much of what the priest was saying, I did make out that he was talking about cancer and me and introducing Chema. Trudi nudged Chema and me to go to the altar for the blessing. It was stifling hot. The priest heroically tried to say the blessing and simultaneously wipe sweat flowing from his brow into the holy water. The blessing was almost as long as the mass. It was past noon when the priest finished, after which everyone immediately stampeded out of the church to go home.

Not one child stayed behind to see the mules.

After the priest blessed Ratón and Dulce and sprinkled them with holy water, we were on our way. Temperatures were already in the mid-nineties and the air so hot and dry I could hardly breathe. Chema didn't seem to mind the heat. In fact, he never seemed to mind anything. Chema was a true Louis L'Amour cowboy. He seemed ageless—a man of the outdoors, fit and lean, with a calm demeanor. His face was neither happy nor sad. His eyes were observant and lively, and his emotions were still and quiet.

Chema and I made our way from the mission to Arroyo de las Parras on the outskirts of Loreto. I walked, Chema rode Dulce, the bigger of the two mules, and Ratón, tethered behind, carried our gear—which was very little, thanks to Trudi's help.

But we hadn't factored in the celebrations of Founder's Day weekend, a popular holiday, and the major event was drag racing—in the arroyo. Everyone in Loreto seemed to be there, partying, drinking, and cooking. The arroyo, an immense gulch filled with sand and debris, was overrun with drag racers and the air saturated with the smell of diesel and propane. Fine desert sand and dust hung so thick in the air that it was hard to see a few feet ahead.

Dogs barking, horns blaring, music blasting, people shouting, children screaming, and beer cans and trash everywhere. What a disaster for a muleteer and a walker!

The mules were skittish, and Chema wrestled to keep control by dropping down the ditch into the dusty arroyo. I continued walking on the road but couldn't breathe in the thick fumes and dust. Chema was struggling in the arroyo, and soon he and the mules came up the steep embankment. He crossed the road, and slowly and cautiously drove the mules down the vertical embankment to the street below. I slid down the embankment on my rear, feet first and off the ground, and followed him and the mules, the mules stirring up even more dust and adding more anxiety to the chaos.

Down below it was a bit quieter and less dusty, but growling dogs were everywhere, running at the mules and snipping at their hooves, snarling and baring their teeth at me. I had my water bottle in a sling and used it to hit approaching dogs on the head, to keep them away. I picked up several large rocks to throw.

I started coughing uncontrollably, my eyes swollen, throat scratchy—an insane environment for lung cancer. "Stop," my raspy voice cried out at Chema above the ruckus. "*Yo enferma!*" I wheezed in my rotten Spanish. I struggled to talk and couldn't breathe.

Chema didn't need to speak English to know the mission walk was finished for the day. He pulled the mules to the side of the road and called Trudi to come pick us up.

She apologized profusely for the bad timing and the carnival atmosphere along the sandy arroyo. Chema headed back to Trudi's house with the mules, and Trudi drove me back to the hotel, where I checked back into my room—which had not been made up, and looked as if I'd just left.

I was right back where I'd started.

17

After the disastrous, failed beginning, I had a restless, sleepless night and lay awake in bed until the alarm sounded at five o'clock. It was dark outside when Trudi picked me up from the hotel. She was still feeling bad about yesterday's fiasco. We drove back to the arroyo, arriving just before sunrise. Chema and the mules were already there, and he was saddled up, ready to hit the trail.

Trudi offered to meet Chema and me at the next mission, in San Javier, and take my overnight gear in her truck to save Chema the time and effort of packing the mule. "Sure, that would be great," I said, although trusting gear with anyone is a taboo for a walker.

Before she took off, Trudi tried to convince me to walk the auto road to Mission San Javier. "Some of the mountain streams may be too deep to cross," she warned. I got the impression she might be testing my resolve to walk the original old mission trail, instead of walking on easier, and often more direct, auto roads.

I looked at Chema, he smiled and shrugged, and I knew we could get across anything in our path.

A missionary described Arroyo de las Parras as a "stretch of sand which reaches toward the mountains . . . without grass, without a tree, a bush, or any shade."[1] He was right. I took off walking down the enormous arroyo, and Chema rode ahead on Dulce, leading Ratón on a tight rope. It was a rough walk in ankle-deep sand. I was drenched in sweat and barely able to walk. There was no shade. No breeze. Just endless miles of deep sand.

Midmorning, the mission trail cut through a rocky canyon and criss-crossed mountain streams for several hours. The walls of the canyon were high and, thankfully, provided shade. I had bought a pair of cheap canvas shoes in Loreto after Trudi suggested they might come in handy to wade across streams and wear in camp. Upon reaching the first mountain stream, I sat down on a pile of rocks and took off socks and boots, put on the canvas shoes, and slung my hiking boots over my shoulder to cross. The water flowed rapidly and expansively but was less than a foot deep. That was the last time I bothered to take off my boots. On a long walk, there is neither time nor energy to change shoes.

Several miles up the canyon, we came to a rocky and very steep dirt road leading up the eastern flank of Sierra de la Giganta. This was the original road built by the missionaries and the first Jesuit road built in Lower California, or *Baja* California. Within seventy years, they would build more than a thousand miles of road from south to north through the Sierras and to a few scattered coastal ports where food and supplies were shipped in from the mainland missions to feed the starving natives and missionaries.

When the missionaries arrived, there was no mule or horse path through this steep canyon—nothing but a precipitous gorge filled with wild grape-vines, *las parras*; thus, the name. The gorge was too treacherous for a mule or horse, so the missionaries came back with a few soldiers and Indians, and "crowbars, picks, axes and adzes." The men "each put in the work of two men," and completed a mule path in a week.[2]

This segment of El Camino Real mission trail was still as rugged as the original old mule path. My feet slipped and slid on loose rocks, and I felt like an inexperienced skateboarder trying to balance and not fall.

I walked for six hours without stopping. My legs were burning. Sweat was pouring from my brow into my eyes, blurring my vision. The glare was intense even though I was wearing sunglasses and the stiff brim of my cowboy hat shaded my eyes.

It was a sweltering and exhausting climb up the mountain road to reach the mesa at the top and a small rancho, Rancho de las Parras. We arrived at noon, exhausted and hungry.

This walk would be so much different from my California walk. Instead of the crowded highways and developed towns and cities that made me long for a stretch of wild, rugged terrain for a bit of peace and quiet, El Camino Real in Mexico is as remote and wild as you could ever get. You must reach the ranchos sprinkled along the trail if you want food or water. These ranchos have been here for years and are often owned and tended by the same families who settled here during missionary days.

At Rancho de las Parras, I depended on Chema to ask the caretakers, Alejandrina and Javier, if we could buy food for ourselves and water for the mules. While they fixed beans, fresh goat cheese, and tortillas, Chema removed saddles and bridles and filled a water bucket for the mules. Chema and I ate outside. A few feet away, the mules munched happily on dry, thorny branches of an almost-dead palo verde tree. Mules will eat essentially anything.

Rancho de las Parras has been here since the time of the missionaries. Years ago, three spinster sisters lived alone here, and each lived to be more than one hundred years old. They did everything themselves—irrigated the small garden and orchard, brined olives in huge earthen vats, and raised sheep and goats.

Mexico has always been known for its strong, beautiful women. Some historians believe California got its name from one. A popular Spanish romance novel written in early 1500 told of a tribe of Amazon women living on a mythical island. Their leader was Queen Calafia, a courageous black giantess, regal and beautiful, who dressed in robes made of gold and precious jewels. The island was made up of the wildest cliffs and sharpest precipices found anywhere in the world, "where an amazing abundance of gold and precious stones are found."[3]

Other historians believe the name California derives from a phrase that is a combination of Spanish and Latin, *callida fornax* (hot furnace) and referred to the suffocating desert heat encountered by early Spanish explorers and missionaries.

I prefer the story of Queen Calafia. It's more romantic and in keeping with the wild nature of Baja California. The story is even more interesting because the natives in Loreto told the first missionaries of a giantess who lived on the other side of Sierra de la Giganta, the enormous three-hundred-mile mountain barrier. The Indians didn't read sixteenth-century romance novels, so one wonders where their legend came from.

After lunch, it was time to keep going. No time for a siesta. I continued climbing up the steep, winding mountain road, facing the blazing hot afternoon sun as I walked west. The sun was low in the sky when I passed a small goat ranch, Rancho Viejo, original site of Mission San Javier. It was too late to stop, and there was nothing left to see anyway. In 1707, a seven-year drought dried up the water and destroyed crops, and hot, dry desert winds blew apart the original crude mission. The missionaries and Indians moved farther south to find water and build again.

A few miles from Rancho Viejo, El Camino Real veered north to Comondú, but I was determined to follow the footsteps of Junípero Serra, and I continued walking south to Mission San Javier as he did. Serra had detoured south to say farewell to his dear friend Father Francisco Palóu, and pick up supplies for his long trek north to San Diego.

After walking ten hours through sand, water, and rock, I was dehydrated—which made me feel shaky and disoriented. The last rays of the sun were fading when we finally arrived in San Javier. Chema rode ahead with the mules to feed and water them for the night—and to look for the hotel where Trudi had promised to meet up with us.

I walked alone down the cobblestone road leading to the mission. I stood a few minutes outside the massive stone walls, marveling at this Moorish fortress of desert stone.

The night was serene and beautiful; not a soul was in sight. Nighthawks circled above the bell towers, and a full moon was rising in the night sky. It was a supermoon, a full moon that occurs when the moon's orbit is closest to the earth and looks oversized. In the moonlight the mission was tinted blue and translucent against the towering black lava folds of Giganta.

The beauty took my breath away. *If I don't walk another mile or see another mission, it will all have been worth it*, I thought to myself, feeling my spirit satisfied and whole.

I finally pulled myself away to walk back down the cobblestone road to find Chema. I soon realized it had become too dark to find my way.

A block from the mission I came upon two men standing next to an old truck. They spoke no English, and I spoke little Spanish, but we managed to communicate. I asked them where the hotel was. "There is no hotel," they answered. My heart began to pound in confusion. *Then where am I staying for the night?* I somehow was able to discern that they were telling me about a woman in town who rented rooms, and they motioned for me to get in the truck and they would take me.

I am a woman alone, and not a soul knows where I am. I didn't let the thought get to me. I jumped gratefully into the front seat of the truck next to two strange men.

We stopped in front of a dark house at the edge of town. Before leaving, the men pointed to the faint outline of two mules in a darkened field a slight distance ahead, and asked if they belonged to me. I had no idea. Mules all looked alike to me—in fact, I couldn't yet tell a mule from a horse. But then I spotted Chema up the street, outside an old vacant shack. His saddle was on the ground, and he was preparing his bedroll to sleep outside under the stars.

Gratitude and relief rushed through me. I scolded myself. *Edie, it's only day two and you let yourself get lost in the dark. You've got to be aware.* I knew we were far from the land of streetlights and alarm clocks, and I would need to learn to heed nature's hours.

A young woman who spoke some English emerged from the house. She was from La Paz and visiting her mother, Rosina, who lived there, and, yes, her mother would rent us two rooms in her home. I walked across the street to the vacant shack and told Chema he didn't have to sleep outside on the ground.

I paid six hundred *pesos* for two rooms, each with a bed, no mattress cover, and a light blanket. The rooms were barren: cold concrete floors and a threadbare cloth over open, glassless windows. Sheep—or were they goats?—silently grazed a few feet from the window.

There was nothing for me to unpack. I had no clothes, toothbrush, or anything—my gear bag had been left in Trudi's truck, and she was not there.

I asked Rosina if I could pay her to fix Chema and me something to eat.

Within minutes, she prepared a skillet of homemade beans and hot tortillas. We ate voraciously.

It was getting late, and Trudi still hadn't arrived. I could barely keep my eyes open. "Can I pay you for soap and a pair of pajamas for the night?" I asked Rosina, her daughter interpreting. Rosina smiled, took my money, and returned with a pair of ruffled pink pajamas that looked new, like a precious gift never worn. She handed me a small bar of slightly used scented soap and a tattered towel.

Rosina's daughter showed me an ancient-looking, decaying shower house with a muddy floor, and asked if I wanted a shower. There was an electrical power cord strung across the ceiling that attached to a small showerhead with a hot water heating unit. I said yes even though I was unable to enjoy the warm shower; my mind was too filled with scary thoughts of electrocution—and creepy scorpions and slithery things that hang out in dank, dark places.

Trudi arrived late that night. I had already paid for her room. The next day, I discovered Trudi was given a room in a separate *casita* with a sink and water. It was luxurious compared to my tiny, barren room. I smiled. Rosina was a smart businesswoman. I was a transient stranger, never to pass this way again. Trudi would come again and bring other wayfarers and tourists.

———

I awoke early, excited to start walking the trail toward the next mission— Mission San José Comondú.

At breakfast, Trudi, Chema, and I pored over Harry Crosby's old trail maps, while Rosina fixed eggs, beans, and tortillas. Although Harry had started in Comondú, past San Javier, he sketched this portion on his map.

Chema and Trudi discussed the map in Spanish. I didn't understand most of what they were saying. Several times, Chema shook his head and said, "*No lo sé*," and I knew that meant "I don't know."

At the end of the conversation, they decided I needed a second vaquero, someone more familiar with Sierra de la Giganta. Also, Chema might need help hacking through two centuries of cactus that covered parts of the trail.

"I wouldn't be surprised if there are parts that haven't been traveled in two hundred years." Trudi chuckled at the absurdity of walking in a cactus patch.

Trudi called another vaquero from a local rancho to lend a hand. The vaquero, José Martínez Castro, knew every trail for thirty miles. José agreed to meet at noon at Rancho El Horno, one of the small goat ranches I had walked past yesterday.

Chema left on the mules and headed for Rancho El Horno.

Since I wasn't meeting up with José and Chema until noon, I asked Trudi if we could spend an hour at Mission San Javier.

The mission door was open when we arrived, but no one was there. Early morning sunlight poured through the glass windows—the first glass windows in California, handmade of sand at the mission. It took fourteen years to build this magnificent stone church quarried from the rock of Giganta.

When Junípero Serra arrived at Mission San Javier in 1769, on his way to San Diego, it was the most prosperous of all the missions. It wasn't always so. The mission was abandoned a year after it was founded when a drought dried up the water. Mission San Javier struggled to be born, was abandoned shortly after birth, and would have died in infancy if not for the arrival of Jesuit missionary Juan Ugarte in 1701. Ugarte's arrival in Loreto was the beginning of a thirty-year heroic story of sheer physical and moral courage fueled by a devotion to Jesus Christ.

At Mission Javier, Ugarte conquered climate and soil to make the mission succeed. Displaying the strength of Hercules, he built a ditch of stone and mortar to channel every drop of water in the arroyo to a small patch of wheat and corn. He imported sheep, and they multiplied until there were two thousand of them grazing in Giganta valleys. He lured a master Irish weaver living in Mexico to teach Cochimí Indians to weave wool into sacks, clothing, and blankets.

Then another drought hit. This one lasted five years, and the arroyo dried up, his crops withered and burned in the sun, and the starving people left to find water and food. Ugarte was forced to abandon the location and find a new home for Mission San Javier.

The Cochimí found a small oasis of flowing water several miles southwest of the original mission. Ugarte started again. He and the Cochimí rebuilt Mission San Javier, this time a bigger church with walls of stone and mortar. They cleared thickets of thorny cactus, removed rocks, and leveled the terrain. They channeled the small stream, and when rain fell they built conduits to make sure every raindrop was collected and flowed onto his small planting field.

Droughts always end, and rain always comes. But so did a hurricane of ferocious winds that tore down Ugarte's rebuilt church and modest dwelling and once again destroyed the crops.

He must have felt like Job, that God was punishing him in order to strengthen his faith. Yet he began building another church.

Ugarte, with all his talent and skill, did not know how to build a church of stone of this magnificence. Almost thirty years after he died, another Jesuit missionary and great builder, Miguel Barco, found an architect willing to live and labor fourteen years in such a remote barren place. Together, they finished building Mission San Javier de Viggé-Biaundó.

And the mission thrived. It blossomed like a slow-blooming desert flower into this beautiful church high in the desert Sierras.

These missions were living testaments to God's grace, because it truly defied the imagination that anyone could make what the friars made out of the sand, brush, rocks, and dirt. They took what was here and transformed it into these beautiful buildings. I was humbled to think of the spirit, the courage, the bravado, the creativity, the inspiration it took to create mission life in this stark desert.

It's impossible to describe Mission San Javier, the greatest of the Jesuit desert missions, with its towering Romanesque façade and windows set in five-feet-thick stone. One must go and stand in its presence. Trudi and I sat in awed silence in the front pew of the vacant church.

She interrupted the silence to tell how, during the Feast of San Javier in early December, Catholic pilgrims from around Mexico come to Loreto to walk or ride mules up the mountain to Mission San Javier. "They sing this song." And her soft, clear soprano voice soon filled the empty spaces.

As Trudi sang, my eyes looked heavenward, following the morning light rays coming through the dome, accentuating the vaulted ceiling and the cruciform shape of the church's floor plan.

I stood up, walked to the aisle, and lay down on the cool stone floor, to get a better look at the ceiling transept in the shape of a Latin cross. The missionaries built churches in the form of a cross facing upward toward heaven.

Modern man seldom looks in wonder at the night sky and the heavens. Maybe that's one reason we feel disconnected from God, and why we feel so big and powerful. We are big inside our boxy buildings, but mere specks of stardust outside.

As I lay looking up at the artwork on the ceiling, I felt the strongest urge to move my arms and legs up and down in the sandy dust on the floor, like a child making snow angels.

Trudi stopped singing and walked to the front of the church with its three enormous wooden altarpieces carved and gilded in Mexico and sent by ship to Loreto. Thirty-two pack mules carried the pieces over Sierra La Giganta to the mission. The three richly gilded and ornate altarpieces honor San Francisco Javier and San Ignacio de Loyola, the two greatest Jesuit saints.

It is fitting that the greatest desert church in Mexico glorifies the Jesuits. A mere seventy years after their arrival, the Spanish king, acting on lies and rumors that they were stealing the riches of the land and hoarding it for themselves, arrested the Jesuits at gunpoint and forced them to leave; many were sent to prison, where they died. They left behind fifteen missionary brothers who lay buried beneath the desert sands of this forlorn peninsula, having devoted their lives to serving Christ and feeding God's children.

At the side of the front altar there was a small board covered with *milagros*. These small metallic charms and personal items are left at church altars at time of prayer, and are often a plea for healing or a token of thankful appreciation for God's blessings. On the *milagro* board was a young boy's sock, a child's toy, a hair ribbon, and many charms—a house, truck, sheep, shoe, heart, brain—too many to count.

In one of my vest pockets, I carried several small metallic *milagro* charms of my own, bought at Mission Loreto, in the shape of lungs, stomach, feet, a man, and a family. I hung my charms on the board and prayed for healing, a safe journey, and for my family.

Before it was time to leave, I walked alone around the mission grounds.

I sat in the shade of the ancient olive tree planted by Father Juan Ugarte, where Junípero Serra rested on his way to San Diego. Father Serra had assigned the mission to his dear friend Francisco Palóu. They had traveled together from Spain to Mexico thirty years earlier, and Father Palóu would eventually join Father Serra in California, where he built the Dolores mission in San Francisco and wrote Serra's biography.

I closed my eyes and *felt* their spirits and the spirit of the place. There was a gentle breeze that cooled my face in the dry desert air. As I sat under the massive olive tree, my spirit, the spirit of the missionaries, and the spirit of the wind became one.

Afterward, I wrapped my arms around a gnarly branch twisting out of the tree's giant trunk, and gave it a good-bye hug. The Greeks believed that the vitality of an ancient olive tree was transmitted through its branches. As I walked away, my body tingled with its energy.

My mother, Dora Emma Looney Littlefield, a hired girl starting at age thirteen, attended college during the Dust Bowl Depression. (1935)

Dressed for church in one of Mama's beautiful handmade flour-sack dresses (1955)

Playing cowboy atop Old Nellie, Daddy's plow horse (1956)

My father, Edmond Varner Littlefield, on our Oklahoma cotton farm a year before his death. (1963)

Our family (Dale, Sarah, Whitney, Stefanie, and Rebekah) a year before my cancer diagnosis (2006)

Dr. George Fisher, Stanford Cancer Center, saved my life. (2007)

Hugs from Stefanie and Whitney during chemo at Stanford Cancer Center (2007)

Walking after liver surgery with Pat Erzinger's cross hanging from the pole (2007)

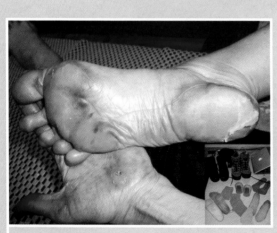

Chemo-burned feet made walking difficult. (2011)

Ten days after lung surgery, I took a four-mile walk to Stanford Dish. (2012)

Day 1: On a rainy February in 2013, at the start of my eight-hundred-mile mission walk, with Dale, Sandy and Ron Briery, and Ron Graham at Mission San Diego

Day 7: El Camino Real follows the Pacific Coast Highway north from San Diego.

Day 4: Family friend Diana Holm greets Whitney, Stefanie, Dale, and me at Mission San Luis Rey.

Day 21: Franciscan Friar Gerald Barron greets Whitney and me at Mission Santa Inés.

Day 11: Meg Grant and her husband, Greg Lecklitner, at Mission San Gabriel for the day's fourteen-mile walk

Day 23: Bell tower of Mission La Purísima in Lompoc

Day 26: Mission San Luis Obispo

Day 40: Lighting candles Easter Sunday at Mission Carmel, where Junípero Serra is buried

Day 45: Deb Dawley and QRandom on a remote mountain road near San Juan Bautista

Day 45: Mission San Juan Bautista

Day 57: El Camino Real bell marker north of San Francisco

Day 58: Arriving at Mission San Francisco Solano in Sonoma, the last mission, eight hundred miles from San Diego

Day 58: Surprise visit from Sally Canfield Coupe, my roommate at Stanford Hospital, at Mission San Francisco Solano in Sonoma

I am forever indebted to the vaqueros
who accompanied me on my journey.

José "Chema"
María Arce Arce

José "Che" Martinez Castro

Raymundo Vargas Mayora

Cesar Villavicencio Aguilar

Carlos Antonio
Villavicencio Lopez

Abraham Villavicencio
Villavicencio and son Adria

Agustín Villa Romero

Gertrudis "Chico" Arce Arce

Patricio A. Ojeda

Carlos Aaron Villavicencio

Tomás Murillo

Francisco "Pancho"
Murillo Flores

Marcos "Chikis"
Medina Arce

Porfirio "Guile"
Aviler Aquilar

Arnulfo Murillo Grosso

Joaquin "Lira" Martorell

Juan Martorell

Jonathan Presiche Meling

Alfonso "Pancho"
María Dueñas Rojas

Day 3: Mission San Javier (founded 1699), jewel of the Baja California mission churches. Sierra de la Giganta is visible in the background. (2015)

Day 9: Mission Purísima Vieja ruins, hidden and undisturbed for two hundred years

Day 12: The mule refuses to climb steep Sierra de la Giganta.

Day 14: Ruins of Mission Guadalupe

Day 16: Summit of Sierra de Guadalupe, looking north to Sierra de San Francisco

Day 16: Vaquero Agustín Villa of Rancho Santa Cruz meets up on the mission trail a day's ride from Rancho San Sebastian.

Day 17: Rock and debris-filled Arroyo Santa Cruz in Sierra de San Francisco

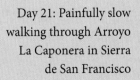

Day 21: Painfully slow walking through Arroyo La Caponera in Sierra de San Francisco

Day 23: Giant cardon cactus through Sierra de San Juan to Santa Gertrudis

Day 23: Saint's Day celebration at Mission Santa Gertrudis

Day 24: Lighting candles at Mission Santa Gertrudis

Day 26: Hot desert through Arroyo Calmalli Viejo

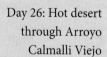

Day 27: Queso after a steep climb to Mesa Las Palmas in Sierra de San Francisco

Day 27: Vaquero Tomás Murillo coaxes mules through the deep-creviced mission trail.

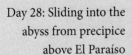

Day 28: Atop rocky peak near El Paraíso

Day 28: Sliding into the abyss from precipice above El Paraíso

Day 29: Dense cactus obliterates El Camino Real in Sierra de San Francisco.

Day 29: Vaquero Tomás Murillo at the summit of Sierra de San Francisco

Day 30: Mesa Compostela overlooking Desierto Santa María and San Borja

Day 35: Beautiful, poisonous water of Arroyo Calamajué

Day 37: Pancho Murillo follows the mission trail through Sierra Santa María

Day 37: Ruins of Mission Santa María, the last Jesuit mission in Mexico

Day 40: In Cataviña, my saddle for the next three hundred miles

Day 40: Resting in shade of giant cardon cactus near Agua Dulce

Day 43: Cenovio Gamboa Lazcano prepares coffee at a desert camp near Cerro Prieto.

Day 44: No relief from blowing sand, zillions of teensy sand flies, and scorching sun

Day 47: Vaquero Joaquin Martorell in rugged Sierra San Pedro Mártir

Day 50: Cold morning breakfast Sierra San Pedro Mártir

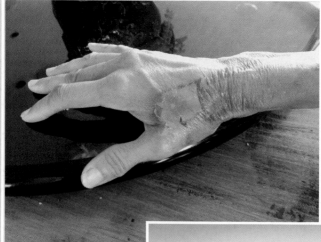

Day 53: I spilled coffee on the hand I burned in the campfire.

Day 53: Valle San Jacinto to Mission Santo Tomás

Day 58: Saying goodbye to vaquero Alfonso María Dueñas Rojas at the Tijuana border

18

I was undeterred when Trudi speculated there might be parts of the mission trail where no one had been in more than two hundred years. Knowing the trail was untraveled and overgrown with cactus made it more exciting, not less. Wilderness is invigorating. A Jesuit missionary observed, "Difficulty itself inflames the desire of an undertaking."[1]

When Trudi and I arrived midmorning at Rancho El Horno, Chema was outside, patiently waiting for José to arrive. Dulce and Ratón were near a small thorny tree, free of saddle and packs and munching away at the spiny branches to which they were tied. Trudi left after promising to meet us in Comondú at the end of the week to pick up Chema. She needed Chema to guide some tourists on a mule trip; afterward, José and I would continue alone to Mission La Purísima. I packed ten days' supply of food and *pesos*, double what was needed to get to Comondú.

It was almost noon, and Chema and I were offered coffee and a mixture of dried beef and beans served with freshly made flour tortillas. Nothing was said about payment, but it was understood that I would pay. Starting at Rancho El Horno, my customary payment at a rancho was fifty *pesos* for coffee and one hundred *pesos* for food. If given a cot, bedsprings, or a mattress to sleep on, which was rare, I would leave an additional fifty or a hundred *pesos*.

When I heard about the *ranchos* of Mexico, I imagined those depicted in

Hollywood westerns—a small but pristine ranch house with a wooden corral and a few bucolic trees. Reality is starkly different. Rancho El Horno consisted of a large, open-sided room with a dirt floor and an aging, thatched palm leaf roof with sunlight coming through. There were two small bedrooms on a concrete slab; an outdoor flushing toilet had recently been added. Saddles, horse blankets, and leather riding gear hung neatly from a beam extending across one side of the large room. On the opposite wall were ropes, halters, bridles, and a few personal items. An old wheelbarrow, a bale of hay, and a discarded, broken table were pushed to the side. Food was cooked outside and served on a counter at the far end of the room, where an aged television sat atop a stand. There were three plastic chairs on which to sit. There were no electric lights and no refrigerator. Natural sunlight filled the space, and a slight breeze stirred the air. Outside, it was hot, but inside was cool and pleasant. Dogs, cats, and sometimes birds wandered in and out.

As promised, promptly at noon, José Martinez arrived. José was saddled up on a stout white *macho* mule, Blanco, with a smaller, dark chestnut-color *mula*, Mongolita, in tow.

So began my first lesson on mules. A mule is a cross between a donkey and a horse. A *macho* mule is a male; a *mula* is female, usually smaller than a male. In a mule, never confuse small for timid or female for docile. During the course of my journey, vaqueros in the high Sierras preferred to ride female *mulas*, especially over lava rock or rough, steep terrain; the female mules were more spirited and agile than *machos*, and responded quicker to a spur thrust in the soft underbelly. *Machos* often carried the heavy packsaddles.

Throughout the day, frequent shouts of "Macho!" or "Mula!" ring out as the vaqueros whip, spur, or cajole the mules into behaving.

I wasn't sure if Dulce and Ratón were *machos* or *mulas*, and I was not inclined to get close enough to look.

I soon learned that it's hard to bond with a mule as with a horse. Mules don't allow it. They care to please no one. Men need mules. Mules don't need men.

Chema loaded my gear pack on José's *mula*, Mongolita. Neither vaquero trusted his bedroll on the pack mule. Instead, bedrolls were wrapped in leather and tied to the back of their saddles. Chema rode Dulce. Ratón was saddled up, ready for me to ride if I became unable to walk.

José and Chema studied Harry Crosby's map, then pointed to the oasis of Santa Rosalillita, famous water hole of the missionaries, as our destination for the night.

When I asked how many kilometers we were from Santa Rosalillita, José looked puzzled. He replied, "*Cinco o seis horas más o menos.*" Five or six hours, plus or minus. Travel in the cactus wilderness is not measured in kilometers, but in days and hours, the journey unknown and never certain, and always "*más o menos,*" plus or minus.

It took five hours to walk to Santa Rosalillita. Chema and José rode ahead, lost in conversation and only occasionally turning in their saddles to see if I was still following.

The old El Camino Real mission trail was in good condition in places, and nonexistent in others. The missionaries and Cochimís cleared rocks from the path and stacked them to the side, making the mission road easy to differentiate from cow trails. Sometimes El Camino Real was less than two feet wide and nothing more than a gully cleared of rock; in other places it was wide enough for a cart or wagon with rocks stacked high and neatly to the side. It went from level hard-packed surface to loose, sliding lava rock; from cactus jungle to scattered thorny bushes and sagebrush; from steep mountain trails to flat mesas; from sandy, rocky arroyos to boulder-filled, impassable arroyos. There was no water, just sand and rock. No trees, just thorny cactus and shrubby mesquite, palo blanco and palo verde. It would be this way the next three hundred miles.

Santa Rosalillita was more of a swamp than an oasis, nothing but a small pool of water filled with tall reeds and surrounded by aging date palms.

When the missionaries arrived, a small *ranchería* of Cochimís lived here, and called the place Ohobbe. Missionaries named it Santa Rosalía, and it became a small visiting mission with a chapel, run by the Cochimí. But smallpox and typhus swept the area, sickening the missionaries and killing the Indians. The stony graveyard became Santa Rosalillita, just another lost place amid rock and cactus. Unknown and forgotten.

Beginning with that first night, a camping routine was established that would remain constant until I reached the California border more than eight hundred miles to the north. We would stop an hour before sunset, whether water was close by or not. The vaquero would quickly remove packs and saddles from the mules and lead them to water if water was available, sometimes walking a mile or more in a dry arroyo. Often there was no water. If no shrubs or bushes were available for feed (there was never grass), he would tether them to long ropes close to our campsite and go in search of a scrawny mesquite or shrub brush to hack with his machete and bring to camp.

The vaquero would remove saddles and harnesses, and the heavy packs containing water and my REI gear bags from the pack mule. I would unload the pommel bag and saddlebags from my mule.

The pommel bag, which hung on the front of my saddle, contained the day's water, my Olympus pocket camera, emergency medicine, pocket flashlight, butane lighter, small combination ax and hammer, pepper spray, and small Camelback UV water purifier. An old blue canvas saddlebag with a broken zipper, borrowed from Trudi, was attached to the back of my saddle and held with a leather cord. It was stuffed with my multi-pocket vest and small nylon zippered jacket, rain poncho, water purifying tablets, Jetboil with instant coffee and sugar, a large enamel coffee mug, and fresh food, if we had any. Vaqueros are never without coffee and sugar.

Immediately after the vaquero unloaded the heavy packs, I would search out a place for my tent, ideally a flat sandy area at least five by seven feet with little cactus and few rocks. Many nights I compromised; it wasn't always possible to find such a place.

Water was most essential.

I carried two sixteen-ounce bottles of drinking water in the pommel bag, and two large ten-liter dromedary bags of fresh water in the mule pack.

The first thing I would do, even before setting up my tent, was prepare the next day's water, and make sure I had enough water to last the night. I filled the two water bottles from a dromedary bag, and when that water ran out, I would refill with water from a waterhole or a mountain stream, using my Camelback UV filter for sixty seconds to purify the water.

After preparing water, I unpacked the large REI gear bag, which contained four small duffel bags—one with nightclothes, wet wipes, and toiletries; one with tent; one with cooking supplies and food; and one with a manually inflat-able air mattress and sleeping bag. It was often windy, and the four duffel bags were used to anchor the ground cover and my tent. Once my tent was set up, I placed the small bags inside, anchoring each corner. One night, the desert wind blew so fiercely that the tent, loaded with bags, rolled like a tumbleweed across a mesa and into cactus.

Wild and beautiful Santa Rosalillita was an awful place to set up a tent. There was no level ground, and my choice was either sloping loose sand or uneven rocks. I chose sand, and all night slept at an uncomfortable angle. My tent could not be secured with stakes, and gravity and shifting sand caused it to slip slowly into an even more awkward, neck-twisting angle.

José warned of mountain lions and rattlesnakes in the area. There was a bright full moon, and during the sleepless night I could hear little foxes sniffing around my tent and see their shadowy outlines. When I awoke in the morning, there were small puddles of fox pee everywhere.

Chema and José had wisely chosen to sleep on rock, not on shifting sand. They spread their bedrolls on mule blankets and slept next to the mules, their presence a deterrent to mountain lions.

We left camp at sunrise. The mules stopped for one long, last sip of water. Chema lay on his stomach and drank from the swamp with the mules.

A twisting cactus-choked canyon led out of Santa Rosalillita. Chema pointed to a cluster of fresh large paw prints. He looked around nervously, muttering, *"Muchas pumas."* He and José spoke softly, and I could not hear what they were saying. José continued riding ahead with the pack mule, hack-ing the overgrowth with the machete. For the next hour, Chema rode a short distance behind me as I walked slowly up the narrow trail.

Sierra de la Giganta has always been known for its mountain lions. When the missionaries arrived, large numbers of lions roamed the area, terrorizing the superstitious Cochimí, who would not kill them, believing if they did the dead lion would bring death to the killer and tribe.

It may be here on this rocky path that a scene unfolded that became part of the famous folklore of the old Jesuit mission trail, a true David and Goliath story. On a narrow mountain trail, Father Juan Ugarte encountered a snarling mountain lion ready to attack. The strong and powerfully built missionary threw a large rock, which hit the lion's head and killed it. He slung the still-warm body of the beast over his mule and brought it to the mission to show the natives. The Cochimí were stunned by Ugarte's strength and courage. When Ugarte didn't die—and, in fact, nothing bad happened to him—they lost their superstition and started to kill the lions, freeing them of their greatest enemy.

The trail became steeper and rockier, until it was all loose lava rock. The cactus became so thick we couldn't see each other; there was just the sound of Chema hacking away with the machete, trying to clear a small path.

We carried only José's machete, and he and Chema took turns using it. In Loreto, Trudi advised me to buy a machete, but Chema said I wouldn't need one. He was used to tourists riding mules on dirt roads and worn paths, not old mission trails.

For the next six hundred miles, often surrounded by impenetrable cactus, I wished I had followed Trudi's advice.

José was prepared for the cactus jungle; Chema and I weren't. José wore thick leather chaps and his stirrups were covered in even thicker leather to protect against the cactus. Chema had no leather chaps and wore Levi denim jeans; the stirrups of Trudi's tourist saddles were open metal and offered no protection.

For three hours I continued to walk, feeling like a human machete, cutting through thorny brush with my body. Chema and José were not as mangled atop the mules, being about six feet taller in the saddle than me walking on the ground.

Cactus tore at my wool-felt cowboy hat, making it hard to keep my head covered and protected. My sunglasses were pulled from my face and broke. Every bush, every leafless tree, every plant was covered in thorns. The only variants were how big the thorn, how vicious and nasty its shape, and how deep its cut. My cotton shirt was shredded. My flesh ripped open.

As we headed up the thorny trail, the lava rocks got sharper and larger and looser. Soon there was no trail, just a sea of rock. I kept walking. The mules moved slower than me, trying to balance and walk across the rocks shifting dangerously underneath their unshod hooves.

A thought flashed through me: *This is foolish. You should stop walking and ride Ratón.* I didn't listen to the little voice within, though, and in a few steps my foot slipped off a rock, wrenching my left ankle to the side. As I fell forward, I cried out to Chema, ahead and hidden behind cactus, "Stop!" I writhed on the ground in pain. There would be no more walking today. Chema lifted me atop Ratón; my sprained left ankle dangled from the stirrup.

I sprained the same left ankle on the fifth day of my California mission walk and walked nearly seven hundred miles with a sprained ankle. There I had cold ice to soak my foot. Here I had nothing.

Chema quickly unloaded the mule to retrieve the emergency medicine. I swallowed three thousand milligrams of Advil. I was out of purified water, and Chema handed me his canteen filled with swamp water at Santa Rosalillita. I drank almost all of it.

We continued on. We planned to stop for the night at Quini, another famous waterhole of the missionaries. It was getting dark and our plans changed. We stopped instead at a place José called Los Frailes, another forgettable dust hole next to a dry arroyo with a small pool of water. Los Frailes, Spanish for *friars*, may not exist. It is on no maps and known only to cowboys.

I quickly unpacked Ratón to set up my tent before it became too dark. I was knee-deep in sand, behind a scraggly bush, anchoring my tent with rocks, when I heard the sounds of horse hooves and turned to see three strange men ride into camp.

There is something eerie about encounters with strangers in the nighttime wilderness. One expects to encounter wild animals, not men.

I quickly scrambled into my tent, zipped it tightly shut, and took out my only two weapons: the pocket ax hammer and pepper spray. Then I dug deeper in my bag to find my emergency satellite phone and leave a voice message for Dale. If those were three serial killers riding into camp, I wanted Dale to have GPS coordinates to know where to dig for my remains.

As I sat in the dark in my tent, I began to calm my breathing. *José must know them.* I soon heard talking and laughing that lasted most of the night. I slipped out of my tent at dawn when I heard them take the mules down into the arroyo for water. Bedrolls, saddles, and blankets were spread out next to a simmering campfire; an empty gallon jug of tequila lay nearby, tossed on its side.

That morning, my left ankle was so swollen I couldn't lace my hiking boots. I managed to take down my tent and pack my gear, crawling in the soft sand to do so. Once again, Chema helped me into the saddle on top of Ratón, and insisted on putting my swollen left foot in the stirrup and not leave it dangling. "*Muy mal camino*," he explained as I winced. Very bad road, indeed.

19

Trudi wasn't sure how long I could keep Ratón and Dulce. After the first week, I wasn't sure how long I wanted to.

Ratón didn't like me. I grew to detest him. He started making noises, first unhappy noises, and then groaning noises. The hotter it got, the more he groaned. He insisted on stopping for shade in the middle of a cactus thicket, wedging me between needles and slowly ripping off thorny bites to eat, refusing to budge until finished. He brushed up against thorns and tried to rub me out of the saddle. He especially delighted in low-hanging, jagged mesquite branches where there was just enough room for him to duck his head and pass underneath; all I could do was fall forward, bury my face in his sweaty, shaggy mane, and latch my arms around his neck. I do believe his groaning noises turned wickedly gleeful.

The trail got so bad I couldn't keep my hat on. Thorns snagged at my hair and pierced my scalp. I crouched forward, molding my body against Ratón's wet neck, and peered through his ears to keep the brambles from ripping my face. Blood trickled down the side of my head. My mouth bled. I forgot all about my swollen, throbbing ankle.

The cactus slowly thinned, and we found ourselves surrounded by towering peaks of lava rock piled one on top of another. The ground was littered with small pieces of glassy black obsidian that resembled broken bottles and was just as sharp. We pushed our mules up and down one peak after another. Here the old El Camino Real was nothing more than a deep trench of rock. Ratón was small—at least two feet smaller than the other mules. *Maybe that explained why he was so ill tempered,* I thought.

To keep Ratón from crushing my legs against boulders as we plunged up and down the mountain, I had to raise my feet, still in stirrups, almost level with my hips. Once again I found myself holding tight to the saddle, bent over Ratón's smelly neck, and peering ahead through his ears, or leaning so far back my head touched his rump.

There was cactus everywhere, growing out of every crevice of every rock. Leafless branches covered with thorns blocked the steep trail and slowed our progress.

Mules plow straight up mountain cliffs, not stopping for anything. There is no turning back on a steep trail less than a foot wide. There is only one way to go, and that is up. If your foot is crushed against a rock, so be it. If your leg is torn off, so be it. If a branch hits the top of your head and snaps your neck, so be it. You are irrelevant. The mule will not stop. Often his body is almost parallel to the ground—and the ground is loose, sliding lava rocks, tearing into his unshod feet and giving way beneath him. If he stops, he perishes—and so do you.

At such a time, it might be tempting to ask, *Why am I doing this?* I never asked. I knew why: I would rather kill myself on a mule than let cancer kill me.

It took hours to reach the highest peak. The mule's hearts were pounding and chests heaving. Sweat poured down their legs in a steamy stream, softening the ground beneath their feet.

My legs were bruised and throbbing.

A cholla cactus head with dozens of spiny needles had pierced my Cabela's nylon cargo pants, and its thorns were embedded in the flesh of my right calf. Chema tried to flick the cholla away with the tip of José's machete. It wouldn't budge. He bent down and took hold of one thin needle between his thumb and forefinger, and tried to pull the thorny head loose from my bleeding leg. Again, it wouldn't budge. A dozen needles protruded from my leg. The area felt as if it were on fire, as if each needle were a smoldering branding iron thrust into skin.

Chema dismounted Dulce and leaned over my leg, carefully taking each thistle between his teeth and slowly extracting it, spitting each out as my flesh released it. The pain and the fire remained.

Several hundred yards from the top was the most treacherous part of the ascent, a sheer wall of lava rock with barely twelve inches of trail for the mule to walk. On a thin ledge jutting out from the rock was a small blue image of Our Lady of Guadalupe, the most precious and venerated religious symbol in Mexico.

"*Un santuario vaquero*," José replied, when I asked later. It was a shrine made by a vaquero. Death can come suddenly in the Sierras. A mule slips. A man falls. One never knows the hour when God calls. He and Chema made the sign of the cross, a vaquero prayer for a safe ride coming up—and going down—the chasm.

At the summit, patches of blue wildflowers bloomed amidst the harsh desert shrubbery. Whenever I see wildflowers, I think of Mama. She always felt wildflowers were God's gift of adornment, a visible reminder of divine grace.

More than a thousand feet below us, nestled between mountain peaks, was the emerald-green arroyo the Cochimí called Comondú, or valley of stones. What we saw from atop the highest peak was not unlike what the first missionaries saw three hundred years ago. The two settlements of San Miguel and San José Comondú are less than three miles apart in a narrow Shangri-la valley of palm trees and lush green fields. Whitewashed adobe houses glistened in the sun.

Our mules excitedly sensed water and grew impatient and agitated.

The old El Camino Real mission trail descended straight down into San Miguel Comondú. At the top, the mission trail was no more than a foot-wide ditch and so deep we were forced to ride with our legs on the necks of the mules.

Ratón plunged down the narrow ditch behind the other mules, squeezing his body and my legs between large boulders. I struggled to hold on to the saddle and bridle and keep my feet elevated. Ratón shook his head trying to dislodge my legs from his neck. I knew that if my feet slipped from the stirrups, I would fall.

For five terrifying minutes I hardly breathed. All I could do was grip the saddle and pray through clenched teeth, "Lord, help me hold on."

Once we descended, Chema and José rode ahead, while I walked silently into San Miguel Comondú, exhausted and only partially aware of the crumbling old stone walls lining the dirt road. Although it didn't look as green as it did from above—nor the adobe houses as white—there was still a wondrous charm about the place and a wild, wilderness feeling.

The two vaqueros came to a stop across the road from the stone ruins of San Miguel and sat patiently atop the mules in the shade as I walked respectfully through the heap of rubble and dried earth that once was a stone church with aqueducts and orchards and fields of crops.

I stepped warily through knee-high brush, wearing nylon rattlesnake gaiters. I did not want to test if they worked. My swollen ankle began to throb. I had forgotten about it until now. Dried blood from the cactus wound soiled my pants, and my leg ached where the thorns had punctured my skin.

I sat down to rest on an edge of the ancient stone foundation and tried to picture what it was like three centuries ago.

San Miguel was a visiting station of Mission San Javier, founded by Father Juan Ugarte. During another drought that lasted four years, Ugarte was again forced to travel long distances from Mission San Javier to find water. The Cochimí brought him to Comondú, where he found a spring of water rising from deep within the Giantess that flowed through a gorge into water holes in the arroyo. Ugarte and the Cochimí from San Javier moved here to live and to build a chapel.

Ugarte, the former president of a college, went to work building ditches, barefoot. He wore the black robe of a Jesuit missionary, a robe made of camel hair that hung to his ankles. He and mission Indians undertook an effort that reached biblical proportions, defying mortal humanness. They filled up the gorge to make a trail, using 22,000 mule loads of rock, and 18,000 mule loads of earth. It is that holy trail that I walked to get here.

Ugarte continued to labor in this land of thorns and barren stone. He wrote that laboring "one year in the cactus patch is as hard as two years in other mission fields."[1] He built a dam and aqueducts to bring water from the tiny stream in the arroyo to crops. He leveled ground for an orchard by filling a ravine with 160,000 mule loads of earth. I can still see faint outlines of his orchard. Intertwined with thorns are a few of his grapevines that once produced the finest wine and brandy of the missions.

I was filled with a tremendous sense of wonder as I mounted Ratón and headed toward Mission San José Comondú on Father Juan Ugarte's old mission trail.

Mama taught us that, through the grace of God, what we can conceive, we can achieve. Father Ugarte's works were a testament of belief. When others saw a gorge, Ugarte saw a trail; when others saw a ravine, he saw an orchard.

Mission San José Comondú was moved twice during times of drought and epidemic. It found a permanent home in Arroyo Comondú, a mere three miles from Ugarte's beloved San Miguel. It was the largest mission church in the desert, with three naves constructed of towering stone walls four feet thick, and an arched roof supported by eight Grecian pillars.

It withstood time, earthquakes, and vandalism for almost two hundred years. In 1930, it was dynamited and its stone used to build a school and private residence. Nothing remains of the original mission church except a small side chapel. I spent less than fifteen minutes at Mission San José Comondú, its spirit too diminished by man's ignorance and stupidity. Destruction of the past profoundly affects our spirits too. "There is a pathos in the ruins of past splendor which casts a shadow over the spirit of the traveler," observed Arthur North when he traveled through here in 1905.[2]

Trudi had instructed José and Chema where to pasture the mules, and we arrived there in the early afternoon of the fifth day, expecting Trudi to show up soon. This was where Chema and I would part ways. Yet there was no sign of her. We waited in the field several hours until a man in a beat-up car drove by and offered to take us to a local hotel for a hundred *pesos*. José and Chema shook their heads. They didn't want to leave the mules, and Trudi would be there soon to drive them to the hotel. My swollen ankle was hurting, and my legs sore from cactus, so I paid the man for a ride to the hotel.

The hotel, La Hacienda Don Mario, was newly constructed—and my room had a hot shower that worked and a toilet that flushed. At 750 *pesos* it was expensive, but for a hot shower and a soft bed I would have paid just about any price. My shirt was torn to shreds from cactus, and the woman at the desk,

Amelia, offered to repair my shirt and clean my clothes for one hundred *pesos*. I hadn't eaten since early in the morning at Los Frailes, and I was starved. Amelia walked with me to a restaurant, which turned out to be her mother's house. Her mother fixed eggs, beans, and tortillas for fifty *pesos* and showered me with loving attention.

I was surprised that Trudi wasn't there yet. I told Amelia that Trudi would be arriving soon, and I would pay for her room, and a room for Chema and José. Then I went to my room and spent half an hour under the hot shower. I was in bad shape. My bottom was blistered with saddle sores, and I spread a quarter tube of Neosporin over it. My legs, arms, and shoulders were bruised and covered with infected cactus punctures that looked like blisters. I used up most of what was left of the Neosporin, dabbing away at each cactus blister. My swollen left ankle had turned several shades of blue, with streaks of black and red; it looked broken.

I took two Advil, slathered olive oil over my body, and climbed into bed. I slept like a baby in the warm, soft sheets.

The next morning, Trudi still wasn't there. "*¿Dónde están los vaqueros?*" I asked Amelia. Where are the men? She shrugged her shoulders; she hadn't seen them. Amelia offered, for two hundred *pesos*, to have her husband, Lorenzo, drive me to the field where I left José and Chema yesterday. For one hundred *pesos*, she said, the mules could stay in her mother's backyard, where there was plenty of grass to eat.

We arrived at the field, and José and Chema were sitting under a small tree, where they had spent the night cold and hungry. Trudi never showed up, and Chema was unable to reach her by phone. They piled into the back of Lorenzo's truck, and we drove back to the hotel. For sixty *pesos* each, Amelia's mother made *machaca*, beans, and tortillas for breakfast. *Machaca* is beef jerky and was hard to chew. My stomach cramped from trying to digest it; my insides were too compromised after liver and colon surgeries, and my stomach swelled. I hoped and prayed this wasn't the beginning of serious digestive issues.

Amelia gave José and Chema a room to take hot showers before heading back to the field with the mules. Trudi had most of my *pesos*, and I was going through cash so fast I was worried I wouldn't have enough to pay for everything.

There was no place to get *pesos* in San Miguel or San José Comondú. We were a hundred miles from the nearest bank or Western Union.

When Chema was finally able to reach Trudi on the phone, she told him she was too busy to drive to Comondú and he should catch a bus to Loreto. She would bring my gear to San Ignacio in several weeks.

I looked at Chema in shock. How could Trudi do this? She had most of my food, my money, my passport, satellite phone batteries, and all my clothes except for the thin pajamas and what I was wearing.

I knew I didn't have near enough money to pay Chema, José, and expenses until San Ignacio. It was two hundred miles to San Ignacio, and several long, difficult weeks to get there.

I talked to Trudi on Chema's phone. She was getting annoyed, and I couldn't blame her. This was her busiest tourist season, and I had shown up, not a well-heeled tourist taking a well-organized weekend saddle trip, but a crazy woman alone, determined to walk two months through the Sierras and deserts on a cactus-covered mission trail.

I knew I was more than she bargained for. She had rented me her two favorite mules for three weeks, and arranged a couple of vaqueros. That was about all she could do. She scolded me for leaving my money and essential gear with her; after all, she had said she was *maybe* coming to Comondú.

She was right, about everything.

The conversation was going nowhere, so I took a deep breath and carefully ended it. I was truly grateful for Trudi. She was my best hope to complete this journey.

José would take me to Mission La Purísima, and we could stay with a lady named Altagracia. Trudi didn't know any vaqueros who could take me beyond La Purísima. Word was out that I was looking for vaqueros, and many needed work. Raymundo, a vaquero raised near La Purísima who now lived in Loreto, might be able to take me from La Purísima to Guadalupe. That's all Trudi could tell me.

I was in God's hands. He had gotten me through cancer. I trusted He would get me through this.

20

José and I set out late in the day. We were both anxious to get to Mission La Purísima. José replied, "*Uno o dos días más o menos*," when I asked how far. One or two days, plus or minus. I was able to walk the first hour, until my swollen ankle made it impossible.

José saddled Dulce for me and put the packs on Ratón. "*Muy mal mula*," he declared. Ratón was now the pack mule and rid of me. He stopped groaning. I think he was happy.

Storm clouds were gathering, and a strong, cold north wind appeared out of nowhere. Two hours north of Comondú we made camp in a sandy mesa with nothing but sagebrush and cactus to protect against the fierce wind. The sky filled with thunderclouds and bolts of lightning.

All night the wind howled and whipped the light tent around me, making sleep difficult. I didn't care. I loved being in the middle of nowhere listening to mules chomping away at cactus, and crickets chirping above the roaring wind.

I awoke at 2:00 a.m., startled, thinking a truck outside was shining its lights into my tent. The inside of my tent was as bright as day. I cautiously opened the flap to look out. It was not a truck. It was the bright moon, and stars, thousands of them, so close I felt I could reach up and touch them. I felt as if I was in God's church.

It took eight hours to get to La Purísima. I alternated riding Dulce and walking when there was hard-packed sand without rocks or shards of knife-edged lava. The more I walked, the better my ankle felt.

We arrived in La Purísima in the late afternoon. Trudi had arranged for us to stay with Altagracia, the widow of a vaquero, where there was grass and water for the mules. Altagracia greeted us like a warm and loving grandmother, and made us a delicious meal of lentils, corn tortillas, and fresh goat cheese; she hovered over us, refilling our plates and coffee mugs.

It was Saturday night. I had been on El Camino Real mission trail a week, but it felt a lifetime ago that I had left Loreto.

I did not know who my next vaquero would be, or where we would meet up.

I did not know where my next mule would come from.

Living with late-stage cancer is living a life of unknowns, and I had become quite comfortable with not knowing. It kept me aware and paying attention. I didn't take anything for granted. Out here, I lived the same way.

———

José was anxious to start the long ride back to his rancho, but he refused to leave until I had another vaquero.

The new vaquero arrived within an hour. His name was Raymundo Vargas Mayoral, and he had grown up on Rancho Paso Hondo, on El Camino Real mission trail between La Purísima and Guadalupe. He arrived with the gear Trudi had promised to bring to Comondú—my passport, a money belt with ten thousand *pesos*, satellite telephone batteries, food, and clothes. Trudi would bring the other half of my gear and money to San Ignacio in the next two weeks, before I got there. I knew I wouldn't make the mistake to trust others with my essentials again.

Raymundo also arrived with his truck, his horse, his mule, and his wife, Rosa. He intended to take all four along with us.

This was not exactly what I had envisioned. A truck would never be able to follow the mission trail through the Sierras.

Rosa, Raymundo, and I piled into the truck and drove into town, looking for gas and old Mission La Purísima Concepción de Cadegomó. No one we asked, not even the local policeman, knew where the ruins of the old mission were located. We finally found a four-foot corner foundation of rock and mortar hidden in overgrown weeds and a small sign staked nearby, "SITIO DE LA MISIÓN," surrounded by trash.

Junípero Serra had assigned this prestigious mission to his lifelong friend and former student, Father Juan Crespí, who was there only a short while before leaving for San Diego. I could imagine them turning over in their graves knowing Mission La Purísima was a pile of rubble, overgrown with weeds and desecrated with trash. The stone mission built lovingly by the Jesuits to minister to and feed the Cochimí *ranchería* of Cadegomó, the Arroyo of Reeds, was unknown and forgotten and unloved.

I was struck by how different this was from California. Harrye Forbes believed there were no greater art treasures in the world than the mission buildings of California, and she dedicated her life to saving them. Forbes and hundreds of volunteers and philanthropists rescued the Franciscan missions from death and destruction and restored them to active parish churches and thriving religious communities. The missions in Mexico were not as fortunate. Here, there were no priests to greet pilgrims and no candles to light. Often there was just rubble and empty chapels.

Raymundo saddled Rosa's mule and Dulce, loaded the gear packs on Ratón, then headed north in the truck, bouncing on rocks, with his horse saddled in the back.

Our mule pack was filled with goodies Rosa had bought in Loreto: strawberry jam and Nutella, a loaf of white bread, goat cheese, apples, dozens of tortillas, canned Spam and tuna, and pounds of dried *machaca* beef. I had packed instant oatmeal and thirty packages of dehydrated survival meals created for United States Army Special Forces "with a twelve-plus-year taste guarantee" that had to last until San Ignacio, more than two hundred miles north.

Raymundo had packed five pounds of sugar, pound-size jars of Nescafé instant coffee and Coffeemate creamer, and a lot of Marlboro cigarettes.

I walked, and Rosa rode her mule with Ratón and Dulce in tow.

It was dusk when Rosa and I reached Purísima Vieja, the original location of the La Purísima mission, which was soon abandoned for lack of water.

Raymundo was waiting for us. He quickly loaded harnesses, saddles, and gear packs in the back of the truck, and then led the mules up the arroyo, where they drank their fill of water and cooled themselves in the brisk mountain air. Raymundo warned us to be watchful for rattlesnakes and scorpions in the underbrush and wild pigs in the arroyo. After his warning, Rosa and I chose to stay on the trail side of the arroyo and watch as Raymundo tethered the three mules to separate mesquite bushes. The sun had set, and the arroyo was dark under the thick mantle of towering palms as we loaded in the truck for the short ride to Rancho Paso Hondo. We knew we would have plenty of time in the morning to explore the mission ruins of Purísima Vieja.

Paso Hondo was no more than a handful of huts and a small church with a weathered sign announcing service times.

Raymundo pulled the truck in front of a dark, two-room concrete block hut with a corrugated metal roof. There was no electricity. I was struck by how dark the nighttime world is without electricity. It was only half past six, but Raymundo's aunt María Luiza and cousin Roberto had already gone to bed. Rosa and I stayed in the truck while Raymundo roused them. He returned with a flashlight, and Rosa and I followed him around back.

Rosa and María Luiza greeted each other with an extended embrace and excited laughter. Rosa had also grown up in Paso Hondo; this was home.

We hadn't eaten since breakfast in La Purísima, and Raymundo unpacked coffee and food from the truck. The kitchen was a separate small thatched hut in the back with a four-burner countertop propane stove, though only one burner worked. The dirt floor was uneven, and the tattered vinyl chair rocked as I sat watching María Luiza and Rosa work by flashlight to boil water for coffee and heat *machaca* beef tortillas on the open flame. Raymundo came in wearing a headlamp and ate with us, but Roberto stayed just outside the open doorframe, playing with a tiny frisky puppy, while farm cats rubbed against his leg.

Rosa and Raymundo made a bed out of a tarp and blankets on the bare dirt underneath a thatched palm porch. Roberto slept nearby, under the stars, on a seat taken from a truck.

I asked María Luiza where I should sleep. She led me inside the concrete block room, where a dim solar-powered light bulb flickered on and off, and pointed to her bed. María Luiza offered to share her bed with me! I was struck by this simple act of charity and kindness and accepted with heartfelt gratitude.

It was an old bedspring with no sheets, just two worn blankets for cover. The small puppy slept in the room at the bottom of three wood shelves supported by concrete blocks. On the top shelf, layered in dust, was a faded picture of a young woman adorned with plastic flowers. A prayer card with Our Lady of Guadalupe leaned against the photo. It was a prayer for the dead. A waning candle flickered nearby. *Who was she?* I wondered, struck by her beauty and María Luiza's humble devotion.

There was no door to the room. A piece of fabric hung from the doorframe and partially covered the opening. The small puppy frequently raised its hind paws to scratch its head, and I was concerned about fleas. I covered myself from foot to head, with nothing exposed but my face. I wore a headscarf called a buff that covered my neck and head, a jacket zipped up to my neck, and pants and socks. There were several concrete blocks stacked next to the bed, and I put my boots on top so nothing could crawl in.

María Luiza slept sweetly quiet through the night, her breathing a soft purr, and hardly turned over.

In the morning, Rosa showed me the outdoor toilet in a small field in back with the goats. It was so dirty and smelly that when Rosa left I relieved myself outside on the ground with the goats.

Raymundo was in a hurry to check on the mules at Purísima Vieja, and we headed back at sunrise before coffee. The mission at Purísima Vieja was moved further south to Cadegomó, a Cochimí *ranchería*, after drought dried up the arroyo. The area was nothing but cactus and desert sand except for the narrow sixty-foot arroyo, which now overflowed with water and reeds. Raymundo said as long as he had been alive and his father and grandfather before him, there had been water in the arroyo. The missionaries had built in the right place—but at the wrong time.

The ruins were not close to the road and easy to miss; they were mostly undisturbed by vandals. Purísima Vieja was everything that Mission La Purísima was not; its spirit and ruins protected more than three hundred years in a distant arroyo off the beaten track.

Rosa and I walked back to Paso Hondo, and Raymundo took the mules in the truck. When we arrived an hour later, Rosa asked to stop at the home of her great-aunt Isabel, who lived in the largest of four dwellings in Paso Hondo. An elderly, toothless vaquero lived there as a boarder and became excited when Rosa told him I was walking the old El Camino Real through the Sierras to San Diego. He eagerly explained that he knew the original old trail from Paso Hondo to Mission Guadalupe and would ride with us if I could provide a mule.

Many times over the next week—as we wandered lost in the Giantess—I thought back to the old man and wondered if he had been God's messenger that I chose to ignore.

After leaving Paso Hondo, I walked several hours while Rosa rode a mule and pulled Ratón. Raymundo drove the truck with Dulce bouncing in the back. His horse was saddled up and tied to the side of the truck with a leather rope. She was a regal, pale-cream palomino with flowing, blonde tail and meticulously groomed mane; she pranced alongside the old farm truck with the grace and bearing of a champion show horse.

Raymundo would drive several miles ahead, park the truck, then ride back to meet us. He rode with the grace and bearing of a conquistador in an expensive white felt cowboy hat and thick leather chaps. Sitting straight in the saddle, he was as handsome as any Hollywood cowboy, with deeper dimples than Tom Selleck's and more masculinity than George Clooney but with the same full head of gray hair.

I believe Rosa came along to keep an eye on him. I can't say I blamed her. However, he was a sullen fellow, rather melancholy, and I can't remember ever seeing him smile.

He didn't have that much to smile about. The road was mostly eroded rock and cactus brush with many twists and turns. El Camino Real crossed Arroyo Agua Verde several times, and the arroyo was a thick mass of rocks and boulders almost impossible for a truck to drive through. The truck would get stuck in the middle of the arroyo, and each time Raymundo had to dig large rocks out from beneath. Often, the truck overheated. Rosa and I would come around a bend, and the truck would be blocking our path, with the hood up and Raymundo underneath, swearing, and banging loudly with a wrench.

And then there was Ratón. Ratón's good behavior was short-lived. Rosa tried to keep him on a short rope, walking directly behind her mule. He would have none of it. He would push and nip Rosa's mule and cause it to bolt to the side of the trail, almost knocking Rosa out of the saddle. At the first opportunity Ratón would jerk the rope out of Rosa's hand and tear off into the thick underbrush.

Raymundo would ride into the thicket to retrieve Ratón, screaming "*Diablo!*" and other choice words outside my limited Spanish vocabulary.

Once Ratón's rope twisted around a large barrel-shaped cactus, called a *bisnaga* (but better known as a "Spanish dagger"). It was over six feet high and studded all over with red, almost black, thorns. At its center the thorns were three inches long and curved like a fishhook. That was where Ratón's head was planted. The rope was wrapped tight around the cactus, pinning Ratón's nose, ears, and face against the deadly fishhook blades. Ratón was kicking his hind legs in all directions trying to free himself.

Raymundo approached slowly and cautiously, speaking softly. He carefully unwrapped the rope, trying not to get his own chest or face too close to the lethal daggers, or get hit in the face by Ratón's wild, uncontrollable kicking.

Had he a gun, I am sure Raymundo would have shot Ratón.

It was almost dark when we arrived at Rancho El Llanito, the last rancho and the end of the rocky dirt road. Raymundo parked the truck under a scraggly mesquite and unpacked a week's worth of camping supplies for him and Rosa. This was the end of the road for the truck. Beyond the rancho it was nothing but a trail of thorns, accessible only by pack mule.

It had been a long, hard day of walking and riding. I was thankful I had been able to walk. There would be little walking in the days ahead. It was hard to ride a mule for hours on end. I could comfortably ride a mule about two hours, and then I had to get off and walk to restore circulation to my aching knees and numb feet.

But there were risks to walking. Earlier today, stepping down an arroyo embankment, I was not paying attention and almost stepped on a rattlesnake concealed in the brush. It slithered quickly away, escaping under the earthen overhang, its shaking tail still visible and terrifying. A muleteer in the Sierras once commented that for every rattlesnake we see, there are several hundred that we don't.

It is one we don't see that strikes.

Snakebite was a frightening, ever-present danger to missionaries and Indians. A missionary wrote in his journal, "Every year several natives are dispatched into eternity by snake bites, and still they have no other protection against it except to tie the injured member between the wound and the heart in order to restrict the blood circulation, or if a finger or hand has been bitten, to cut it off."[1]

Rattlesnakes were in such abundance that "a person is never and nowhere safe because they glide up a flight of stairs or the walls of a house."[2]

Once the missionary discovered a five-foot rattlesnake on the top shelf of his bookcase when he reached for scissors. Another time he woke up to find one on the inner edge of his windowsill, a few inches from his head. The missionaries were always cautious when stepping outside because the vipers frequently hung out beneath the doorstep.

Rancho El Llanito was a small, very poor rancho. When Harry Crosby had ridden by fifty years earlier, it was a deserted goat ranch. When we arrived, an elderly woman, Señora Tirsa Arce Meza, lived there alone with a young vaquero, José Manuel Ceta, hired to help with the few cows. The Sierras are losing their children. Along El Camino Real many ranchos were deserted, and it was not uncommon to find very old men and women living alone, their children having left harsh rancho life for jobs along the coast.

There was not enough room for us under the palm leaf shanty Señora Meza called home, and we pitched our tents in sand near the cows. The mules were tethered nearby, eating cactus; Raymundo's horse was next to their tent, contentedly eating a small bale of hay from the back of the truck.

We were too tired to fix food. Rosa boiled water on the woodstove, and I made instant oatmeal. The young vaquero brought a gallon bucket of fresh warm cow's milk and freshly made cheese.

The next morning, I found my tent crawling with ants. There were thousands of ants everywhere. I wore deerskin gloves to pack up the tent, and stopped frequently to shake crawling ants loose from my arm and glove.

Later, I dropped my water bottle on the ground to load the pommel bag on Dulce. When I reached for it, I almost grabbed a giant centipede that was suspended in midair almost underneath me, its grotesquely segmented upper body reaching for the water bottle and my leg. It must have crawled in my pommel bag the night before. Missionaries were always on the lookout for these noxious, stomach-churning night crawlers, measuring more than nine inches long. They found them in their beds at night and in the folds of their coats.

I kicked the vile creature away, horrified. I couldn't shake the image for weeks, until an even worse horror took its place. It was one horror after another on the old mission trail.

After years of battling late-stage cancer, I thought I knew all about suffering. I soon found out there was more to learn.

21

We rode north into Sierra de la Giganta with a sense of adventure and filled with a spirit of romance. Raymundo led the way on his horse, riding tall in the saddle and wearing thick leather chaps, looking like a *soldado de cuera*, a leather-jacketed soldier of days past who rode ahead to cut a path through the wilderness.

Cactus and brush obliterated mountain trails; Raymundo was soon lost in a morass of steep ravines, called *cañadas*. His machete grew dull from hacking away at thick cactus, and he stopped several times to sharpen the blade on rocks.

In late afternoon, we arrived at a small waterhole in the middle of nowhere. Rosa called the place Arpillera.

"Many mountain lions were here this morning." Raymundo pointed to fresh tracks in the sand and spoke rapidly in Spanish. He took the machete from its saddle holster and tucked it in his waistband. "We may hear them tonight when they come for water."

Nevertheless, we decided to make camp for the night. He did not believe the mountain lions would bother us. "The mules will get agitated, but I will tie them next to the tents and the lions won't come too close."

It was very windy, and I struggled with my tent. The wind picked it up and threw it against the sharp lava rock. Rosa helped me secure it with the heaviest rocks we could find.

I crawled painfully into the tent. My legs and knees were heavily bruised, my arms torn and bleeding from cactus thorns, and my neck was sore from ducking under mesquite. Sometimes the top of my head would hit a branch, popping my head back like a rear-end collision.

Cancer had brutalized my body, and now the desert sierras threatened to do to the outside what cancer did to the inside.

El Camino Real was indeed "*muy mal.*" We had struggled for more than eight hours that day, and I wasn't sure how far we had come.

In the morning, I was up an hour before Rosa and Raymundo, but not before the mules. During the night, they stayed so close to my tent I feared they might knock it over. Raymundo had cut a large thorny branch for them to eat, and I could hear the dry thorns snap between their teeth most of the night.

We left camp before sunrise, and Raymundo walked ahead leading his horse. In the soft sand he pointed to three sets of mountain lion tracks. "*Muy grande.*" He put his fist next to a paw print, and it was much bigger than his fist.

We were now in Sierra de Guadalupe, no longer in Sierra de la Giganta, although the only thing that changed was the name. The trail slowly ascended up a steep canyon, and the shrubby mesquite and cactus became so thick we couldn't see a few feet ahead.

For six hours we kept moving, not even stopping for a drink of water.

Raymundo kept desperately hacking away with his machete, leading us up and down steep gorges and across arroyos. Three times we came to the top of a mountain and there was no trail—we had to turn around. When you go up a steep mountain ravine through all the thorns and cactus and then must come down through them again, it's a double shock, like being freed from a torture chamber and then sent back.

El Camino Real trail was here somewhere underneath two hundred years of thorns. But I believe when Raymundo left the Sierras and Rancho Paso Hondo to move to the city, he lost his wild instincts and ability to follow a sierra trail through thorns. He could ride a horse as magnificently as before, but he had lost his vaquero instincts. We were lost in a purgatory of thorns of every size and shape imaginable—cactuses named fishhook, snake, pincushion, prickly pear, bayonet, and dagger.

We would get to what we thought was the top of a mountain and discover another peak in front of us. "Here in the Sierras at the top of every mountain is another," Raymundo lamented.

Life is the same, I thought wryly.

Shrubby trees ripped our flesh. When the Old Testament prophesied, "The land will be covered with briers and thorns"[1] it was describing this land of leafless trees.

Heinous vines called devil's claw tore my pants and pierced through my boots. Devil's claw vines grew along the ground and, like a sinewy snake, wound through the brush. Its tendrils ended in curved, prong-like claws. The curved claws clasped onto the mule's nostrils and forelegs and latched on to boots and pants. One clawed tendril tore my wrist as I bent down to disengage another from my torn pants leg.

The most hellish of all was the innocent-sounding teddy bear cholla. It was straight out of a horror film. The cholla came apart, and each fuzzy joint was covered with fangs that seemed to jump and latch onto bare flesh, saddles, and mule packs.

Cholla is the terror of the desert. A missionary, out of curiosity, counted the thorns on a single piece of cholla about the size of his fist. He counted 1,680 thorns. A cholla contained seventy or more branches. "It is easy to see that, according to my calculation, a single plant carries more than a million thorns," he observed.[2]

When a cholla clump attached to my gloved hand, my other hand could not free it. I had to clench each thorn between my teeth and jerk, being careful not to sink my lips into the clustered thorns. My hand couldn't free thorns from my leg. Raymundo pressed the machete blade underneath the thorns and quickly jerked them out. The pain almost paralyzed me. My arms and legs were covered with raw blistered spots that stung and ached but would not heal.

I frequently lost sight of Rosa and Raymundo. I could hear them, but I couldn't see them. The cholla cactus was too thick. The sun was bright, and each cholla thorn glistened like a glass needle.

I found myself unable to breathe. Dehydration and exhaustion clouded my senses, and I felt sheer terror, overcome by my phobic fear of needles. I became woozy and lightheaded. I was hallucinating, and vaguely aware of what was happening, but I couldn't stop. I felt faint and could barely hold on to Dulce's saddle. I began to shake uncontrollably.

I started to cry, loud heaving sobs of pain and fear.

The act of crying stopped the hallucination. It also stopped Dulce right in the middle of the cholla cactus patch.

I felt embarrassed and looked around to see if Rosa or Raymundo were near enough to hear me. They weren't.

With a shaky voice I called out, "Rosa, where are you? Raymundo?"

There was no answer, and I yelled louder.

"*Aquí!*" yelled Rosa. Here.

Dulce and I fled from the cholla and followed the sound of her voice. Only the tip of Raymundo's white hat was visible above the cactus. It looked oddly like a halo.

It was over ninety degrees, but Rosa wore Raymundo's leather jacket. Her hands were wrapped in the pockets for protection from thorns. The cholla pierced straight through my thin deerskin gloves, but still they provided some protection as I pushed away thorny branches. My light denim cotton shirt was shredded, with four gaping holes where cactus had clawed through the fabric. It was my only shirt. My other shirt was in the gear bag that Trudi was bringing to San Ignacio in two weeks.

Raymundo's machete broke. The blade snapped loudly. He continued to hack away with what was left. The jungle became too thick to ride through. Raymundo dismounted and led his horse, and tied Rosa's mule and my mule to the horse.

We slowly descended the mountain. The trail was so steep my head touched Dulce's rear, and I clung to the saddle for dear life. My saddle slipped forward, and the metal cinch tore a hole in Dulce's soft underbelly. The wound left a thin trail of vivid red blood. I turned to look back and a mesquite branch hit the top of my forehead, wrenching my head back, and my neck made a crunching sound. It was a painful reminder to never look back and never lose focus.

Raymundo anxiously led us through the dense brush until the narrow ravine exited into a small valley of lava and sand enclosed by lofty copper-colored ridges that rose steeply above the sides and blocked the scorching sun.

We finally arrived at a small *tinaja*, a stagnant pool of brackish green rainwater collected in bedrock near an ancient deserted ranch, Rancho El Saltito, here since mission days. All that was left of the rancho was a decayed wood wall and a few rocks surrounded by a large rock corral.

Rosa and I quickly unpacked the mules, while Raymundo built a campfire. Rosa boiled water on the campfire, and I prepared a package of dehydrated lasagna, which we spread on the remaining bread. Rosa and I nervously ate spoonfuls of Nutella and strawberry jam straight from the jar, giggling like misbehaving schoolgirls. Raymundo sat, unsmiling, with his back against the rocky wall that formed a semicircle around the *tinaja*. His eyes roamed the thicket in front of us for movement, ever watchful for mountain lions, his broken machete within reach.

We were in our tents before dark. I had a lovely bath with Pampers baby wipes, and squeezed the last remaining droplets of Neosporin on inflamed and blistered cactus wounds all over my body. I felt almost human—despite filthy, shredded clothes and knotted hair.

The next morning, Raymundo was not happy. He encouraged me to forget about following El Camino Real to Rancho San Martín. "*El camino es muy malo,*" he insisted. The road is too bad.

"It has been a very bad road for days but we've made it this far, and it will be just as hard to turn back as to go forward," I argued in broken Spanish. Raymundo relented and agreed to press on.

The next day wasn't much better.

We rode steep mountains between crevices cut through stone. My legs squeezed Dulce and my bruised thighs slammed against the saddle, throbbing in pain. My feet were torn from the stirrup by thorny branches and large boulders. It was very hard, at a ninety-degree angle on the back of a mule, to get my feet back in the stirrups, but critical that I do so.

Often, we were trapped in boulders too large for the mules to tread, and we had to turn around.

It was too steep for Raymundo to ride his horse. He plunged forward on foot through the dense vegetation, leading his horse and Ratón. Rosa followed on foot behind him, leading her mule. I stayed on Dulce and held tight to the pommel. My sprained and bruised left ankle was too swollen and painful to walk through dense underbrush and devil's claw vines. I was afraid of twisting it again—and breaking it this time.

After hours of slow climbing, we came to the crest of a steep ravine, and our eyes followed the arroyo below to a lush green knoll and two small thatched huts surrounded by palm trees. It was Rancho San Martín. We had finally made it!

An older man, César Villavicencio Aguilar, lived alone in one of the huts; the other was deserted. César, like his great-great-grandfather before him, was born on the old El Camino Real mission trail and knew every inch of the old road for forty miles. César's family had lived there since the missionaries.

I was too exhausted for another lost day with Raymundo, and I offered to pay César to ride with us the next morning. He was delighted to join us and immediately agreed.

Rancho San Martín was a beautiful oasis surrounded by desert. A mountain stream flowed from deep in Sierra de Guadalupe through Arroyo San Martín, and, next to my tent, the water collected in lava troughs where the blazing desert sun heated it to hot tub temperature. The sound of the water was soft and hypnotic and lulled my mind into deep, restful sleep. Palm trees provided privacy and shade, and were haven to nesting songbirds. I longed to stay awhile, to rest my battered body and soothe my senses.

It was not to be.

I was awakened before sunrise by César's yelping dog, and César dragging a dead cardon cactus across the pitted lava rock. César lived a modest, self-sufficient life: cactus carcasses for firewood; lentils cooked on a wood fire; and cilantro and chiles in a small garden. Other than the woodstove, the only furnishing in the thatched palm hut was a mattress on a raised platform and a wood rack for harness and saddle. A few clothes hung from nails, but there were no personal items.

César was not a man to waste time or words. Raymundo, Rosa, and I had barely finished packing up camp when César loaded Ratón and took off on his mule. He was on his way, and it was up to us to keep up.

He quickly led us through several small ravines to a clearly defined trail.

"*Este es El Camino Real*," he announced proudly. This is El Camino Real!

The old mission trail was in excellent condition, but terrifyingly steep. The missionaries had chosen a rocky gorge where only a few scraggly mesquite and cactuses could take hold and root. The trail ascended rapidly up a series of steep switchbacks on the edge of a narrow ledge less than two feet wide. One misstep and the mules would have plunged a thousand feet to the valley below.

César rode behind our mules, pushing them forward, while pulling Ratón behind him up the steep mountain trail.

The entire morning, César had struggled with Ratón. "*Esta mula no es buena para las sierras*," he declared. This mule is not good for the Sierras.

Raymundo almost smiled.

I paid César two hundred *pesos*, and he was very grateful—and so was I. With an old-timer like César as my guide, I could have ridden from La Purísima in a few days, almost as fast as Junípero Serra, and would not have been bruised and blistered from cactus.

Down below Pie de la Cuesta stretched the largest arroyo in Baja, meandering for seventy miles through the valley of Guadalupe and into the Pacific Ocean. For centuries, it had been known as Arroyo de Los Ángeles; on modern-day maps it is called Arroyo Raymundo. El Camino Real would cross the immense arroyo many times as I walked north to Mission Guadalupe.

By midafternoon, we arrived at our destination, Rancho El Represito Uno, where a new vaquero would take me to the mission. I paid Raymundo and said a tearful good-bye to Rosa.

The couple who owned Rancho El Represito, Felix and Marisela Villavicencio, descended from goat herders at Mission Guadalupe.

Marisela fixed the first real meal I had eaten since leaving La Purísima—chicken soup, beans, tortillas, and rice. Food never tasted so good! In the kitchen was a small chest refrigerator that worked, but it was not for food. It was where Felix kept his Tecate beer.

Felix's nephew was my new vaquero, and he arrived in time for dinner. His name was Carlos Antonio Villavicencio López of Rancho La Presa, and he was eighteen years old.

I had misgivings about Antonio's age and experience. But the next morning, after less than an hour on the old El Camino Real mission trail, I realized what a treasure he was.

———

Antonio came prepared. He wore thick leather *chaparejos* to protect his legs against cactus, and a dark felt western hat to protect his head. A long, freshly sharpened machete was thrust in the side of his saddle, and he rode atop a magnificent *macho* mule.

He was born on Rancho La Presa, next to the old mission ruins on the original cattle ranch of Mission Guadalupe. Antonio loved the old mission and El Camino Real mission trail. Occasionally, we had to detour off the mission trail because of erosion or flooding in the arroyo. He would apologize and point out the original old road from afar.

He rode quickly and was in complete control of the mules. Even Ratón behaved.

I was able to walk most the day through a narrow valley of small ranchos. Antonio wrote the name of each in my pocket journal—San Estanislao, El Carpintero, La Angostura, Iguasines, San Juan, Los Pozos, El Mesquital, and El Aguajito. He took delight in telling me about each rancho. He knew every person and was obviously a favorite of all. As he rode past, the ranchers would stop work and wave, and he often stopped to talk.

Ranchos communicated with shortwave radios, and everyone heard every conversation. It brought them close together, though they lived miles apart. Everyone knew about my mission walk and was thrilled to help out. It would be that way the next three hundred miles.

Antonio and I arrived at the Mission Guadalupe de Huasinapí ruins at dusk. He reverently removed his hat and held it briefly over his heart as we entered the ancient ruins. We tethered the mules in a thicket of cactus and brush while he showed me the rock foundation of the mission church and pointed out where the missionaries lived.

Afterward, we silently rode through the ruins to Antonio's home, Rancho

La Presa. It was in the back of the mission grounds, and we rode alongside the stone irrigation channel built by the missionaries. This was still the source of water for his family's small pasture and animals. While Antonio unpacked the mules, his father, Heliodoro, proudly walked with me to the arroyo where the missionaries built a dam and stone aqueduct to channel water to the rancho and to the mission grounds.

Antonio's mother, María, cooked outside on a woodstove, and we ate a simple meal of *machaca*, beans, and tortillas. There was no electricity. We ate in the dark underneath the thatched palm roof with enough moonlight peeking through to see our food. Antonio insisted that I sleep in his small room, where there was a bunk bed he shared with two younger brothers away at school. There was no bedding, just a single sheet over a bare mattress. I slept in my sleeping bag, thankful for a room to shield my broken body from the cold mountain air and a soft bed to lie in.

In the morning, while Antonio was packing Ratón and saddling Dulce, his mother showed me a very old adobe and thatched-roof shack next to their house.

"This was built by the missionaries," María said in Spanish, pointing to the adobe wall. The adobe was weathered but in excellent condition. The side-walls were crumbling thatched cane. A thatched palm roof looked old but solid. Like the mission trail, the shack was still in use.

While his mother fixed breakfast, Antonio playfully bantered back and forth with her to borrow her watch. Hers was the only watch on the rancho. We had a long ride ahead, over towering *cuestas* and through deep canyons, to get to Rancho San Sebastián by nightfall, and Antonio wanted to make sure we made it.

Before he mounted the mule, Antonio sharpened his machete on the waist-high stone wall and hammered the heels of his boots. I was soon to learn why.

22

Antonio was in the saddle and about to leave when María came running out of her thatched-roof kitchen, waving her watch. He bent down and took the watch and gently caressed his mother's face with his hand.

Antonio had a vaquero's soft heart and a love of tradition and family. I doubted he would leave for the city and lose his way.

The night before, he had sketched out the route we would take to Rancho San Sebastián in my pocket journal. It followed the old El Camino Real mission trail deep into Sierra de Guadalupe over several mountain peaks and a steep *cuesta* called El Barranco that dropped precipitously into an arroyo.

I walked when I could, but the trail soon turned to loose lava rock, and I was afraid of further damaging my still-swollen ankle. Antonio rode fast, and Ratón galloped close behind his mule. When Dulce galloped, it felt like riding in an old jalopy bouncing up and down on rocks. The constant jarring was painful, and I pulled back on the reins to slow Dulce to a fast walk. Antonio would patiently wait for us to catch up and immediately spur his mule and take off again like a rocket.

The mules came to an abrupt halt at the top of an immense rocky gorge leading down into an arroyo.

"El Barranco," he sighed, as my eyes followed his gaze down the thousand-foot plunge.

Antonio started down slowly, his mule sliding underneath him on the loose rock. Pulling Ratón was a blessing because it kept his mule from sliding too fast and losing control.

Dulce and I were halfway down when she panicked on the loose, sliding rock. Somehow, the mule turned herself around, almost stopping in the middle of the steep descent to do so. I was whipped back and forth in the saddle and unable to control her, barely able to hold on. It was too steep for her to climb back up, but she was too afraid to go down.

Antonio was almost at the bottom by the time his mule and Ratón stopped sliding. He dismounted and tied the two mules to a tree, and then crawled on hands and knees up the steep trail to where I was barely hanging on to Dulce's back and saddle. Antonio reached us and grabbed for the reins. He leaned on Dulce with all his weight to steady the frightened mule while I dismounted. I was trembling and fearful that my boot would catch in the stirrup and Dulce would slip and break my leg.

Antonio waited for me to slide to the bottom of the slope and out of danger before he attempted to turn Dulce around. She was a big *mula* and weighed a ton, and the two of them fought against each other like two wrestlers unwilling to concede defeat. Ultimately, Antonio was victorious: he got Dulce turned back around, then walked in front of her as they slid down the embankment, grabbing at bramble along the way to slow their descent. His presence seemed to calm Dulce, and they were almost to the bottom when Antonio slipped on rock and the heel of his boot broke off.

We were all badly shaken when we reached the bottom. Antonio walked the mules to a small clearing alongside the arroyo and removed saddles, bridles, and packs.

I spread a sweaty mule blanket on the rocks underneath a mesquite tree and unpacked the Jetboil to boil water for coffee. It was stifling hot even in the shade, but the coffee tasted good, and I knew the ritual would calm our spirits and get our wits together before we continued on. Antonio had packed canned Vienna sausages, and we rolled the sausages in María's homemade tortillas and nervously ate half a dozen.

Our troubles weren't over. The mission trail between El Barranco and

Rancho San Sebastián was overgrown with cholla higher than a man on a mule. Straggly shrubs covered with thorns towered above the cholla and draped over our heads. Antonio had to bend backward in the saddle to hack the branches and clear a path. Antonio called the cactus *garabatillo*. The thorns resembled meat hooks, and some were larger than his thumb. For hours Antonio never sheathed his machete; it was a constant struggle to clear the trail.

It was nightfall when we reached Rancho San Sebastián. It was a very warm Sunday night despite being high in the mountains, and as we arrived, the ranch was bathed in festive atmosphere, with families and small children eating and laughing and listening to music. They rushed outside when they heard our mules. Children crowded around, and the women piled plates of warm food in front of us.

Little girls followed me around and playfully fought each other to help me set up my tent on the outside porch. They ran to get plastic chairs from the kitchen for my things so nothing was on the ground. They asked to see the inside of my tent, and gleefully turned the LED lights on and off. They held my emergency satellite phone and gasped in wide-eyed amazement when I turned it on and showed them how it searched for a satellite. There was a big world (filled with strange creatures like me) out there waiting for them, and they delighted in all its wonder.

Soon, the children and families left for home, and it grew quiet. It was dark, and the night was soon freezing. I did not have warm-enough clothes for the Sierras, and my sleeping bag was too light. I spent a miserable, shivering cold night trying to stay warm.

Rancho San Sebastián was prosperous and clean, with a sink with luke-warm water and a toilet that flushed—two rare luxuries in the Sierras. I washed my face for the first time in a week, luxuriating in the feel of warm water rinsing desert sand from my eyelashes and brow.

Two families shared the house, Bernardo and Celsa Villavicencio and their middle-aged son, Abraham, and his family. Abraham agreed to be my next vaquero.

I was sad to say good-bye to Antonio. I paid him for his time, and his mule, but he refused to take money for the food. *"Esa es mi regalo,"* he said. That is my gift.

The most exceptional men are ordinary men of character and integrity. Antonio is an exceptional man.

Abraham's fourteen-year-old son, Adrián, was going to accompany us, and we planned to meet up with another vaquero from Rancho Santa Cruz somewhere along the old El Camino Real.

Everything about Abraham Villavicencio was professional and competent, and Adrián was a carbon copy. They wore matching white felt western hats; the brims had the same upward bent and their leather chaps the same intricate leather detailing. They rode in silence, slightly slouched in the saddle. Sometimes they rode side by side, but most often, Adrián swung his mule behind me to coax Dulce to pick up the pace.

We were in the high Sierras on the northern edge of Sierra de Guadalupe where it slopes and eventually ends, while Sierra de San Francisco rises. At the summit of San Venancio, we stopped the mules to rest for a moment, and the view took my breath away. In the distance, as far as I could see, were the abrupt, awe-inspiring peaks of Sierra de San Francisco silhouetted against the skyline.

This was wilderness. This was the West of myth and legend, of mystery and poetry. It may be disappearing in California, but not here.

I breathed in the indescribable beauty of this Wild West, and my breath felt lighter than air.

We soon stopped at a rancho for coffee and to give the mules a much-needed rest. The old rancho was surrounded by elaborate stone corrals and fences buried in a dense thicket of mesquite and palo blanco.

The owner of the ranch was proud of his land.

"The missionaries and the Cochimí built everything. There are two more corrals up the trail, and a cave painting less than five miles from here." He offered to ride with me, but I declined. I didn't have time to stray that far from the trail.

Abraham, Adrián, and I reluctantly departed the cool porch of the rancho. The sun was blistering hot. An hour later, on a beautifully preserved stretch of the old El Camino Real, a man on a mule rode toward us. He was my new vaquero: Agustín Villa Romero from Rancho Santa Cruz.

Abraham was happy to see Agustín. Meeting up this early in the afternoon gave him and Adrián time to ride back to Rancho San Sebastián before nightfall. I quickly paid Abraham, and they rode off at a much faster pace than we had come, unburdened by Dulce, Ratón, and me.

Agustín Villa, like all the men of the Sierras I met on El Camino Real, was tall and handsome, and neatly attired. He wore a white hat without a trace of dirt, snakeskin cowboy boots with sharp pointed toes, and lightweight chaps. His handmade leather saddle was intricately designed, and he had a matching leather canteen. He had the hands of a vaquero, a workingman's hands—strong, but worn and snarled and deeply wrinkled. His hands resembled the bramble brush that lined the old mission trail.

The vaqueros' hands reminded me of my father. Mama loved Daddy's hands, and when he died she took a photo of his hands and gave one to each of his children. Daddy worked hard on the farm up to the day he died, and his hands were gnarled and calloused from a lifetime of physical labor. I was thirteen when he passed away peacefully in his sleep without physical pain or torment. Mama said God came for him quickly. It was God's way of saying, "Well done, good and faithful servant."

"He may not have told us how much he loved us, but he showed us every day of his life, with his hard work and Christian living," she said.

Daddy was gentle of spirit, never arrogant or conceited, and of a kindly and quiet nature. He never drank. He never smoked. He never gambled. He never swore. He had a choice to do these things as all men do, but he chose not to. He never considered himself poor, and we never felt poor. We weren't. For we were raised to understand that poverty is not measured in money and material possessions but in spirit and character. Daddy was rich in both.

Agustín rode ahead and never looked back. I could have become lost in the cactus jungle and he wouldn't have known. He expected me to take care of myself. He didn't have a machete and wore no gloves. He brushed cactus and thorny shrubs aside with his bare hands.

Agustín's parents owned Rancho Santa Cruz, and their sons and families lived there. We arrived before sunset. For centuries, the rancho has been known for its cattle. Its bulls are among the biggest and meanest in Mexico. As we approached, I stopped walking and mounted Dulce. Enormous three-thousand-pound dagger-horned bulls were everywhere on the trail, and they wouldn't budge. Agustín cautiously steered our mules around them. I was thankful to be riding Dulce and not walking.

Rancho Santa Cruz was large but poor. When we rode up, Agustín's wife, María, was outside cooking on a wood fire. Their daughter was using a grindstone to pound beef jerky. Two bashful toddlers hung on to María's leg. A little girl had a shoe with no sock on one foot, and a sock with no shoe on the other. A little boy, barely old enough to walk, was barefoot. Both were covered in dirt from head to foot and having a grand time. A young woman, whom I assumed to be the children's mother, came over and took the children so María could finish fixing dinner.

Another daughter, who looked to be in her late teens, grabbed my gear bag and motioned me to come with her. "*Usted puede tener mi cama,*" she said. You can have my bed. Jesus smiled in her eyes.

Her bed was in a one-room wood shack with a dirt floor and a cloth over the doorframe that only partially covered it. There was no cover on the soiled mattress, just several wool blankets. I slept in my sleeping bag and wrapped the wool blankets around me for added warmth. I could see stars through the partially covered roof, and all night I heard animals running above my head. I tried to brush horrible images of rattlesnakes, scorpions, and giant centipedes from my mind.

When Junípero Serra stopped midday in Santa Cruz on his journey to San Diego, there was nothing here except a rocky arroyo. That night, he slept on the ground under the stars and heavenly sky. I didn't have it so bad.

I was up before sunrise, and María was already in the kitchen, preparing breakfast. There was no refrigeration, and refried beans left over from last night were still on the table alongside three small flowers in a clouded water jar. María warmed the beans outside on the wood fire and added fried pork fat. The fried pork fat tasted rancid, but I was hungry and ate it.

"There is no sauce like hunger," a starving desert wanderer wrote in his journal.[1] I felt sick to my stomach for two hours afterward. I could only imagine what was happening inside my digestive system, eating pork fat after gallbladder, liver, and colon surgeries.

Agustín's twenty-three-year-old son joined us for breakfast. He had a cell phone and proudly showed videos of Rancho Santa Cruz rodeo bulls bucking off American cowboys. He said that Bushwhacker, the most famous bucking bull on the planet and the baddest bull of all time, descended from one of their bulls. I believed him. When we rode into the rancho last night, the bulls had all looked like Bushwhacker's big brother.

After breakfast, Agustín and I rode off in the hot morning sun, past giant cardon and equally large pipe organ cactus. El Camino Real followed Arroyo Santa Cruz and meandered for miles. This was the tail end of Sierra de Guadalupe. Mountains were everywhere, and I wondered where one sierra ends and another begins. Is there a line in the sand that I cross over and Sierra Guadalupe becomes Sierra de San Francisco?

When one is walking, or riding a mule, the land changes slowly. The size and shape of every rock on the trail is noticed and felt, as is every thorny bush and weed. All are potential threats and must be respected. A stumble or slip on a rock, or a branch hitting my face or neck, could mean death.

We all live closer to death than we think.

The arroyo was bone-dry and immense. It was an open page of a tragic history book. Uprooted trees and large boulders told of massive floods, ruined crops, and drowned animals. Household items—pans, harnesses, chairs, tables, and doorframes—wedged in the rock told of despair and ruin and lost dreams. A lifetime of hard work had been swept away in an instant.

We passed old Rancho Agua Verde, the front yard sunken into the edge of the arroyo. More than a hundred years ago it was built on high ground. Floodwaters found it.

Agustín abruptly stopped and pointed high up a cliff. He spoke rapidly in Spanish. "There are many carvings and paintings. They are everywhere here."

He dismounted and climbed up a ledge. Agustín was tall, over six feet. Towering high above him on the face of the cliff were deep carvings that resembled Egyptian hieroglyphs. *How did the person who carved the cliff reach such heights?* I wondered. He motioned for me to climb up and look. I struggled on the loose rock. Agustín removed his spurs and chaps, slid down, and took my arm to steady me.

There are thousands of ancient carvings and paintings in Lower California, extending six hundred miles from the cape to the northern Sierras. They are on granite and lava cliffs and in caves that rise hundreds of feet above the ground, impossible to reach, impossible to carve. *How could people possibly do this?* Man seeks answers to all riddles. Perhaps, some say, lower buttresses of rock have crumbled away. Others have suggested people used rope ladders.

When the Spanish arrived, Cochimís said the carvings and paintings were the work of a giantlike nation, which had come there from the north. These giant men once lived in the mountains, long before their coming. Missionaries found one inscription that resembled Gothic letters interspersed with Hebrew and Chaldean characters.

A Jesuit missionary in San Ignacio, José Mariano Rotea, heard of a gigantic petrified skeleton and had it dug up. He found all the backbone, a long bone, a rib, several teeth, and a large fragment of the skull. The rib was about two feet long. Rotea, a master builder and architect well versed in math and measurement, calculated the man must have been eleven feet tall considering the rib, backbone, and size of the skull. Scientists find this preposterous because no race of people have been found whose height average more than six feet.

I stood below the carvings etched deep in stone and wondered who carved the rock. *What were they saying?*

One of the meanings of the Greek word *hieroglyph* is "sacred engraved words." Language is sacred whether written or spoken. It is who we are. It endures and becomes who we were. These carvings are who they were. I couldn't help but wonder if our words would become lost as we surrendered to technology.

God carved the Ten Commandments on stone for a reason.

23

After almost three weeks of weaving in and out of rocky arroyos, Dulce was done.

She stopped at the top of a deep embankment twenty feet above an arroyo and refused to go further. No amount of coaxing or threatening or pleading would get her to budge. I now understood where the saying "as stubborn as a mule" had come from.

Unperturbed, Agustín tied one end of rope onto his saddle and the other around Dulce's neck and dragged her down into the arroyo. Agustín was willing to drag her all the way to San Ignacio, but Dulce figured Agustín was more stubborn than she was and finally started walking again. I walked alongside her most of the afternoon.

About four o'clock, we saw a vaquero on a mule coming across the desert toward us.

Agustín recognized him. "*Es Chico Arce.*"

Vaquero Gertrudis "Chico" Arce of Rancho San Luis would take me to San Ignacio and perhaps further. We made our hellos, and then Agustín was anxious to turn around and start back to Rancho Santa Cruz before nightfall.

Chico explained that we were close to his rancho, Rancho San Luis, and could stay the night, but we were only two hours from San Ignacio. Though it would be after sunset and dark by the time we got to San Ignacio, perhaps it would be worth it?

I was exhausted and hungry and leery of riding a mule in the desert after dark, but the thought of a warm bed and hot food was too tempting. I reluctantly agreed to ride to San Ignacio.

It was a bad decision.

It was *not* a couple of hours' ride to San Ignacio. Maybe for Chico riding alone. But with a pack mule and me, it was much slower. It became a five-hour ride in the dark in the desert. There was no moon. The night sky was overcast; there was not even starlight. We were in the desert, surrounded by cactus and thorns, and it was pitch-black. I couldn't see.

Chico said there was a shortcut through the desert to San Ignacio and took off galloping on his mule, pulling Ratón behind him. Dulce and I followed nervously. A short while later, I was hit across the face by a mesquite branch and felt warm blood trickle down my cheek. I was terrified. Riding through cactus and mesquite during the day when you can see is terrifying; at night, when you cannot see, it is horrific.

Where was Chico? I couldn't hear his mule or the jingle of his spurs.

"Chico!" I cried out.

Nothing.

"Chico, I can't do this. This is not good." I was beginning to whine. I hated that.

I thought back to the dark days of fighting cancer. *Don't whine*, I would scold myself. *Cry or scream if you have to, but don't whine.* Whining can quickly lead to self-pity and self-victimization and passivity, which make things worse, not better.

In a crisis it is necessary to be constantly aware of what is happening and to get a grip before things get out of control. Do something! With cancer, when you start vomiting, figure out how to stop it or slow it down. When diarrhea is like a rushing river, figure out how to keep from getting dehydrated. In chemotherapy, don't just sit there and let your dry mouth develop blisters and sores. Do something!

It is not safe to ride a mule through desert cactus at night, so stop. Don't do it!

My voice became firm and resolute. "Chico, I am not doing this."

I stopped, unwilling to ride further.

I soon heard Chico; he took Dulce's reins and slowly led us through the cactus. We came to a dirt road. From there it was another three hours of riding on the dark road to get to San Ignacio.

I had been walking and riding a mule through desert hell for almost twelve hours. I was exhausted, hungry, and riding against a freezing north wind. I started shivering and knew I had to calm myself to get through this. I couldn't allow myself to give in to hypothermia, hyperventilation, or hyperanxiety.

A year ago, when I discovered cancer had returned in my left lung, I was sitting in the lobby at Stanford Cancer Center, waiting to meet with my doctors to discuss what to do. I felt despondent.

My friend Joyce Blue Summers, a mission walker, shared a short, affirmative prayer that transformed my life. It was three simple words.

"Edie, relax and say, 'All is well,'" Joyce suggested. "And all *will* be well," she promised. I tried it. I closed my eyes, took a deep inhale, and let the breath out slowly. "All is well." I felt peace and a sense of well-being.

Riding Dulce through the dark desert, I could hear Joyce's reassuring voice: "Just say, 'All is well,' and all will be well!"

"All is well," I whispered.

I carried on a silent conversation with myself. "I am doing exactly what I want to do. I am exactly where I want to be. I am wrapped in the arms of God and am utterly, completely safe."

Slowly, I began to feel at peace. I would never be here again. I would never again experience being on a mule at night in the thick of desert, in complete darkness. No moon, no stars, no light. No seeing. Just *feeling*—just *being*.

I started humming the tune of the old gospel song. *It is well, it is well with my soul.*

I was hungry, exhausted, and freezing, but—remarkably—happy.

We finally saw lights and arrived in San Ignacio after ten o'clock. Trudi was in San Ignacio to pick up Dulce and Ratón for her tour group. Chico and I rode to a rancho where the mules would stay the night. I said a sad good-bye to Dulce and even Ratón; I'd grown quite fond of the cantankerous little mule.

Trudi picked us up and took me to a hotel. She had leftovers from dinner in the truck—a small piece of fish and half-eaten chile relleno—and gave them to me.

I checked into my hotel room. I was literally worn ragged and filthy. I hadn't had a bath in two weeks, and had washed my face once at Rancho Sebastián. I was too exhausted to even take a shower. The leftover food looked delicious. The only thing I had eaten since the pork fat beans at breakfast was a bean burrito. I didn't have a spoon or fork in the hotel room, but I was so starved I ate with my fingers, shoving food in my mouth in a couple of handfuls. I felt wonderful, eating the food with my fingers as fast as I could, exhausted, laughing at myself, and falling into bed filthy. Having a real bed with real sheets felt so wonderful.

"All is well," I whispered before falling into a deep, dark sleep.

———

I planned to sleep late, but a loud knock on my door woke me early. It was Trudi.

"Edie, you have a problem. The old El Camino Real goes through an area where there are cave paintings, and you don't have a permit." She was worried.

I had no idea what Trudi was talking about. She soon explained that all tourists going into a protected area of Sierra de San Francisco where there are cave paintings must get a permit from the Department of History and Anthropology, known as INAH, in La Paz. In addition, someone working for INAH must accompany tourists through the area. The rule was to protect the cave paintings from vandals and miscreants. I was neither, but INAH didn't know that.

Trudi was nervous. She could lose her license to run a small tour-guiding business if she broke the law. Trudi had rented me two mules, which made her liable for my conduct and responsible for applying for permits. She had gotten an angry call from a very upset woman named Lucera who worked for INAH in La Paz, demanding that I immediately stop my walk and go through proper procedures to obtain a permit. It could take weeks or months to get a permit.

I listened in disbelief as Trudi explained the predicament.

"You may not be allowed to go further." Trudi was serious. "Lucera is fuming and demanding that we call her immediately. No one loves the cave paintings more than Lucera, and she is determined to protect them. I am a tour operator and should know better, but you aren't in a tour group. I guess I messed up."

Two people worked for INAH in a small office in the old Jesuit wine cellar of Mission San Ignacio. I quickly got dressed, and we drove over to the mission for a conference call with Lucera.

When Trudi and I arrived, the INAH employees began filling out a pile of forms and making copies of my passport and travel documents. One of the men, Jesús, was very polite and spoke excellent English. Trudi told him about my mission walks, that I was walking the old El Camino Real, and assured him I was trustworthy and had no interest in cave paintings.

Finally, Lucera called on the office speakerphone. For half an hour she scolded Trudi. She was speaking loudly enough for everyone in the wine cellar and down in the arroyo to hear. I understood enough Spanish to know she was refusing to let me go further. Trudi was soft-spoken and hardly said a word other than to profusely apologize for our bad behavior and promise to never do it again. After thirty minutes of venting, Lucera calmed down and said that she *might* allow me in the protected area, but she had to approve my vaquero, *and* one of her INAH employees had to accompany me.

Chico Arce was sitting quietly in the INAH office with us. After exchanging a few words with Jesús, Chico suggested that he be approved as the vaquero. Everyone loved Chico. He played the accordion and sang locally, and always had a smile.

Trudi was stunned when Lucera agreed.

Soon it was determined who from INAH would accompany Chico and me, and then Trudi and I went to lunch to celebrate.

"Edie, I just witnessed a miracle," Trudi said as we sat down, the smells of delicious food making my belly rumble. She had never known Lucera to give an inch. "These cave paintings are as precious to her as children, and I should have informed her earlier. Believe me, I will never do that again!"

I was starved. Really. My belt had five notches. In Loreto, I fastened the second notch. I was now on the fifth and last belt notch, and my torn and dirty cargo pants were almost falling off. I ordered three plates of food: huevos rancheros, carne asada with rice and beans, and a large plate of grilled vegetables. I ate it all and was still hungry.

Then it was time to do some shopping. "This is your last chance to buy supplies for four hundred miles," Trudi warned. I needed sunglasses, fleece clothing, flash memory for my Olympus camera, medicine for my cholla-infected legs and arms—and a lot more Neosporin.

Afterward, I walked to Mission San Ignacio de Kadakaamán and spent several hours marveling at the beautiful old mission.

Though I didn't know it at the time, Junípero Serra had also arrived in San Ignacio in the dark, at 3:00 a.m., after riding through the desert all night. Riding through the desert in the dark of night, he, too, must have cloaked his fear in the mantle of God's protection.

It was Father Serra's first trip to Mission San Ignacio, more than two hundred miles from Loreto. He had not been this far north. The stone church was under construction when he arrived, and it would be another twenty years before it was completed. He saw only walls without a roof.

José Rotea, the Jesuit missionary who examined the giant-size fossilized skeleton, only had time to build the church walls before the Spanish king expelled the Jesuits in 1767. None of the Jesuits were told why. Rotea was native-born in Mexico, but the king banished him to Europe and into misery. A missionary expelled with Rotea wrote of his anguish, "He was not even told whether the construction of the church or something else was responsible for his banishment."[1]

Rotea and the other Jesuit missionaries had fallen victim to a power struggle between king and church being played out six thousand miles away in Madrid, Spain. Lies circulated in the royal Spanish court that the missionaries had amassed a fortune in gold, silver, and pearls; lived like kings; and were becoming too powerful.

In 1767, the king ordered the missionaries arrested, imprisoned, and exiled. The general sent to arrest them cried and asked for forgiveness when he found the impoverished missionaries living in "a sandy waste sown with thorns and thistles."[2]

The arrested missionaries must have cried, too, in the darkness: "Dear Lord, why hast thou forsaken me?"

The Jesuits were among the most educated and hardy young men of Europe. They were the entrepreneurs of their generation, possessing amazing skill and superhuman courage. Each man was a self-taught explorer, adventurer, and mapmaker, builder and craftsman, farmer, rancher and vintner, weaver and tailor, teacher and preacher.

I felt the missionaries' suffering. I felt their hurt. I felt their despair. Every day on the mission trail, I paid humble homage to their sacrifice, especially when I arrived at a mission, stood in ruins molded with their hands from sand and rock, and marveled at what they had created. Each day I walked on trails made holy with their toil and tears, and each day I gave thanks to the God of Abraham and his Son, Jesus Christ, whom they had given up their lives to serve.

———

Chico arrived the next morning riding a chocolate-brown *macho* mule named Gato (cat). He had a smaller *mula* for me named Voya. It was love at first sight.

Voya was an iridescent light auburn color, and her color matched perfectly with the copper-hued lava rock of Sierra de San Francisco, as if God had used the same color palette for both.

Chico didn't have a pack mule. He arranged with a local vaquero to deliver a burro. I had finally figured out the difference between a burro and a mule and could even tell them apart, sometimes. A burro is a full-blood donkey, usually small, with a mouth full of really large teeth that, next to their hind legs, is their most feared weapon. A mule is half horse and half donkey and usually more handsome and well-mannered. Of course, there were exceptions, like Ratón, whose genes weighed heavy on the donkey side. Vaqueros dislike burros, and the feeling is mutual. Mules hate them too. Burros are inherently wild and untamable and will escape at the first opportunity—even heavily loaded with supplies—and disappear into the wild. Wild burros were a common sight in remote places along the old mission trail. They delighted in sneaking up behind us, biting our pack mule on the rump, and causing a wild commotion.

Half an hour up El Camino Real, we met the vaquero, Gerardo Valensuela, walking alongside a motley brown burro and dark horse. Neither animal was tethered, and both followed closely to his side like obedient children. Gerardo had the kind eyes of a saint and a gentle smile. He asked if he could pray for me. He took my hand, closed his eyes, and said a prayer. It was very beautiful and touched my heart. The warmth of the prayer stayed with me for days.

The burro behaved until Gerardo was out of sight. This was my first encounter with a burro. I soon understood why vaqueros hate them. Chico tethered the burro tightly to his mule, but it was a constant struggle to control him. He would kick both hind legs up at the same time, rising on his forefeet with butt in the air, and kick his hind legs into Voya's nose. My poor *mula* was kicked half a dozen times, and terrorized, by a burro half her size.

For twenty miles we rode across a plain scattered with massive piles of lava, through forests of giant cardon and barrel cactus, and across mountain *cuestas* and arroyos the missionaries had named Satancio, Lucifer, and El Infernio, hellish places from which there seemed to be no escape.

Cactus pierced our legs, but the sides of the mules must have been thicker than bull leather, because they plowed straight through it and gave it no mind. A ferocious wind blew across the plain. Gato and Voya walked slowly and hesitantly over the sliding lava rock, and Chico struggled to keep them moving. When my hat flew off, the lava rock was too sharp to dismount and get it. Chico bent over in the saddle and used the tip of his machete to pick it up.

At sunset we arrived at Rancho El Carricito, home of Norma and Rafael López, Chico's relatives.

Norma's house was immaculate, which is almost impossible in the desert. She was a stout, strong woman, like my mother. I watched as Norma labored to wash eight huge buckets of dirt-drenched farm clothes, and it brought back memories of my youth.

When electricity came to rural Oklahoma in the mid-1950s, one of the first things Mama did with her egg money was make a down payment on an electric wringer washer. Before her electric washer, washday was the hardest and longest day of the week: it required her to heat water in a large bucket, pour the scalding water into the washtub, and use a scrub board and hand wringer to wash. Mama never cared much for electric clothes dryers, preferring instead to hang clothes on the clothesline to let them dry in the sun. Our clothes always smelled fresh and deep clean. Mama said the clean smell came from the sun's ultraviolet rays acting as an antiseptic. To this day, I can close my eyes and hear the lulling, meditative sound of clothes flapping gently on the clothesline, and Mama humming gospel softly underneath her breath.

I imagine that's what heaven must sound like.

That night, I slept in a dark concrete shed in the back of Norma's ranch house next to the clothesline and fell asleep to the rhythmic sound of clothes drying in the desert wind, and dreamed of Mama.

Chico and I followed Arroyo Santa María, where there was less cactus and lava rock. There were long stretches of hard-packed sand with fewer rocks, and I walked about ten miles.

When I wasn't walking, Chico and I ambled slowly along on Gato and Voya, in no hurry.

"The mules need a rest after yesterday," Chico advised in Spanish. I didn't speak much Spanish but was beginning to understand what was said.

Chico was a lovely young man in his thirties. He sang. He whistled. He hugged the burro after yelling at him.

I had given him a thousand *pesos* for food in San Ignacio, and he'd bought three dozen bean burritos, fresh melon, six cans of tuna, and a saddlebag full of Snickers candy bars. Two or three times a day, he reached behind Gato into his saddlebag. He unwrapped one Snickers bar at a time. He tore it in two, reached over Gato and Voya, and handed me the smaller piece. He flashed a big smile full of mischief and fun, hoping that I wouldn't notice and not caring if I did. His smile revealed a gold front tooth.

We arrived at the famous missionary water hole of Rosarito in the late afternoon. Chico took the animals down an embankment to water before spreading his bedroll on bare ground under a leafless palo verde tree that looked dead in the dim light of sunset. He was careful to avoid the vicious thorns that hung down ready to tear open an ear or lip.

A man on a mule rode into camp. His name was Patricio Ojeda. He was a friend of Chico's—though everyone is a friend of Chico's. He had ridden four hours from Santa Marta. He worked for INAH and accompanied tourists to see the cave paintings, and Lucera had sent him to ride with us, to make sure we didn't go near the caves.

Government jobs in Baja must pay well. Nothing on him, or his mule, looked worn. His saddle and harness were polished, and his saddle blankets looked new. A shotgun in a polished leather sheath was attached to his saddle, as was a machete. Patricio wore a snow-white hat and a clean white shirt, and his leather *chaparejos* were thinner and stylishly cut. His silver spurs glistened in the light of the campfire. Chico eyed everything with his characteristic smile, but his eyes were not as bright. He was younger than Patricio, but he was worn. Patricio was new.

Patricio set up his clean-looking bedroll on the other side of Chico's palo verde tree, and I heard them talking around the campfire until late into the night.

Unable to sleep, I lay awake in my tent, writing in my journal and reflecting on the walk.

The mission walk mirrored life. When young, we focus on the trail, on our objectives—our jobs, education, buying a home. We realize no one cares where we've been; they just care where we are going. At midlife, our focus becomes the people in our lives, the blessings and heartache others bring to us; people come and people go, even people we love. Sometimes we have to move others out for us to move on, and that is painful. As we grow old, life is about the journey. We reflect on the journey of our life and what has been gained, what has been lost, and what remains; of those who have come before us; of what we will leave behind.

Life can be bittersweet, even brutal; nonetheless, it is a beautiful gift, and the long mission walk was allowing me to unwrap it slowly, one soul-felt step at a time.

24

By midafternoon the next day, a dark rain cloud gathered above us and sat in the center of blue sky. We were close to Tres Vírgenes, an active volcano, and I wondered if the volcano influenced the peculiar cloud formation. The day had been dry and stifling hot; now raindrops fell from the dark cloud directly above us, soon followed by thunder. The rain couldn't come at a worse time.

El Camino Real was about to climb steep and narrow Cuesta de Tagualila. Missionaries had cut the old road into the side of the mountain and piled loose lava rock five feet high on the sides.

In the rain, our mules kept sliding on the wet rocks. When the lead mule stumbled, the other mules plowed into him. There was nowhere to go except up. We were packed together as tight as an accordion until the lead mule moved.

The Tagualila trail was treacherous but breathtakingly beautiful. The lava rock was a deep maroon red made even darker with rain. Scrubby cactus bushes swelled to collect each raindrop, and green colors of the desert deepened around us. Leafless, thorny palo verde trees and shrubs came to life. The rain softened their thorns, and for a few hours we suffered no stab wounds or torn flesh.

We reached a mesa, and the trail leveled. It was getting late, and it was still raining and cold. There was no place to set up camp other than the middle of the trail. Chico had no tent, only a thin calfskin ground cover for a top blanket. Thorny shrubs were so thick the ground underneath was dry.

I set up my tent in the freezing drizzle. There was less than a foot of bare ground on the worn old mission trail, and a tight squeeze to wedge my tent between shrub and rock. My tent was soaked, and the outside of the sleeping bag was damp but dry inside. I quickly inflated the air mattress, and stepped outside to boil water in the Jetboil.

It was too wet for a campfire.

Rain dripped from Chico's face as he drank the hot coffee. Patricio had his own food and sat on a rock, eating. I brought him hot coffee, and he smiled gratefully.

I opened a can of tuna, and Chico pulled out the three-day-old burritos. He peeled a melon with his machete, and cut it in half. Both halves slipped out of his hands and dropped on the rain-soaked ground. He smiled, picked both pieces up with the blade of his machete, flicked off the dirt, and handed one to me. I ate it.

I was headed back to my tent when Chico pushed me quickly aside. He grabbed a rock and threw it at a large rattlesnake that was crawling along the edge of my tent, less than a foot in front of me. The wounded snake slithered underneath a small brittlebush branch in the middle of the trail. We watched it coil, and the brittlebush shook. Before it had a chance to strike, Chico threw a larger rock and hit it squarely on the head. When it stopped coiling and moving he used his machete to pull the snake from under the brush to make sure it was dead.

I shuddered as I stepped over the dead snake to get to my tent. It was still in the middle of the old mission trail when we left camp the next morning.

We awoke to sunshine, and both vaqueros were in a great mood.

Patricio liked to sing as much as Chico. For hours they sang and harmonized, their loud baritone voices amplified in the dry desert air. The mules picked up the pace too. Even the burro was happy.

"*Muy contento,*" Chico said as he playfully rubbed the burro's nose and gave him a hug.

After a few hours, Patricio and Chico had exhausted their songbook, and Patricio stopped singing, but not Chico. He sang at the top of his voice; he sang in whispers; he sang happy Mexican folk songs and sad cowboy ballads.

He sang to everything. He sang to the mules; he sang to the burro. His voice got hoarse, and he stopped singing and started whistling. When he could whistle no more, he took his machete and thumped a song on his chaps.

Dark clouds gathered and hid the sun. A few raindrops fell. Only then did Chico stop singing. He doesn't sing in the rain.

We wove for hours through Arroyos El Carrizo and San Casimiro, and Sierra de San Juan. On the side of a steep cliff, the burro slipped and fell on his right hind leg, scattering our gear all over the trail. A few minutes later, Voya slipped and lurched forward, lost her balance, and almost knocked me off. My neck snapped backward and my bones crunched. My throat throbbed in pain.

I took two Advil and prayed there was no damage. I walked and focused on keeping my stiff and painful neck in straight alignment above my shoulders. Stiffness and pain slowly melted away as clouds disappeared and the sun ignited the desert sand, radiating warmth.

At nightfall, we came to a small clearing under a dead mesquite tree next to an old rock corral.

"This is Tinaja de Guadalupe," Chico said as he dismounted. "We will camp here."

Patricio took the mules to water, and Chico managed to spark a slightly green palo verde branch. Once lit, the fire roared to life. The three of us stood with our backs toward the fire and slowly stopped shivering.

Patricio was packed and ready to leave before dawn. We had one last coffee together, and Chico and I stood watching until he was out of sight.

We were five hours from Santa Gertrudis and still had one last peak of Sierra de San Juan to climb. Most of the time there was no trail, just endless thickets of stinging thorns, mostly matacora—an evil, shoulder-height bush with black, snakelike limbs. Instead of leaves, it is naked like the devil and covered in thousands of crooked thorns resembling devil horns. The thorny limbs reached out to snare Gato and Voya and the burro. It was a ride through hell.

Time and time again, the burro got the *alforjas* holding my gear bags tangled in the dense matacora, and Chico had to rescue him. *Alforjas* are large, crate-sized side bags vaqueros make out of tough rawhide, using old wooden orange crates as molds. The burro delighted in rubbing the *alforjas* off his back against thorny bushes that embedded a thousand needles into the rawhide, making it almost impossible for the vaquero to reload.

Chico was tired. He didn't sing as much. Or whistle.

A trail reappeared, and instead of copper-colored lava rock, it was white stone. From Google Earth, this small section of the old El Camino Real looks like a long white scar. It is one of the most visible parts of the old trail.

For a while, we were safe from thorns, and I was able to walk at a faster pace. Nothing could penetrate the white stone, not even cactus. It was as hard as concrete, and contained mica that shone with "whiteness so intense that it is dazzling."[1] The missionaries pulverized the stone and made whitewash for tombstones and mission interiors. It was so brilliant it had to be softened with glue.

I rediscovered once again what the missionaries learned three centuries ago: in this godforsaken desert, even a blessing is cursed.

The crystalline brilliance of the noonday sun against the white stone was blinding. It hurt to open my eyes, even to squint. I didn't have to worry about thorns, but I couldn't see. For the next hour, I rode Voya with my eyes closed, trusting her to follow closely behind Chico and Gato.

We made it to Santa Gertrudis by early afternoon, and the tiny pueblo was filled with trucks and people celebrating. Since every town is named for a saint, every day there is a celebration somewhere in Mexico.

We had arrived at Mission Santa Gertrudis on her feast day. It was also Chico's birthday, and he was ready to celebrate! In Mexico, a child is often named for the patron saint of his or her day of birth. Chico was, unfortunately, born on the feast day of a female saint. Thus his name is Gertrudis Arce.

There wasn't much in Santa Gertrudis. It was in the middle of the desert and inaccessible by the lack of roads. Not many outsiders came here. There was no hotel, no restaurant, no plumbing or electricity, just a few scattered homes, mostly old RVs, generously called ranchos. What it lacked in amenities, though, it made up for in authenticity and hospitality.

Just the kind of place I loved.

Chico and I stopped at Rancho La Chinga on the outskirts of town, and quickly unpacked the burro and unsaddled Voya and Gato. A small crowd was gathered in a dirt yard in front of the horse stable, and live music blasted from large speakers in the back of a farm truck. The celebration had been going on for two days and was winding down. The owners, Kiko and Maty Medina, had an ice chest of Tecate beer and large pots of pinto beans, beef, corn tortillas, and fresh salsa. Their two sons were playing guitar and singing. Chico grabbed a beer and an accordion and sang along.

I ate, and ate, and ate.

The Santa Gertrudis saint's day ceremony was going on at the old mission church. Kiko thrust a large banner with a picture of Santa Gertrudis la Magna in my arms and said, "*Vámonos.*" Let's go.

I was filthy and smelly. No one seemed to mind.

Chico and the Medina family lined up behind my banner and we walked a quarter mile up the hill to the mission.

We arrived just as several dozen celebrants were walking in a solemn procession led by the priest and four men carrying a platform with a beautiful gold and porcelain statue of Saint Gertrude the Great. I joined the back of the procession, carrying the large Santa Gertrudis banner. We arrived at the barren arroyo and, next to an old windmill, the priest prayed for water and abundance.

After the prayer, the crowd quickly dispersed to celebrate.

It was time for Chico to return to Rancho San Luis, and he introduced me to Cenovio Gamboa Lazcano, a retired schoolteacher from San Quintin, hoping Cenovio could help me. The schoolteacher had grown up dreaming of being a cowboy. He was passionate about vaqueros, ranchos, the missions, Baja California culture—and Facebook. He had twenty-five thousand Facebook friends and wanted to post videos of me and share my walk.

Cenovio belonged to a network of horse-loving men who rode in *cabalgatas* between missions on saint's days. *Cabalgata* riders hire local vaqueros and take trucks along for hay and water for the horses, and food and tequila for the riders. Cenovio knew most every rancho and vaquero on the mission trail between Santa Gertrudis and the California border, and he promised to help me finish. We planned to meet up again two hundred miles north of Santa Gertrudis, at a remote truck stop in the desert, called Cataviña.

After the saint's day procession, Kiko and Maty took off with their two sons in the truck with the speakers. They invited me to set up my tent on a concrete slab next to an old RV they slept in. Chico asked for three hundred *pesos* of his pay, and I didn't see him until the next day.

The next mission, San Borja, was ninety miles north, through the spine of Sierra de San Francisco—and through the hottest and driest area of one of the hottest and driest deserts on the planet.

I went to bed not knowing how I was going to get there. Cenovio had introduced me to several vaqueros at the mission. None wanted to take me.

The wind howled all night, and it was freezing cold. The cold ate right through the four layers of clothes I slept in. I was wearing every item of clothing in my gear bag, including a heavy fleece jacket and pants purchased in San Ignacio. I hoped it wouldn't get colder as I walked north toward the infamous Sierra San Pedro Mártir and deeper into winter.

Coyotes kept me up most of the night. My tent faced Arroyo Guadalupe, and hordes of coyotes run through the arroyo during the night, scavenging for food. Where I grew up in rural Oklahoma, the coyotes ran through creek beds at night, yelping and prowling for food, too, but these coyotes sounded different, like ravenous swarms of four-legged hairy locusts devouring everything in sight.

Chico had been out partying and singing all night. He had fallen asleep in his clothes on an old cot in the stable. But I soon learned he'd also been with Cenovio rounding up a couple of vaqueros to ride north with me. They soon showed up: Tomás Murillo and Aaron Villavicencio of Rancho Santa Cruz Norte. Aaron agreed to ride two days to Rancho Los Corrales, where I would meet up with Tomás Murillo.

This was how my journey progressed. On faith and the goodwill of people willing to help out. Yes, of course, I would be paying them, but I was so thankful that no vaquero left me alone, on my own, to fend for myself. They always looked out for me.

At least so far.

After Chico left with Voya, Gato, and the burro, I had the rest of the day to myself. I scrubbed my clothes by hand on a rough rock and hung them to dry.

A son and daughter-in-law, Gladys, lived in a second RV parked at an angle to the other. An open patio with a dirt floor and thatched-palm roof was between the two RVs. There was no refrigeration, and food from the two-day celebration was still on the table and stove. Flies were everywhere. Gladys fixed a large breakfast with eggs, beans, and onion and tomatoes, and served real milk. For more than a month, my only milk had been artificial dairy creamer. At midday, she fixed ceviche made with octopus, tomato, cucumber, and onions, and crisp tostados, which we smothered with mayonnaise and doused with hot sauce. I was so hungry I could hardly stop eating. I knew it would be the last meal of the day. No one eats three meals.

After the meal, Gladys and I walked to the mission and past old stone corrals built by the missionaries. All that was left of the original mission was a gray wall of rough-hewn rock and mortar. The inside had been robbed of its treasures centuries ago. The church was rebuilt in 1997, and now a parish priest conducts weekly mass. Outside the chapel were five shelves containing candles; I lit a candle and said a prayer.

Mission Santa Gertrudis was originally called La Piedad, the pure and pious, and its success was largely the work of one man of extreme piety and faith. Andrés Comanaji was a blind Cochimí, and his zeal and spiritual purity were legendary among his tribesmen and the Jesuit missionaries.

Several decades before founding Mission Santa Gertrudis, missionaries rode forty hours from San Ignacio to baptize the natives. Comanaji was instrumental in converting his people. He was their teacher and spiritual inspiration. Six hundred Cochimí were baptized before the mission was founded, and more than fourteen hundred were baptized in the first few years. Comanaji displayed exemplary integrity and possessed great charm. He had a gift for explaining the mysteries of God and faith and Jesus's teachings. He gained respect and veneration from his people by patiently overcoming the influence of witch doctors whose power was threatened by Christianity.

This pure and pious blind man built the first crude mission church. His touch was substituted for the lack of sight. He had no hammer or nails. He framed the rustic building in wood and made walls of mud and small stone.

When the buildings were finished, a Jesuit missionary from Germany,

George Retz, who had been at Mission San Ignacio a year to learn the Cochimí language, came in the summer of 1752 to establish Mission Santa Gertrudis.

It was a constant struggle to feed everyone. There wasn't much here, just a narrow valley, a rocky arroyo, and a sometimes-running spring. The ability to grow food was poor.

When he was not teaching or working in the fields or hewing stone, the devout blind man was in the mission church, praying with great humility.

Andrés Comanaji continued to toil beside his native brothers and Padre Retz until the expulsion of the Jesuits. When the Spanish king ordered the Jesuits to leave, Father Retz had a broken leg and could not walk. His Cochimí Christian friends carried him on their backs to Loreto.

Retz died of a broken heart a few years after being arrested and expelled to his homeland. There is nothing written about what became of Andrés Comanaji.

25

People of the desert "do not die but gradually dry up and blow away,"[1] wrote a gold prospector passing through Santa Gertrudis in 1849. It took him three weeks to get from San Ignacio to San Borja. Two horses died. He almost died.

There is no water, just endless desert sand. Even the air is thirsty.

North of Santa Gertrudis, Harry Crosby pieced together a map of the mission trail using vague historical sources and local vaquero knowledge. I carried Harry's maps and hand-drawn maps from missionary journals and latter-day explorers and adventurers. In places, El Camino Real was in such good shape a map wasn't necessary. Sometimes there wasn't even a cow path, just ancient names of ranchos, arroyos, and waterholes.

Every two or three hours I turned on my emergency satellite phone and pinged our location. Dale was following my pings on a digital map in San Diego. He was better informed than I was on where I was.

Aaron Villavicencio, my new vaquero, had arrived early in the morning in Santa Gertrudis with two horses and a mule but no riding saddle for me, no packsaddle or *alforjas* for the mule, and no machete.

I was to suffer greatly for his lapses.

Aaron gave me the larger horse, a beautiful, spirited roan beauty with no name. I would have been much happier with a dispirited old mule. The horse wanted to run through the parched dry desert.

I wanted to live and not break my neck.

Since Aaron didn't bring a saddle for me, I was told to choose a saddle from a rack at Rancho La Chinga. I knew nothing about saddles, and I chose one that was less worn than the others.

As a walker, I learned early on there is a reason a road is less traveled, and I never go there. Now I know to never choose a saddle that is less worn.

After an hour in the saddle, I knew something wasn't right. The saddle was small and narrow, the stirrups were short, and the stirrup coverings, called *tapaderas*, were six sizes too small for my wide hiking boots. Unfortunately, I had picked a child's saddle. My feet were numb, and my entire body ached. By then it was too late to do anything about it.

The lack of a packsaddle and *alforjas* for the mule was a constant headache. But it was Aaron's headache, not mine. Aaron did his best to tie and twist rope around the gear bags and around the mule's belly and buttocks, but it kept sliding off and under the mule's belly.

Without a machete, there was no option but to plow straight through cactus and thorny trees. I saw ocotillo cactus, known as devil's chair, for the first time. Ocotillo was wicked. Thorny whips more than ten feet high lined the old mission trail. Its snakelike limbs swayed in the wind and lashed out at us, with razor-sharp needles that dug into clothes and skin. It would be a terrorizing presence the next three hundred miles.

Aaron was a vaquero, not a tourist guide, and what he lacked in packing skills he made up for in tracking skills. He was an outstanding vaquero and knew every inch of the terrain. Although he had no schooling beyond the primary grade, he slowly, and with great pride, printed names of arroyos and ranchos in my journal.

He liked to talk, and spoke at length about the desert and the trail and who knows what. He knew I spoke limited Spanish. He didn't care. He was just glad to have someone to talk to.

He drank from waterholes and didn't carry water in his saddlebag, only Coke. He was only thirty-two but was missing several teeth, which made him look older. He was as unselfconscious of his missing teeth as he was of his lack of education.

Aaron's toothless smile, jovial banter, and good humor when the gear pack slipped off the mule warmed my heart, and it was easy to overlook his mistakes. Like all the vaqueros of the Sierras, he loved the old El Camino Real mission trail and was proud of his cultural heritage.

I walked off and on through the day as we wove through three arroyos— Guadalupe, Purification, and Piedra Blanca. We arrived at Rancho La Unión at dusk. I had briefly met the elderly couple who lived there, Gilberto and María Rojas, at the mission church in Santa Gertrudis. María was outside cooking a pot of beans on a woodstove when we arrived. She had a modern kitchen and butane stove but preferred to cook on her old woodstove, fueled with dead limbs of pitahaya cactus. Everything María served was made by hand: the refried beans, cow cheese, tortillas, even the brined olives. She lived a simple life and had lovely black hair without a touch of gray. They had a bathroom sink but no water. I took a cup of water from my water bottle and used it to brush my teeth and wash my face and hands. In a country where water is scarce, every drop is treasured. It amazed me what I could do with one small cup of water.

The next morning, Gilberto saddled up his horse and rode with us an hour, until we came to the end of Rancho La Unión.

The sun was brutally hot. A fierce, dry desert wind slowed the horses. My lips peeled, and flakes of dead skin irritated my eyes. Brush-lined arroyos cut deep through the sand and provided our only relief from the hot wind.

We had seen no water for two days, except a small spring at Calmalli Viejo that had been a reliable waterhole the past two hundred years. The horses stopped for a long drink of water in the shallow pool and to cool their hooves.

Aaron had a toothache and didn't talk much. When we sat under a small mesquite branch at lunch, he explained his quick and efficient way of treating toothache. This was told in rapid Spanish, which I didn't understand a word of, and also in sign language, which I understood completely.

"I wrap a thin piece of tightly braided rope around my tooth," he explained as he opened his mouth and pointed to an aching tooth, and pretended to wrap it. "I fasten the other end to my saddle, and I whip the horse."

I winced at his description, and my mouth hurt to think of it.

I was often asked about walking alone. *Aren't you scared?*

Cowboys don't get scared. They don't bother anyone, and they don't tolerate anyone bothering them.

My favorite cowboy story took place here in Calmalli. Arthur North, a storytelling adventurer, told it a hundred years ago.

When gold was discovered in Calmalli, gold seekers from all over the world descended on the area to stake claims. One was an American woman from Arizona, who arrived alone on a mule with a gun strapped to her waist. She wore overalls, a felt sombrero, and heavy boots. Her arrival caused quite a stir. She was all business. "I come from Tombstone," she asserted in perfect Spanish, "Tombstone, Arizona, where three times a day the coroner makes his regular rounds, and I have always done my modest share in furnishing him with employment. I do not want any of you bothering me." And with this she nodded in a most cordial manner, swinging forward the holster with her formidable revolver. "I do hope, *caballeros*, there will be no misunderstandings." There were no misunderstandings. She left with her fair share of the three million dollars in gold taken from Calmalli.[2]

I didn't carry a six-shooter, only the puny hatchet hammer from Home Depot, but if I had to use it, I hoped I would fight like a she-lion of the Old Testament and make the lady from Tombstone proud.

We arrived at Rancho Los Corrales at sunset. It was the only rancho from mission times still inhabited. The vaquero, Francisco, and his wife, Ana, greeted us at the gate.

It was the end of the road for Aaron, the two hungry horses and pack mule, and the child's saddle. The new vaquero, Tomás Murillo, arrived at night.

The next morning, I watched as Ana fixed breakfast. A small table with lit candles and a picture of an elderly vaquero next to a large statue of Jesus dominated the room. In the candlelight, Ana warmed food that had been left out overnight, scrambled fresh eggs from her hens, and whipped up several dozen tortillas in just a few minutes.

The three vaqueros—Francisco, Aaron, and Tomás—sat at a wood table, drinking Nescafé instant coffee sweetened with Coffeemate and heaping teaspoons of sugar. Ana and I sat together at the end of the table, eating in silence, listening to Aaron and Francisco. Tomás didn't say much.

I loved not speaking the language—just sitting and not talking, not understanding much, but enjoying the conversation nevertheless.

Once we got on the trail, I soon learned that Tomás didn't talk or smile. He rode far ahead on a stout *mula* and never looked back.

The mule I would ride for the next several days was a large macho the color of moldy cheese. "What is his name?" I asked Francisco before Tomás and I set out.

Francisco shrugged. "Queso," he suggested. The name fit perfectly.

And thus began my love-hate relationship with Queso, the toughest mountain mule in Sierra de San Francisco.

Queso knew where he was going and didn't need any vaquero or *mula* to show him. He refused to follow the trail. He often found a better route—for himself. Sometimes the route that was best for him was not best for me. He plowed through thick mesquite brush and ducked under low-hanging palo verde branches that bloodied my mouth and cheek and ripped the pocket off my cargo pants. He didn't respond to "Whoa!" or "Stop!" or "Ouch!"

Queso had no fear of mountains or vaqueros or death. Several times I wished I had that six-shooter—or the nerve to use my Home Depot pocket hatchet.

On the dark side of a mountain ravine we came upon two riders traveling in the opposite direction. As they came closer, Tomás recognized them. It was Gilberto's daughter from Rancho La Unión, Josefina, and a vaquero from her rancho. Josefina carried a shotgun on her sidesaddle, and she looked like she knew how to use it. I wondered if her great-grandmother came from Tombstone, Arizona.

Tomás shook hands, exchanged some pleasantries, and kept riding.

After eight hours of riding without stopping, Tomás and I were exhausted and hungry. We camped atop Mesa Las Palmas, an enormous mesa covered in thorny brush less than a foot high. Hot, dry desert winds in the Sierras can go from zero to more than fifty knots in a few minutes and are strong enough to uproot trees and even carry away grown men. Here there was nothing to stop the wind, and I struggled to keep my tent and myself from blowing across the desert.

Tomás removed the saddles, tied the mules to a mesquite branch, unfolded his bedroll on the ground, and lay with his head propped on his saddle, waiting for me to fix dinner. He had packed no tortillas, no canned Spam, no Snickers, no nada.

It was obvious he was done for the day, and there would be no campfire tonight.

I was riding a macho mule and riding with a macho man.

Tomás was a tough, hardened, no-nonsense man of the Sierras. He was fit and thin, about five feet tall, with piercing dark eyes and a touch of feral wildness. He smoked Marlboro cigarettes and wore faded Levi jeans. He didn't wear gloves. His hands were as tough as the side of a mule, and his face as weathered. He never smiled and didn't talk much. He had a slight speech impediment and pronounced *w* as *th*, which made it difficult for me to write location names in my pocket journal. Over the course of a week, the only personal information he was willing to share was that he had seventeen brothers and sisters, and he was the middle child.

Still, I was delighted to boil water in my Jetboil and cook a package of dehydrated macaroni and beef for Tomás. I had used only two of the dehydrated survival meals since the start of my walk in Loreto. I hadn't found one vaquero who would eat it. The poor pack mules had been carrying the stuff for four weeks.

I cheerily prepared the macaroni and beef, poured it into his soiled campfire coffee cup, and handed him the sugar spoon.

He took one bite, spit it out, and glared at me.

I'm glad he didn't have a gun.

I was a hundred hours from nowhere in the middle of the desert Sierras with twenty pounds of survival food that Tomás refused to eat. It didn't take rocket science to figure out that no food equaled no vaquero.

I remembered a couple of leftover burritos that Aaron hadn't eaten. In the desert sun, meat turns green in eight hours. These burritos were three days old. They were partly green but mostly black, and smelled like rotting chicken flesh.

I gave them to Tomás.

He ate them.

Apparently satisfied, he wrapped himself in his bedroll and fell fast asleep.

Tomás had mentioned there were mountain lions in the area, so I ate the entire double serving of macaroni and beef. I didn't want to leave a trace of scent for a hungry lion. I felt wretched all night. My surgically compromised digestive system had no problem digesting fried pork fat, but it threatened massive rebellion after being stuffed with macaroni.

———

There was nobody out here in this remote and wild desert wilderness of northwest Mexico.

People had been here and their remains were here. We passed deserted ranchos, and Tomás told me the names: La Joya, El Rancho, El Rodeo, Las Quivitas, and San Juanico. Rubble and decay were the only reminders that these were once homes.

No one had lived in this desert for decades. There was no water. Water comes in a flash, and disappears just as quickly, and so does man's livelihood. Man must move on in search of a different life, leaving generations of hard work behind. If water returns, man clears the rubble and rebuilds in a never-ending cycle of hope and despair.

I thought of my father.

Daddy was born in the Texas desert in a decade of drought. His father was born a rambling man, filled with a hunger for riches and adventure, and too often unable to control his red-hot temper and sharp tongue.

Grandpa Littlefield might have learned to control both if his young life had not been upended by drought.

He was twenty-six years old when he left a small cotton patch in southwest Tennessee and moved Grandma to rural Jones County, Texas, miles from nowhere.

Grandpa was full of dreams of cheap fertile farmland and hopes of a better life.

He found neither. Instead, he found loose, sandy soil unsuitable for farming. His Texas farmland was covered with shrubby mesquite trees with needle-sharp thorns and deep roots that sucked up what little water was in the ground.

Within a year, a severe and prolonged drought hit the area. Grandpa stubbornly tried to hold on, but the drought held longer.

Without rain, the crops failed, the topsoil blew away, the cistern dried up, and Grandma's milk cow became so thin and emaciated it stopped giving milk. Prairie dogs and jackrabbits depended on for meat died off; thousands of withered carcasses were strewn across the dry windy Texas plains. Everything Grandpa had sweated and worked for was lost. Gone, too, were five years of youth and vigor.

With his family facing starvation and the land still besieged by drought, Grandpa sent Grandma back to Tennessee and hopped a train headed to California. He was gone a year. When he returned, their family life in Tennessee was happy and stable the next few years.

But Grandpa was as much a hot prairie fire as a rolling stone. When times were tough, Grandpa would leave. When times were good, he would leave to find something better.

Daddy managed to attend school for five years before Grandpa's wandering spirit once again uprooted the family. After that, Daddy went to school when he could, which wasn't often. More than anything in the world he wanted an education and a way out of a life of hard labor. It was not to be.

Daddy never felt sorry for himself or blamed anyone. Instead, he was determined to educate himself. At night, after a hard day's work on the farm, he would sit for hours and study the World Book Encyclopedia and read the Bible. He was one of the smartest, best-educated men I have ever known.

In the desert Sierras, a man is but a wind that passes and does not return.

The desert doesn't need water or man. It quickly erases man and reclaims itself. Where man is unable to survive, thorns thrive. Cactus and leafless desert trees may die, but their thorns remain.

Sierra de San Francisco is a massive prehistoric barrier formed from violent volcanic eruptions. Nightmarish scenes from *Jurassic Park* surrounded me. Only here, pterodactyl and plesiosaur talons had morphed into cactus thorns two inches long and an inch thick.

We reached the top of one jagged peak only to discover another. And then we came to the end of the world.

"El Paraíso." Tomás said the words slowly, without impediment, as he turned in his saddle to face me. He was a preternaturally calm man, but there was nothing calm in his eyes.

We had reached the abyss. El Paraíso—paradise—was a half mile straight down below us. We must pass through hell to get there.

We were atop the deepest, most severe plunge on El Camino Real. For centuries, this drop through hell had frozen the hearts of strong and fearless men.

Queso had been here before. You could see it in his eyes and the stiff erectness of his body. He stopped at the cusp of the abyss and refused to go further.

Tomás dismounted the *mula*, removed his spurs, and held Queso's reins, trying to quiet him. Queso wouldn't stand still; he was jittery, and his body rippled with the nervous energy of a gladiator entering the arena. His ears pointed almost straight back, and his tail was tucked. Sweat glistened on his forelegs. He was poised to escape, but Tomás took the reins and held on tight. The big *macho*, afire with adrenaline, almost lifted Tomás off the ground. Queso was spooking the pack mule and the *mula*. All three mules started pulling away from Tomás.

"Go!" Tomás yelled at me between clenched teeth, and I moved quickly away from the mules.

"You go first," Tomás commanded, again.

I knew he meant business, but as I stood at the edge of the abyss, looking down, I felt sheer terror, and the blood drained from my heart.

Below me was a dark labyrinth, a two-thousand-foot plunge to a valley below. The first two hundred feet were almost straight down, a vertical drop.

In the wild there was always that one moment—that Indiana Jones moment—when you stopped resisting and totally surrendered. It was the moment in between breaths when you committed or turned back. Once committed, it was as hard to go back as it was to go forward, so you went forward.

I hesitated, shaking.

"You go first." Tomás was more insistent.

A small opening, barely wide enough for a mule, was visible between the massive rocks on either side.

"Lord, have mercy on me," I prayed as I slid down the precipice, grabbing at cactus to slow my descent.

I could hear my parched, pleading voice, "Lord, have mercy," joining the echoes of every other sojourner—missionary, Indian, vaquero, gold seeker, explorer—who had passed through here.

I slid for more than a hundred feet and came to rest on a small ledge.

I could barely see Tomás. He was still above, holding the reins of the three mules, trying to keep them calm until I was safely out of the way.

Now it was his turn. He motioned for me to stand back, out of the way. Animals are unpredictable, especially a scared or angry mule. Antonio, my vaquero through treacherous El Barranco, had warned that mules hardly ever scare, but when they do, all hell can break loose, and usually does.

Tomás was a fifth-generation Sierra San Francisco vaquero and understood mules. He had been down El Paraiso and knew how to get himself and mules down safely. Though I doubted if he had ever gone down with a crazy American woman, a fully loaded pack mule, and two saddle mules in tow.

He wasted no time, quickly moving Queso around to the front, and maneuvered the pack mule between Queso and his *mula*. Queso's ears stood straight up, rigid and defiant.

Tomás whipped Queso in the face with a thick leather strap, and positioned his lightweight body in front of the heavyweight mule. Queso didn't budge. His ears tipped forward, like a mad bull ready to charge. Tomás threw down the reins, tightened his hold on the reins of the *mula* and pack mule, and from a half-sitting position slid down the steep drop to the first shallow ledge below. Queso followed behind.

I wedged my body against a boulder out of the way, and Tomás and the mules came crashing by, not stopping. He kept them moving by sheer force of will and vaquero skill. He didn't stop until they were halfway down, and only then to wait for me.

It took us two hours to get down the vertical drop. It was so steep I had to hold on to whatever I could find—cholla, prickly pear, palo adan, palo verde, mesquite shrub—to slow my descent and keep from plunging headfirst into cactus hell.

Cactus closed instantly over the path left by the mules, so it was impossible for me to follow Tomás. I had to make my own trail. Cactus was so thick I couldn't see even a few feet ahead, or my feet. I shivered at the thought of stepping on a rattlesnake or into a patch of devil's claw vines and breaking a leg. I kept yelling out to Tomás, "*¡Hola! ¡Hola!*" He would answer back, and I would follow in the direction of his voice.

Then I would pray softly, "Lord Jesus, have mercy on me."

Soon, I saw that Tomás had stopped the mules so I could catch up and get water. I smiled and thanked him, our eyes meeting over the water bottle. We both knew what we were doing felt crazy. But what were we to do? This was where the trail went. We had to follow.

Tomás plowed ahead, and I looked down at my hands. The inside of my deerskin gloves were filled with cactus. The outside looked like a pincushion with thorns sticking out all over. Once cactus embeds in a glove or buries into flesh, it is hard to get out. I tried to remove the major cactus pieces and pull the thorns out of my glove with my teeth. Then I painfully removed one glove at a time, as thorns inside the glove dug into my skin; it took several more minutes to pull thorns out of my hand with my teeth. The inside of my gloves was bloody, and my fingers, hands, and mouth were raw and swollen.

The next time I caught up with Tomás we finished the water. I soon felt light-headed and slightly tipsy. I didn't know whether it was from dehydration or shallow breathing or both.

Months later, the memory of El Paraíso haunted me. Hardly any maps exist of Sierra de San Francisco or El Paraíso. And then I came upon an old trail map. At the top of the abyss above El Paraíso someone had written "Cañón Misericordia"—Canyon of Mercy.

I laughed when I saw that. I knew then that hundreds of people before me had also prayed the Jesus prayer coming down the impossibly steep precipice. They were frightened too.

It is only with God's mercy that one can make it through the abyss.

We are born into a world that is alienated from God. When we aren't right with God, peace is elusive. Many identify with Vladimir Nabokov's nihilistic lament, "The cradle rocks above an abyss, and common sense tells us that our existence is but a brief crack of light between two eternities of darkness."[3]

I believe the baby lies in a cradle locked in the abyss, waiting for an angel to come from heaven with the key to free him from darkness.

Life has a way of knocking us back down into the abyss.

Prayer guides us out.

26

The next morning, I needed an angel's help to get out of El Paraíso and up the other side of the abyss.

El Paraíso was lush and green and looked innocent and inviting. It wasn't. It was solid cactus. Cholla and prickly pear grew like trees, taller than the mules.

The only way out of El Paraíso was to follow the ridgeline. It took the entire morning to claw our way to the top, and once there, we were perched on the narrowest possible trail on the side of a steep face.

The sun blazed overhead, sucking our breath dry. Heat rose from the sand as intense as a burning oven. Sweat streamed from every pore until we became so dehydrated we ceased to sweat. We rode for hours, stopping briefly to unload the mules and remove the sweat-soaked saddle blankets. There was no shade. We sat on our saddles in hot sand, while I boiled water and made coffee. Along the trail were large pitahaya cactus sprouting blueberry-sized fruit buds, and Tomás stopped and picked several handfuls, sharing with me. He ate them with gusto, but they were too bitter for my taste and didn't sit well in my stomach.

Late afternoon, we came to old Rancho Compostela, between Las Cabras and Mission San Borja, where missionaries and cow herders spent the night. Only an adobe wall and partial rock fence remained. It was a flea-infested sand hole, with a trickle of water in a rocky arroyo.

Tomás was dark and moody. He complained he wasn't getting enough food, so I fixed him two survival meal packages—enough for four people. He still wasn't happy. He took his bedroll and slept with the mules near the water.

The air was dry and thirsty. I was dehydrated, weak from hunger, and lightheaded. There was nothing left of my body but bones, and my bones hurt. All I wanted was to crawl in my tent and not wake up until I was whole again.

I felt like crying, but cowboys don't cry.

The sun was setting rapidly, and it was getting dark. I looked around for a level place to set up my tent. The bank of the arroyo was filled with every thorn imaginable, and the sand was full of rock. I started kicking aside small rocks and debris and hollowing out a space for my tent.

An old campfire with a charred piece of mesquite was in the way, and I kicked hard with the toe of my hiking book to dislodge it. I paused for a minute to catch my breath, and in the muted light I noticed the sandy ground around my feet was moving. I froze in horror.

Scorpions were everywhere, their brownish-yellow bodies, smaller than the size of my thumb, were clustered together and crawling over each other. Their stinging tails were wound tightly, but beginning to loosen and straighten.

They were the same color of the sand and perfectly camouflaged. In the dimming light, my eyes could not visually separate sand from scorpion, but my senses could: sand does not move; sand does not crawl.

Nothing terrifies me more than a scorpion. As a child, one little scorpion walking across the floor of our farmhouse could cause me to quake in fear. It wasn't an irrational fear but one based on firsthand experience of the pain they could cause.

Once, when I was four years old, my family and I used the cellar to escape a particularly fierce and fast-approaching tornado funnel. The funnel cloud was less than a quarter mile away and coming straight toward the house.

Daddy ran up from the cotton field, yelling for us to get in the cellar as Mother lifted the heavy corrugated metal door. All nine of us plunged into the damp, musty-smelling earthen cellar. Barefoot, I hesitated, trembling at the top of the dark stairs, recalling nighttime horror stories my older sisters delighted in telling about the cellar—about dead bodies buried there, and snakes and other creepy crawling things lurking in the blackness.

The most awful nightmare turned into reality as my sister grabbed my hand and forced me below. I descended no more than three stairs down before I stepped on a scorpion, its sting surging from my foot to my heart—almost stopping it, so great was the terror. It was a small scorpion, the kind with the most painful and deadly sting.

Mama was carrying our baby sister on her hip but she managed to scoop me up and hold me close in her arms as we sat on the cold, wet stairs, waiting to hear the storm rain pelt against the metal cellar door, our signal the tornado cloud had passed overhead and we were safe.

My small foot swelled to the ankle and turned dark around the sting. No fuss was made of it, other than my mother wetting a cotton rag with a bit of turpentine to bathe the foot. Mama and Daddy worked too hard to fuss much over us.

Within a single instant of the scorpion's sting, I developed a lifelong, pathologic, irrational terror of scorpions, and to this day I still fear stepping out of bed onto the floor at night in the dark. And here I was on the old mission trail in Baja Mexico, standing in the middle of dozens of scorpions. My heart was beating so fast I thought it might shut down from the pace.

Stop it! Stop panicking. Breathe.

The scorpions were now fully awake, their curved tails curling forward over their bodies, moving into attack position.

I started dancing in place like a small child, kicking my feet, although none had crawled on me. I thought about picking up a rock and pounding them, but I didn't want my bare hands near them.

I stomped and stomped until the sand stopped moving.

And then I ran to my gear bag and dragged it to the other side of the campsite. Trembling and panting, I set up my tent, threw everything inside, and dove in, boots and all. I zipped my sleeping bag over my head and slept in my clothes and boots.

I was still shaking the next morning when Tomás came up the arroyo with the mules. I tried to explain what happened, and showed him where I stomped. There were pieces I clearly identified as scorpions but they looked like nothing more than tiny dry twigs in the desert sand.

I refused to fix coffee until we moved further up the trail. The clear light of day is always the best tonic for fear. I took a deep breath and drank the soothing coffee. I said to myself, "All is well," knowing and believing all would be well, and it was, though it took hours for my breathing to keep pace with my pounding heart.

At every corner something was testing my will, my will to keep coming, my will to press on, my will to believe that God would take care of me.

I tried to hold steadfast to faith, but I felt it slowly slipping away.

———

That afternoon, we reached Mission San Borja, built on the side of a hill facing south, a site chosen by the missionaries to enhance its spiritual effect coming from Mission Santa Gertrudis. As we approached, thickets of thirsty cactus hid it from our view. Then, at the end of a long roadway of piled rocks, we turned the corner and there was the mission, dazzling white in the noonday sun, a vision straight from the Bible, just as the missionaries intended: God's Word built on a hill—a city of light to glorify our Father in heaven.

The long mountain road from Santa Gertrudis to San Borja is inaccessible except on a mule or on foot. No tourist enters the way we came. A modern auto road traversing the peninsula approaches from the back, and that is how tourists arrive today. There is no mystery, no light, just an old stone church enclosed in a chain link fence—an oddity in the middle of nowhere. The impact of the mission seen from afar is unknown to modern travelers.

Is it any wonder that modern man has lost his way?

Tomás and I rode into the mission, and my spiritual rhapsody was replaced with the unsightly reality of a ramshackle outhouse with no door directly facing us. The outhouse was in the middle of the old mission road and the first thing we saw as we entered the mission grounds.

A family lived there, direct descendants of Cochimí mission Christians. The father, José "Angel" Gerardo Monteon, came outside to meet us. For generations, long before the missionaries built the mission in 1762, Angel's family has lived in Adac, the Cochimí name for this tiny green valley. A hot spring seeps slowly from below lava rock and provides enough water for the family to live, and the mission attracts a few tourists who arrive primarily on motorcycles and ATVs.

His twenty-one-year-old daughter, Nonnih, would open the fence and give a tour of the mission for a fifty-*peso* donation. They had constructed some rough-looking one-room shacks for rent, furnished with a miserable bed, no sheets, and an open window without a covering. Despite visions of centipedes and scorpions crawling through the window at night, I rented two rooms for Tomás and me. I asked Nonnih how much a room costs, but she was vague and said she would figure it out later since we probably wanted food too.

I unpacked my things in the rental shack. I was weak from hunger and walked to the main house, an open veranda with a couple of old couches and several truck seats. Angel, Nonnih, and her mother, Ana Ilicia, were in the kitchen eating. Only after asking, "*Comprar comida de usted?*"—Can I buy food from you?—did they invite me to eat. They gave me a plate of barely warm rice and beans and a cold tortilla, but it tasted delicious after not having had real food for a week. I noticed chickens pecking around the house and asked Nonnih if I could pay for eggs for breakfast. I would die for coffee and fresh eggs for breakfast, and warm tortillas.

As I sat eating the food given me, I worried about where I could go from here. Tomás was expected back at his rancho and could take me no further. Angel's sons were working in Mexicali and not available. I used my emergency satellite phone to call Cenovio Lazcano, who promised to help me in Santa Gertrudis. He was trying to find a vaquero, but it might take a week or longer. I was getting worried. It was the end of November, and I had to be back at Stanford Cancer Center on December 30 and didn't have a week or longer to wait.

I was reluctant to pay Tomás until I knew who was coming next. I didn't want to be stuck in San Borja and the middle of nowhere without a mule. Tomás seemed happy to stick around while I paid for him, the mules, and all the food and Coke he could eat and drink at the mission.

Cenovio called the next day with good news. Tomás's brother, Pancho Murillo, was working as a vaquero on a nearby ranch and was available to take me to Mission Santa María. Pancho would arrive the next day.

I couldn't thank Cenovio enough for making my mission his own. What an angel he was!

Finally, I paid Tomás for his time and the three mules. His food and Coke bill at San Borja (plus a dozen egg and beef burritos to take on the road) were almost as much as his pay. I gave him a generous tip just to see him smile. I hesitated because he hadn't been willing to even light a campfire at night, but he had gotten three mules and me safely through El Paraíso, and that's what mattered most.

Adac was a busy place, located at a crossroad halfway between the Gulf of California and the Pacific Ocean. This was the narrowest part of the peninsula, and from a hilltop behind the mission I could see both.

Nonnih appeared to enjoy my company, and we hung around together most of the day. She had never been to school but spoke, and wrote, excellent English. She had an iPad and spent hours on Facebook. Like everyone in the world on social media, she worried about how she looked and asked my help choosing between twenty photos for her profile page.

Nonnih tried hard to convince me to pay five hundred *pesos* to ride with her in Angel's truck to see ancient cave paintings. I was more interested in cleaning my filthy clothes and taking a bath, and Nonnih accompanied me to the hot mineral baths in the arroyo beside the mission.

The missionaries had built two of them, and I used one, while Nonnih used the other. The old baths were constructed of elaborate stone and mortar over the water, which was bath temperature, not hot. It was clear until I stepped on the bottom and sank into soft slimy muck, and stirred up centuries of debris. It was a terrible, hog-wallow kind of feeling.

I awkwardly shampooed my hair and bathed, holding on to the sides and not letting my feet touch bottom. I tried not to think about the prehistoric life forms lurking in its dark, bottomless depths.

The sulfurous odor was noxious. A missionary had once declared that the sickening odor went away, that it became drinkable once the water was cooled.

Nonnih encouraged me to drink the water. "It will cure your cancer," she promised.

I drank it.

The water tasted faintly of stale Alka-Seltzer and mothballs, and like the taste in my mouth during chemotherapy.

I closed my eyes and slowly took another sip of the warm, clouded mineral water in my cupped hands. It wasn't the craziest cure I had tried. A friend of a friend swore that drinking swimming pool chlorine had healed her early-stage melanoma, and after my lung and liver cancer came back, I figured it was worth a shot. I had also encouraged bees to sting me on my walks in the canyon in order to stimulate my immune system. And, truthfully, after five and a half years and 820,000 milligrams of cytoxic chemotherapy, what did I have to lose?

My inner parts moaned, or maybe it was the dying cancer. Only God knows.

It was dark when I walked up the hill to the one-room shack. I quickly brushed my teeth outside using unfiltered water from a water spigot in the middle of the dirt yard. If the slimy mineral water hadn't killed me, nothing would. Ants covered my bed and were all over the shack. I brushed them off and slipped into my sleeping bag. It was a warm night, but I zipped it to the top to keep out ants and who-knows-what. Light from the full moon streamed through the open window, and I thought about getting out of bed and taking a photo of the beautiful old mission in the light of the full moon, but was too exhausted.

A coyote chorus in the arroyo sang me to sleep. They howled all night and kept the dogs excited. These coyotes sounded different—more of a sad and forlorn wild yelp than the ferocious flesh-ripping groans of their starved cousins in Santa Gertrudis.

———

The next morning, I walked over for one last, loving farewell to Mission San Borja. I closed my eyes and felt the promise and pain of the old Jesuit mission.

A wealthy European duchess had endowed this mission. Shortly before her death, María de Borja bequeathed her fortune not to family and friends but to establish Christian missions in the "most remote, inaccessible place in the world."[1] The Jesuits knew just the place—the Central Desert of Baja California. The three missions they established with the duchess's inheritance were San Borja, Calamajué, and Santa María; they'd planned to open more but were exiled before the adobe at Santa María had time to dry.

A tireless Jesuit missionary from Austria, Wenceslao Linck, founded Mission San Borja. The mission grew to cover an area of 4,200 square miles in a desert so sparse and inhospitable there was fewer than one person per square mile.

Before Linck arrived, the German missionary from Mission Santa Gertrudis, George Retz, built a ninety-mile road linking the two missions, a crude church, dwellings for the missionary and soldiers, a warehouse, and a hospital. He sowed corn on a small amount of land to make sure it was arable. There was no timber, firewood, or pasture. No rain fell for seven years. Food and supplies from Loreto kept them alive.

Among the supplies from Loreto were wood doors for the stone church later constructed at Mission San Borja. A century later, gold seekers, passing through the desert, sought shelter in the old church. They built fires on the stone floor and burned broken pieces of the wood doors. One fortune hunter audaciously marveled at the intricate workmanship of his firewood: "The doors were four inches thick and made of small pieces of very hard wood ingeniously dovetailed together. We wonder where the padres got the wood and how and by whom all the work was done."[2]

One hundred fifty years after the mission was built the American Geographical Society called San Borja and the Central Desert to the north "the least known territory of the world except only the polar regions."[3] The vast, parched desert is still as remote, inaccessible, and wild today as it was then.

I took a breath, thankful for being right where I was. I would rather be on the rugged El Camino Real mission trail, living my dream of being a cowboy, than anywhere on God's green planet. But I still had more than four hundred miles to go before I reached the California border.

The Jesuits were just starting to build El Camino Real north from San

Borja when the Spanish king forced them out in 1767. Neither the Franciscans (who left within four years for California) nor the Dominicans who took their place were road builders.

In 1843, a naïve twenty-six-year-old gold seeker from Pennsylvania discovered, much to his peril, that north of San Borja, "for the distance of at least 100 miles, there is not so much as a drop of water."[4]

I knew I had difficult days ahead of me.

27

Tomás's brother, Francisco "Pancho" Murillo, arrived at noon. Pancho drove an old white pickup truck with two large mules and an even larger burro squeezed in the back. The saddles, harnesses, and his gear were tied to the top of the cab. I was packed and ready to go, with forty liters of water and two dozen bean burritos purchased from Ana Ilicia.

Pancho saddled up the light brown *macho* mule for me, and he rode the dark *mula* beauty. I asked Pancho what my mule's name was, and he shook his head. "I don't know." He had rented the animals.

I stroked the mule's creamy light brown, sun-weathered hide, glistening with sweat and immediately thought of hot chocolate. "His name is Coco," I declared.

We rode silently past the mission cemetery; nothing remained there but three unmarked stone crosses atop weathered piles of mortared rock. When I'd asked Nonnih who was buried in the graves, she shrugged. "Nobody knows."

Coco was a bit slow and sluggish and just the perfect temperament for me. But the saddle was painful, and the uneven and crude stirrups held my feet in contorted and painful positions; I dismounted and walked at every opportunity.

I never knew what gear I was getting. The vaqueros had a hard enough time rounding up mules. I paid the same price for a mule regardless of saddle, so the vaqueros didn't pay much attention to the saddle that came with the mule.

North of the mission there is scant vegetation, but what little there is grows in bizarre shapes and sizes—cholla ten feet high, grotesquely twisting cirio, naked cardon, and deformed torote trees.

My skeleton body felt right at home here.

We set up camp in sand and rock near a dirt road. There was no water for the mules, and wouldn't be for days. Pancho lit a roaring fire, something Tomás never did, and I sat close beside it as if with a dear old friend. That night, Pancho took out his pocketknife and adjusted the saddle and stirrups, trying to get them to fit comfortably.

Pancho Murillo was the best of the best, a vaquero par excellence. A north wind blew strong against us for five days, but somehow Pancho always managed to coax a roaring campfire out of dry mesquite, even in a gale-force wind. He respected the animals and stopped often to reposition saddles and blankets. He could find water in the middle of the barren desert and food for the animals. And he would eat anything.

Even after Pancho's attempts to fix them, the stirrups were too mismatched, and I found them excruciatingly painful. I rode for an hour and then walked until the terrain gave me no option. I always walked unless there was simply no choice: barbed-wire cactus, razor-sharp stone, or knee-deep sand. Even in the roughest parts, my feet hurt less on the ground than in the stirrups.

The desert was miles of sameness, miles of nothingness, and looked like a moonscape of white sand. The only thing that changed was the names of the arroyos—Verde, Palo Chino, Huguay—as we moved north through the barren plains of San Julian. It was a sullen, desolate place. There was some green, but mostly gray and brown and white. Even the cow dung was parched white and looked petrified. Much of the cactus was dead, the trees were leafless and barren, and there weren't any sounds. I noticed at night there were no night sounds, no crickets, and in the morning there were no birds.

But there was evil.

The old El Camino Real mission trail follows arroyos, and arroyos have always been hiding places for outlaws. The United States State Department advises against travel to Baja because of the violence of the drug cartels. The

Mexican drug cartels transport cocaine north through the Central Desert to Mexicali and the California border.

Pancho pointed to tire tracks veering in and out of the arroyo; the tracks were deep with no blown sand in the tread marks. They looked fresh from the night before or early that morning.

"*Narcos.*" The word was enough to seize hearts with terror. Drug smugglers.

Further down, there were strange tracks in the sand, like a pushcart, that led to the arroyo. "*Espera aquí*," Pancho advised—wait here—and I took the burro. Pancho called her *burra*, but suggested I call her Paloma, since she was dove-colored, and the name fit nicely, so I did.

Pancho charged down the rocky embankment and quickly came back up. "*Dos grandes contenedores en el arroyo*," he said. There are two large containers in the arroyo. I didn't know the significance of that.

"*Muchos problemas aquí, muchos narcos*," Pancho said in a low voice, looking nervously toward the arroyo. "*Muchas personas en la noche.*" Many people at night.

Innocent vaqueros and mission walkers can stumble upon a *narcofosa*—a narco cemetery—out in the middle of nowhere, strewn with carnage: *encobijados*, or headless bodies wrapped in a tarpaulin and taped, and *encintados*, mutilated bodies bound and blindfolded with tape.

"*No vemos nada y no decimos nada.*" Pancho advised, his voice barely a whisper. We see nothing, and we say nothing.

Yes, I said to myself, *and pray that we aren't in the wrong place at the wrong time.*

We came to a paved highway, the first cars and paved road I'd seen in five weeks. Coco stood firm and erect. His stance reminded me of Queso at the top of El Paraíso. Coco's ears pointed slightly forward in a warrior pose, sensing danger. I shuddered to think what would happen if a truck were to round the curve and come upon me and a frightened Coco in the center of the road.

Pancho and Paloma crossed quickly. Coco refused to cross, and Pancho hurried back, grabbed the rope, and pulled us across. Mules don't like strange things, and paved highways with cars and trucks are strange to these desert creatures.

By late afternoon, the mules were getting restless for water. Pancho said we were close to a rancho and water. And yet we were still riding when it became dark.

Finally, we approached what appeared to be the rancho.

We heard cows, but it was too dark to see them. Two vaqueros came out with flashlights and helped us lead the mules to water. It was a small rancho with only a few cows. There wasn't enough well water to support more. We were slightly west of the famous missionary waterhole of Yubay, where Junípero Serra had spent the night. "*No hay agua en Yubay*," the vaqueros told Pancho. There is no water at Yubay.

The vaquero hut had a small kerosene lamp and a propane burner. They boiled water, and I fixed a survival meal of spaghetti. The vaqueros warmed several tortillas on the open flame. Pancho and I poured spaghetti on tortillas and ate quietly and quickly in the dark.

The vaqueros and Pancho talked in low, guarded voices about drug smugglers.

"*Están aquí en el desierto*," one warned. They are here in the desert.

Our route would pass near a desert landing strip that had been used by *narcos* to smuggle cocaine from Colombia. The vaquero pointed his finger to the sky, tapped his ear, and shook his head. If we heard anything, we shouldn't go further.

The vaquero let me sleep on his bed. The two vaqueros and Pancho slept on the floor.

There was no pasture and no trees or brush to feed the mules. The vaqueros shared their hay. I tried to pay, but they would not accept the money.

Paloma, our poor burra, was in bad condition and hurting. She had bolted loose and had run wild into a large cholla cactus patch; her left eye was swollen and red, with a big blood blister in the center. All morning her eye bled, and blood dripped down her face onto the sand.

The sand deepened the further north we rode. It would trap my feet, like quicksand, and pour into my high-topped boots. When I sat down to empty sand out of my boots, I sank so low it would spill into my cargo pants. My belt was so loose the waist hung open.

Walking thirty minutes in knee-deep sand is like walking two or three hours on normal dirt. I walked an hour and then rode the mule for an hour. Later in the day, the sand became too bad, and I changed to walking thirty minutes and riding an hour.

Paloma was a wild, free spirit, and Poncho was too exhausted to control her, so he let her loose, without a lariat. She walked just far enough ahead of me to kick hot sand in my face; the sand swelled my dry lips and blurred my dry eyes. I was certain Paloma was born of Satan's seed.

We didn't see anyone for days.

And then one morning, suddenly, two dirt bikes came roaring across the desert. After the Darth Vader–looking motorcycle riders roared by, it took half an hour to calm and settle the mules. It took all day to unclog the dust in my suffocating lung.

In the desert, miles are not counted, only places where water is available for man, and brush is available for mules.

There was no food for the mules. Pancho hoped to find a bush or tree they could eat, but there was nothing. There was not a single stick of firewood for a campfire, and we, too, went to bed hungry.

My air mattress had a puncture—probably from a cactus thorn from my pants. Each morning, the air mattress was flat. My air pillow no longer stayed inflated. There was no comfort to be had for my tired bones at night.

Pancho, a man of the desert sierra, didn't have a problem with cactus or wind. He made himself a rather clever tent with the tarpaulin cover he used for the pack burro; the smelly mule blankets provided soft ground cover, and his saddle was his pillow.

In the stillness of the desert nights, I quieted my breath and strained my ears for any sounds of life. Other sojourners had listened, too, and heard nothing. A desperate soul wrote: "One might well think there was a curse resting upon this region, this perfection of eternal desolation. In the whole expanse not a living thing save the never failing cactus, which itself is a curse in many forms."[1]

The desert climate is characterized by extremes, hot days and freezing nights, and I almost froze at night. My dry, taut skin barely covered my bones, and there was no body warmth. During the night, the ferocious winds blew moist air from the ocean. We woke up freezing wet—in the middle of one of the driest deserts on earth. My tent was sopping wet, both the outside and inside layers. I had to pack it wet.

The sun came up, a hot ball of fire. In less than an hour, the desert turns from freezing cold to sweltering heat, and from wet dew to parched air.

Several days before, coming down a steep arroyo embankment, a mesquite branch had torn the sunglasses off my face. The mules slid in the loose sand and covered them; Pancho and I were unable to find them. Now wind blew the brim of my hat straight up, exposing my eyes—just more misery that must be endured. Ash-gray mountains appeared in the distance, and Pancho pointed to the right. "Calamajué," he said with a sweeping gesture toward the mountains. "Sierra de Calamajué."

We rode hours through a sandy, bleached-out arroyo that slowly transformed into a kaleidoscope of intense, vivid color—green palms and reeds, orange and gold shrubs, red clay earth, and burnt copper and cinnabar red mountains. The arroyo narrowed between two mountains, and there was water.

Calamajué's beauty was spellbinding, and water was everywhere. But it was undrinkable.

When the missionaries arrived, the Cochimí had a yellow and sickly appearance.[2] I knew what that meant. When cancer attacked my liver, my skin and eyes looked yellow, a condition called jaundice. Yellow is the color of liver failure and, eventually, death.

The wretched water flowed from a mountain of copper, iron, saltpeter, mercury, antimony, and other toxic minerals. It contained so much salt and soda that thirst-starved men had died drinking it. The salty water didn't quench or satisfy thirst; it increased it, and in some places the water was poisonous.

It caused instant and explosive bowel eruptions.

Paloma and the two mules drank the disgusting water slowly and frequently. They were unbothered by foul taste and toxicity. The stomach of a mule could probably digest acid.

Rather than being sickened by the foul water, Paloma was invigorated. Coco continued to plod along, slower than a slug. I often wondered if he was sleepwalking.

Pancho stopped the mules in front of a small trickle of water dripping from the side of a steep cliff. This small mountain stream had been the only source of drinking water for the mission, more than a mile away.

Pancho dismounted and filled his canteen. *"No más agua por dos días."* There would be no water for two days, and he advised me to fill my water bottles.

I cupped my hands to taste it. After sniffing, I tasted with the tip of my tongue and spit it out, almost gagging from the memory of chemotherapy and the disgusting taste of the curative water at San Borja. I knew my intestines could not handle another sip.

I would rather die of thirst than from angry bowels. I still had one dromedary bag with at least a gallon of water, and decided to ration water rather than drink from the sulfuric spring.

The bad water sealed Calamajué's fate even before the missionaries' hastily constructed palm and adobe church was finished. Calamajué was an impossible place to live, and in less than a year the mission was moved fifty miles northwest to the Cochimí village of Cabujakaamung, where there was sweet water and a grove of palms. The mission was renamed Mission Santa María and was seven months into construction when the Jesuit missionaries were expelled.

We stopped just long enough in Calamajué for Pancho to fill his canteen and for us to eat the last moldy bean burritos from San Borja.

Pancho delighted in finding things along the trail. He had the heart and curiosity of a tinkerer. He found an old bicycle pump that still worked and gleefully tied it to his bedroll. Heaven knows what he would do with a bicycle pump, but I was sure he would make use of it.

Hours later, we reached the mountains. Pancho wove along the base out of the wind. He had spent a lifetime riding these trails. There was one small cluster of palo verde on this naked sandy plain, and he took us right to it.

The mountain protected our campsite from wind, and the palo verde provided food for the mules and Paloma. Pancho made a roaring fire between my tent and the mountain slope. The fire felt like a warm furnace, and we huddled around it. I had only dried scrambled eggs and chili left. I saved the chili and fixed the detestable scrambled eggs. They were awful. But they were better than not eating.

Pancho was sitting on his saddle next to the fire in the dark, and I was brushing my teeth when he motioned for me to be still.

"*Un truck en el desierto*," he whispered loudly, and pointed to headlights coming slowly toward us, about a mile away. The desert was pockmarked with old mining roads, and it was impossible to know where the truck was coming from or where it was going.

"*No luz. Narcos!*" He motioned for me to quickly turn off the light in my tent and stomped out the campfire. We were camped in a secluded dust hole far from a deserted mining road, but someone could easily see the campfire from miles away.

The truck passed, slowly and in low gear, about half a mile from us.

Strangers are not welcome at night in the desert, especially this desert of *narcos* and smugglers.

That night, I took out my bear spray and my Home Depot pocket hammer hatchet and laid them next to my deflated pillow. They were a bit of a joke, but reassuring nonetheless.

I began to have intestinal cramping and pain around my stomach and liver. Any time I have pain, the fear of cancer fills me with dread. *Please, not yet*, I prayed. I fell asleep, massaging my stomach and dreaming of the future. I longed to be with my family and see my friends. When I got to the California border, I couldn't wait to take hot baths and sleep in warm beds. *In the future, I want to live in a campervan in the wilderness and never see another tent in my life*, I thought to myself as I fell asleep.

I was awakened in the night by howling wind, and what I thought was the low sound of a truck motor in the distance. I groped in the dark for my hammer hatchet and held it tightly against my chest until the morning.

28

Pancho and I received a lot of love on the day's walk. For three hours, the mission trail followed Las Arrastras and San Francisquito, where a road was under construction linking the two coasts. There was heavy, slow traffic and lots of dust. Paloma was still untethered and caused quite a stir, stopping traffic, posing for photos and videos, and acting the clown. Most were American tourists heading for Baja beaches for the holidays. Pancho and the mules were an oddity. People held phones outside their car windows to take videos and pictures. They gave us cold drinks, snacks, and chocolates. A couple from Alaska gave us fresh canned Copper River salmon and fresh tomatoes. Pancho took the food and put it in his saddlebags to save for dinner.

The food was a godsend. Pancho told me that morning my dried scrambled eggs were making him sick. I wanted to suggest it might be his canteen water from Calamajué, but my Spanish was too limited.

All too soon, we turned off the road into a wide arroyo that seemed to go forever. It was sweltering hot, and the mules needed water. Pancho was familiar with the trail and knew there was water at a place he called La Palmetta. The sun was low in the sky when we saw palm trees in the distance, and Paloma started running, holding her nose in the air, sniffing the water, our gear bouncing on her back. Coco woke up from his two-day stupor and bolted after her, almost knocking me off the narrow trail. Coco drank for twenty minutes nonstop, filling up with water like a camel.

Not Paloma; she was running wild into the desert in less than five minutes. A burro can go without water for days, survive water loss of up to 30 percent of its weight, and completely rehydrate after a few minutes of drinking.

From La Palmetta we followed Arroyo Santa María north for an hour until it was too dark and the wind too cold to go further. Pancho found a lone palo verde tree to provide protection from the wind, and I squeezed my tent under its low-hanging branches. It was too windy for a campfire, and it was too dark to search for firewood. We shared chocolate and canned salmon from Pancho's saddlebags for dinner.

We were hours from Mission Santa María and a day or two from Cataviña. In Cataviña, I would say good-bye to Pancho, Coco, and Paloma, and meet up with a new vaquero and fresh mules. I fell asleep hoping the new vaquero would take me all the way to San Diego. I was getting very tired.

It would have been a restful sleep but for the mules eating. The hard, brittle twigs of palo verde snapped with each chew, like splintered glass, and the sound magnified in the clear desert air, keeping me awake.

Before sunrise, Pancho had a roaring fire going and water boiling in our cowboy cups for coffee. I stood with my back to the campfire and watched my breath become warm fog in the cold morning air. Vaqueros never stand facing a campfire. It took me a month to notice. I quickly learned that warming your backside warms your entire body, and smoke doesn't get in your eyes. Pancho and I slowly sipped our coffee in silence, facing the morning sun. I felt its warm embrace even before it rose above the mountains.

"*Sierra Santa María es muy difícil*," Pancho warned as he tied an extra rope around Paloma and our gear. We had to cross Sierra Santa María; it was the only way to get to Mission Santa María from Calamajué and San Borja.

Junípero Serra called El Camino Real to Santa María "a most grievous road."[1] But he was a man of few words and lived the hardened life of a missionary.

Others were more descriptive. "The worst mountain of the earth," proclaimed a gold prospector in 1849.[2] However, he purposely bypassed El Paraíso, having been forewarned of its horror. I have been through both, and

Sierra Santa María is terrifying, but it didn't compare to the purgatory of El Paraíso.

What no one wrote about was how beautiful it is. To me, the remote and wild places are the most beautiful. They are the places that haunt us and call to us. This was a road untraveled and unblemished.

It was an excruciatingly painful and difficult day, but it was exhilarating too. Constantly up and down one steep slope after another, peak after peak of bare, burnt rock. There was not much cactus, just occasional cholla, but twenty-foot-high ocotillo cactus wands swayed across our trail like burning rods in the wind—their thin, thorny branches hitting us with hot, smoldering flames of fire.

Violent volcanic eruptions formed Santa María's jagged peaks and deep canyons; these threw rock and brimstone everywhere, in all shapes and sizes. El Camino Real was a minefield of rock—sliding rocks, sandy rocks, big rocks, little rocks, lava rocks, granite rocks, smooth rocks, razor-sharp rocks. Pancho struggled to find the old mission trail, and the weary mules struggled to keep going.

Paloma slipped on ragged rock and lunged forward, losing her balance. She landed on piercing flints of lava stone with her slender legs tucked underneath. It was an unfamiliar and awkward position for a *burra* and unladylike for proud Paloma.

Paloma struggled to get up but couldn't. There was a small gash on her right hind leg, and blood soiled the ground. Pancho gently stroked her neck and removed the gear and packsaddle from her back. That was all the help she needed, and she sprang up. But the rest of the day, Paloma was unsteady on her feet, and so footsore on the sharp lava rock Pancho could barely coax her over the trail.

From atop a ridge I saw palm trees far ahead in a distant arroyo. I asked Pancho, "Is that the mission?" hoping and praying it was.

He shook his head and pointed to the east. "*Dos horas más.*"

I didn't know if I could make it two more hours. But I did.

When I got off Coco in front of the mission ruins after five hours in the saddle, my feet were numb and my knees buckled underneath me. I sank to the ground. It took several minutes to stand and another minute to walk.

Mission Santa María de los Ángeles, the last Jesuit mission, sits upon a small shelf of barren ground in the middle of immense granite boulders. Nothing remains except an outline of weathered adobe in dry sandstone. Ghostly palms tower overhead and soften the sadness of the crumbling ruins.

This desolate and gloomy place was filled with life and hope when the thirty-year-old Jesuit missionary in Calamajué, Father Victoriano Arnés, decided to move the mission here and build anew.

I couldn't imagine why the Jesuit missionary built here in this godforsaken desert. Pancho and I had seen only one occupied ranch since leaving San Borja a week ago. Santa María was as unsuitable for a mission as Calamajué.

But I am of a different age and time. I live in an era dominated by science, not faith; an era of probabilities, not possibilities.

The enchanting tropical forest of palms and lush sedge grass seduced Father Arnés. The only level ground was less than an acre and located in the opening of a narrow canyon between high cliffs of bare granite. There was no pasture or firewood. Not even edible cactus. Arnés was filled with youthful enthusiasm, and his Jesuit oath was a commitment to endure harsh conditions. He overlooked the poor alkaline condition of the soil and the scarcity of water to irrigate crops.

If faith can move mountains, then faith can sow wheat in bad soil. With faith and infallible will, bad soil can be replaced with good soil. Didn't the legendary missionary Juan Ugarte move the earth at Mission San Miguel to feed Christ's children? Victoriano knew the story; he knew that Ugarte had covered rock and desert with a hundred thousand mule loads of good earth.

Undaunted, the young Spanish missionary with innocent brown eyes built a stark church of palm wood covered with palm leaves and planted a tiny patch of wheat and cotton near the stream. Other missions donated cattle, but there was no pasture in the mountains, and they were kept with the herd at San Borja, more than one hundred miles away. Soldiers resented the remote solitude and were disagreeable and sullen. Fierce mountain lions roamed the arroyo, terrorizing the natives, and rattlesnakes abounded in its rocky crevices. Arnés's faith never wavered.

Victoriano Arnés might have done it; he might have transformed the inhospitable arroyo into a garden of Eden. But seven months after the founding of Mission Santa María, a messenger of the Spanish king arrived with a letter ordering Father Arnés to leave without an hour's delay. He could take no personal possessions except his black Jesuit robe, his liturgy book, and two books: one on theology, the other on science.

The young, highly educated Spanish missionary was arrested like a common criminal and taken at gunpoint to Loreto to be returned to Spain and imprisoned.

His Jesuit brothers, George Retz, the German-born missionary at Santa Gertrudis, and Wenceslao Linck, the Austrian missionary at San Borja, were arrested and returned to the protection of their homelands, barely escaping the devil's claws of the Spanish king.

Arnés, a Spanish citizen, suffered a long imprisonment in Spain. When he was released, he was deported to Rome, where he died and was buried. The brokenhearted missionary was fifty-two years old.

Victoriano, did they kill your spirit too? I wondered.

The chorus of the wind replies, "No." Spirit can remain strong, even when one's heart is broken. Kings are not to be feared. *Do not fear those who kill the body but cannot kill the soul.*[3]

Franciscan missionaries arrived at Mission Santa María five months after Arnés was arrested. They built a tule roof on Victoriano's half-finished adobe church, a two-room dwelling, and a small shed for mission tools. The useless soil never produced more than a bushel and a half of wheat. Food was brought by ship from Loreto and other missions. Franciscans abandoned the mission a few years later and moved everything fifty miles north to Mission San Fernando.

When the Franciscans left, Santa María became a haunt of wild creatures by night and serpents by day, an everlasting waste. No man has dwelled here since, and few men sojourn here.

Pancho didn't want to linger long at the mission ruins. He was anxious to get to Rancho Santa Inés and Cataviña. It was five hours from Santa María on a fast mule; our mules barely breathed.

I was tired and hungry and begged to stop for coffee. We hadn't eaten for hours, and I had one last survival package of scrambled eggs. We added a tin of Copper River salmon, but the eggs still tasted terrible. We picked out the small bits of salmon and tossed the eggs in a trash sack in the saddlebag.

The trail leading out of Santa María was as bad as the Sierras coming in.

Pancho drove the mules hard. Riding on the back of a galloping mule is sheer agony. To keep Coco and Paloma moving, Pancho cut a twenty-foot ocotillo limb to poke their hind ends. Pancho would barely touch Coco, and the mule would jerk awake and lurch forward in a shaky gallop. Every inch of my body—back, shoulders, feet, knees, and legs—begged for relief.

What was supposed to be a five-hour mule ride from Mission Santa María to Rancho Santa Inés took four hours galloping and running the mules at top speed the entire distance. We never slackened the pace. Pancho took shortcuts through the cactus and through rocky arroyos and never slowed down. He would sometimes sing to the mules and coax them in a soft singsong voice to keep up the pace. When that failed, he waved the ocotillo spear and instantly got their attention.

The sun was almost down, and it was windy and freezing cold. There was no place to camp, we had no food left, and Pancho knew he had no choice but to get us to Rancho Santa Inés. He knew I was in pain, and he softly talked to me about how wonderful it was going to be when we got there. "*Comida.*" There is food, he promised. "*Cama.*" There is a bed. "*Hotel y restaurante.*" There is a hotel and a restaurant at Rancho Santa Inés.

These promises kept me going. I was so thankful for his care, that he noticed my waning spirit and encouraged me—and gently prodded the animals.

It was pitch-dark when we arrived at Rancho Santa Inés. Not a soul was there.

There was a restaurant, but it was closed and locked up. There were a couple of old trucks, but no people. Pancho said the owner must be with tourists in the desert.

There was no food. There was no bed.

I felt worse than Coco and Paloma looked.

I couldn't talk. I couldn't move. I could no longer feel. I could no longer think. All my mind would register is that it was freezing cold, and the wind was so strong I couldn't stand up. My body screamed at me. And then I started to move.

"Melancholy is useless here," a lonesome missionary yearning for companionship wrote to his family in Germany.[4]

We got to work unloading the mules and Paloma.

Pancho searched for water, while I dragged my camping gear under the porch of the dark restaurant and started to set up my tent.

I tried to reach Dale on the emergency satellite phone, but the battery was too weak, and it shut off before dialing. I made one final attempt, and it connected.

"Edie?" I heard his voice, the sound of home as I shivered in this no man's land.

I had no time to chitchat. The satellite could drop at any second.

"Dale, we are at Rancho Santa Inés, but no one is here. Please, call Cenovio. He will send help; I know it."

An hour later, a police car pulled up with two policemen who greeted us warmly.

Cenovio pulled through for me again. What a godsend that man was becoming!

Pancho and I left the mules and our gear and drove with the police to the only café in tiny Cataviña. We each ordered two meals and gorged on food and hot tea. The café was dark inside. They had a noisy electric generator, but the small ceiling light kept flickering on and off, so they finally turned the generator off and lit a few candles.

Four men sat at another table; the waitress said they were archaeologists excavating Mission San Fernando. We struck up a conversation and learned one of the men was Nonnih's brother from Mission San Borja. It had only been a week, but felt like a lifetime ago since Pancho and I left San Borja. It seemed otherworldly that we were sitting in Cataviña, talking to Nonnih's brother.

After we ate, the policemen took Pancho and me back to Rancho Santa Inés for our gear, and then to a hotel.

Cataviña was a block-long truck stop without a stoplight. There was little there except for an expensive hotel called Hotel Mission Cataviña that took credit cards and catered to truck drivers and tourists who were passing through. It had toilets, sinks, and showers that worked. There was also a small rustic motel that didn't take credit cards and probably the shower or toilet or sink didn't work, maybe all three. The police took us to the rustic motel, and I would have preferred to stay there but didn't have enough *pesos* left to pay for two rooms. So Pancho and I ended up at Hotel Mision Cataviña.

The hotel clerk had a message from Cenovio: "I have not found a vaquero to get you to Mission San Fernando, but I am working on it. Good night."

I had somehow made it more than six hundred miles through the desert and Sierras from Loreto, and I was only a three-day walk from Mission San Fernando, the only mission in Lower California founded by Junípero Serra and the Franciscans.

After Mission San Fernando, I hoped to continue walking north to the California border, following the same route Father Serra took to San Diego and beyond. I had faith that somehow I would get there.

I fell asleep on top of the bed in my filthy clothes, too exhausted to unpack and take a shower.

I awoke in the middle of the night, took a hot shower for a full thirty minutes, and climbed back into bed—the first real bed and hot shower since San Ignacio more than three weeks ago.

I fell asleep dreaming of the Jesuit missions, but the missions were not old ruins or old tourist relics, but holy places clothed in light. In my dream "the burning sand [had] become a pool, the thirsty ground bubbling springs. In the haunts where jackals once lay, grass and reeds and papyrus [had grown]."[5]

The air was thirsty no more.

29

I waited in Cataviña for three days while Cenovio found a vaquero.

But he didn't show up with just a vaquero and a pack mule. He showed up with a truck, two vaqueros, and two horses.

My experience with Raymundo in Sierra de la Giganta had convinced me that trucks are expensive, inconvenient, and completely unnecessary. Mules are far superior to horses in mountains and deserts where water and food are scarce. I pack light, and one vaquero is all that is needed; however, I could be convinced that two vaqueros are better than one, if there was a good reason.

I tried to reason with him.

"Thank you, Cenovio, but I need only one vaquero and a saddle mule and a pack mule."

"Mules are slow and stubborn. You need a horse," he countered.

"Okay, then I need a horse, a pack mule, and one vaquero."

"The horse must have hay and water. You are going into the desert where there is no water and nothing for horses to eat. You will need a truck to carry the hay and water for the horse. You don't need a pack mule because you have a truck. You need two vaqueros—one to ride with you, and one to drive the truck," Cenovio explained with the patience and surety of a primary school teacher.

I knew there was no use trying to reason with him.

For better or for worse, I had two vaqueros, two horses, and a truck.

The horses looked old and tired, and not up to a trek through Sierra San Pedro Mártir, the steepest Sierra in the peninsula. One horse was thin and its rump bones protruded. The other stood with its right hind leg elevated off the ground. Both were listless and stared at the ground, their heads drooping.

My two vaqueros were Marcos "Chikis" Medina and Porfirio "Guile" Aviler.

Chikis was to be my vaquero the next seventy miles, from Cataviña to Rancho El Pozo, and Guile would drive the truck; they would then switch, and Guile would be my vaquero to Rancho El Coyote, seventy-five miles north of El Pozo.

Cenovio was a bit vague when I asked how the truck would navigate the old El Camino Real through the mountains that Junípero Serra took to San Diego, which does not follow any roads. "*No problema*," he assured me, and repeated it for emphasis. "*¡No problema!*"

I knew there would be problems.

Cenovio had graciously loaned me his prized *cabalgata* vaquero truck, a ragtag converted Ford pickup with oversize tires and high suspension springs that lifted it four feet off the ground. By the time it was fully loaded, it was less than six inches off the ground.

The four of us piled into the truck and drove to Arroyo Cataviña to fill with water a large plastic horse tank that took up half the back of the truck. Afterward, Guile and Chikis worked for an hour to fit six bales of hay, a twenty-gallon plastic gasoline container, extra tires, three lawn chairs, an old propane stove, a grilling grate, an army surplus cast-iron pot big enough to feed a battalion of *cabalgata* riders, and tents, tarpaulins, and who knows what else.

We were carrying more food for us than hay for the horses. After the bad experience with Tomás, I wasn't going to be without food for my vaquero, so I had bought a thousand *pesos*' worth of canned Spam, Vienna sausages, and tuna, plus a half dozen Snickers candy bars, at the small roadside convenience store in Cataviña. I had the café in Cataviña make two dozen assorted chicken, egg, cheese, and bean burritos. Cenovio had bought even more food—some canned meat, plus Tecate beer for the vaqueros, ten pounds of sugar, two one-gallon jars of Nescafé instant coffee, and dozens of eggs.

"I love adventure!" Cenovio said, gleefully happy, "and what you are doing is a true adventure."

I enthusiastically agreed. We were kindred spirits.

"We are so rich," Cenovio gushed, and I vigorously shook my head up and down agreeing with every word. "We have the wind to cool us, the sun to keep us warm, stars to light up the night. We need nothing more than what God provides, what nature provides!" Then he presented me with a 3,700-*peso* bill for food, hay, and gasoline.

We laughed; we both knew God's treasures were free, but man's were not.

By the time Cenovio's old pickup was loaded, we looked like the Clampetts heading out from Bugtussle, with Jed driving the overflowing truck, Jethro riding a horse, and Granny walking.

Chikis rode quickly ahead on the skin-and-bones horse and led my horse on a rope. I walked an hour alongside the highway past Cataviña. When the old mission road turned into the desert, I climbed on my horse, the old gray mare, and she lumbered along in the stifling desert heat, slower than a mule. She had a bad right hip and raised her hoof when we stopped, which was often. Chikis had no patience with her and tied a rope around her neck and pulled us behind him.

By midafternoon we were starving hungry but had no food because we had no pack mule. Everything was in the truck, and heaven knew where it was. I took a Snickers bar from my saddlebag and shared it with Chikis. As Chico had done a month earlier, I carefully divided it in half and gave Chikis the smaller half.

It was sunset when we arrived at Agua Dulce—sweet water—one of the most famous waterholes on El Camino Real. In missionary times it was the best water between San Borja and San Fernando, a distance of two hundred miles. The Indians called it Keita when Padre Linck camped here. They had never seen white men or horses and were frightened. When Father Serra camped at Agua Dulce three years later, the Indians, still frightened, fled from him and rebuffed his attempt to talk to them.

Guile was parked near a scraggly, half-dead palo verde tree at Agua Dulce. He took the horses and greeted Chikis with, "*No agua. Nada.*" There was no water, nothing. The famous, tiny spring had been dry for years.

Guile had set up the propane stove for dinner and had hay ready for the horses. I was beginning to feel good about the truck.

El Camino Real from Cataviña to Mission San Fernando and then northeast to San Juan de Dios is well-documented. Wenceslao Linck, the Jesuit missionary at San Borja, explored the area in 1766 and kept detailed notes. Junípero Serra had carried Linck's diary. I carried Linck's map.

The next day, I walked for hours and rode the old gray mare when the sand got too deep or the road too rough. Chikis kept me entertained. He reminded me of the Waylon Jennings song "Mammas, Don't Let Your Babies Grow Up to Be Cowboys." He loved to talk, and I loved to listen. He was in his mid-twenties and had two children by different mothers.

He rode half sideways in the saddle, turned toward me, talking with a Marlboro cigarette dangling between his lips and ashes dropping onto his worn Levi's. "I've worked a month sunup to sundown without a day off," he volunteered, speaking slowly in Spanish and repeating himself several times, and using hand gestures, to make sure I understood. I was impressed with his work ethic. "It's work, and I'm grateful to have it," he said.

It was a long day. A vaquero at a rancho said we were two hours from Mission San Fernando, but it was sunset and too late to go further, so we camped in the sandy plain of Buenos Aires near a ghost town called Pueblo Viejo (old town). It was completely deserted, and the houses weren't that old-looking, but most were missing walls and roofs. There was a school with no windows. The ghost town looked apocalyptic—a world of houses and schools and yards but no people.

Guile was waiting in the truck, parked on the side of the road across from the ghost town. Nothing was unpacked. No food cooking on the stove greeted us; there were no lawn chairs to sit on and recover from a long, hard day.

Chikis turned in his saddle to face me. "There is a restaurant up the highway."

The dirt road to the restaurant was a different direction, far off the mission trail. I never turn back when I'm walking, not a quarter mile, not a block. I am on a straight line to where I need to go.

I believe a long walk is like life: Know where you're going. Walk the straightest line to get there, and don't look back. Otherwise, you never get where you want to go.

"No, let's camp and eat here; we have plenty of food." I was firm.

Chikis was disappointed, but he made a large campfire while Guile opened a can of Spam. Chikis turned on a small portable radio that was barely able to pick up a station. He sat alone in the truck late into the night, drinking Tecate beer, and singing along to the scratchy music.

I fell asleep listening to the wind—so loud it drowned out Chikis's music—hoping the spirits in the ghost town were friendly ones.

Things started to fall apart the next day—fast.

Chikis was distracted and kept complaining of ailments. His tooth hurt. His head hurt. His neck hurt. He kept popping pills.

It was supposed to be two hours to the mission, and walking or riding a horse shouldn't have mattered that much timewise. After four hours, I knew we were in trouble. Chikis had no clue how to get to Mission San Fernando.

Chikis studied my map. I felt we were going too far west and should have been going north. He was certain we were going in the right direction. For three hours we rode through canyons, and arroyos, and up and down mountains. Chikis fastened one of his spurs on the right heel of my hiking boot so I could get my old gray mare to go faster. She was old and tired, and didn't respond to spurs. She was deaf and couldn't hear my coaxing and pleading.

At the top of a mountain, Chikis stopped.

"¡Problema! ¡Problema!" he exclaimed. Using sign language and rapid Spanish he explained the problem: "My horse needs new shoes. He can't walk on the rocks."

Yesterday at one of the ranchos Chikis had put new horseshoes on my horse, and hammered his. What he was saying sounded kind of fishy to me.

Chikis told me to dismount, and he tied my horse to a giant cardon cactus.

"You wait here while I find the truck." He spurred his horse and took off galloping across the mountain.

I was left at the top of the mountain, alone, in freezing wind, wearing nothing but a light jacket. The only shade and shield from the wind was a cardon cactus. I was terrified to move rock and dead cactus to clear an area to sit, remembering the last time I moved a large piece of wood I awakened a bed of hibernating scorpions.

The more I thought about it, the more unlikely Chikis's story sounded. Why didn't he get new horseshoes for his horse yesterday at the rancho? Why did the horses need new horseshoes? Raymundo had ridden a horse for a week across the lava rock of Sierra de la Giganta and never had a problem. Why did Chikis have so many ailments? Why was he popping pills?

I was certain Chikis had *muchos problemas.*

I was almost certain that Chikis did not know this area of the Sierras and was lost. I suspected he left me here while he found the truck and could ask someone how to get to Mission San Fernando.

I had nothing to eat. For breakfast I had a two-day-old bean burrito bought in Cataviña and warmed on the campfire. That's all I had eaten since Spam and a tortilla the night before.

The absurdity of the situation made me laugh. I had wanted a wild, crazy adventure, and I was getting what I asked for.

I decided to clear a spot underneath the cardon, scorpions or not, and rest and wait. First, I made sure there weren't any rattlesnakes sunbathing nearby; I threw several small rocks into the thorny brush to alert them to my presence.

Three hours later, I heard an old truck in the distance and saw Guile and Chikis headed down a road at the base of the mountain. Chikis's horse was trotting alongside the truck. I jumped up and waved to get their attention, grabbed my horse, and slid down the mountain.

Even though they were two crazy vaqueros, they were my crazy vaqueros, and I was helpless without them.

Chikis was sitting in the truck, holding his head, complaining of a tooth-ache. I popped some Vienna sausages in my mouth and got in the truck—and Guile drove one hour in the opposite direction to get to the mission.

I pitched my tent on a secluded spot in Arroyo San Fernando, down the hill from the ruins of Mission San Fernando. Chikis took off in the truck, saying he needed medicine for his tooth, and asked if I would buy him a pack of cigarettes.

Guile made a large campfire and scrambled eggs. We warmed tortillas on the campfire. It was simple food but delicious.

"*Necesitas un nuevo vaquero*," Guile confided. You need another vaquero. We agreed he would try to contact Cenovio to see if there was a local vaquero available.

I slept happily a stone's throw from the ruins of the old Franciscan mission; the moon was like a streetlight hanging above the tent, and wind through the palms played a soft lullaby.

―――――

The same lie that imprisoned the Jesuits destroyed their missions. For two hundred years the sad adobe and stone churches were chipped and hammered by treasure hunters looking for the vast hidden wealth of the Jesuit missionaries. It was the king's lie, a preposterous falsehood that refused to die, and is still alive today. It goes like this: The Jesuits were in Lower California not to feed and clothe and minister to the destitute natives, but to plunder the country of its riches. The outside world was denied entry for seventy years while the Jesuits accumulated stockpiles of gold, silver, and pearls. A secret messenger warned them in advance that the Spanish king had discovered the truth and was going to arrest them and seize their fortune. They were told to hide their treasure, which they did.

Fortune seekers tore apart the old missions, looking for treasure. When they found none, they concocted another theory, a tale of lost missions. Depending on who told the story, the lost mission was called either Santa Clara or Santa Isabel; the latter is used more often. The Jesuits needed a place to hide their gold, silver, and pearls so not one trace would be found. To do so, they built one last mission, Mission Santa Isabel, in a deep mountain gorge north of Santa María. For months mule trains carried vast amounts of treasure from the missions to Santa Isabel. The tale became even more preposterous: Right before their arrest, the masterful and cunning priests closed off the entrance to the gorge by means of a landslide. The treasure is still there waiting to be found. Erle Stanley Gardner, creator of the best-selling Perry Mason mysteries, wrote several books in early 1960 popularizing the myth and feeding the frenzy.[1]

There was never a Mission Santa Clara nor a Mission Santa Isabel in Lower California.

There was never any treasure.

The treasure of the Jesuits was in their hearts and in their sweat and toil in a barren land of rock and sand. Their treasure was *stored in heaven where no thief can break in and steal it.*[2]

Mission San Fernando was the end of the Jesuits in Lower California and the beginning of the Franciscans in Upper California. Wenceslaus Linck discovered the site, and two years later Father Junípero Serra founded the mission.

It is where men and supplies were assembled for the long journey to San Diego. When Father Serra arrived in Velicatá, soldiers were waiting for him and gave him a grand reception. They had been there three months and built five adobe and palm-roof huts. One of the huts was cleaned out and an altar prepared for mass. Soldiers put on their full uniforms with leather jackets and shields, and Father Serra consecrated a new mission, the first and last Franciscan mission in Lower California. He named it Mission San Fernando de Velicatá. Naked and hungry, Cochimís started arriving immediately. Father Serra and Gaspar de Portolá, the first governor of California, departed the next day, leaving missionary Miguel Campa to begin building, planting, and teaching.

The missionaries toiled for fifty years, but the desert never adequately fed its people. Droughts and epidemics took their toll, and the mission closed in 1818.

Forty years later, a desert traveler described the despair and desolation: "The old ruin is a miserable place. There are four root-eating Indians living in a corner of the church where they have patched the fallen roof with cane leaves . . . Others appear to have no houses and live around like wolves or jack rabbits."[3]

That is how the Jesuit missionaries found the desert people in Loreto in 1697, and how the Franciscans found them in San Fernando de Velicatá in 1769, and why they gave their lives to feed and clothe them and show them God's love.

Chikis was up before sunrise lighting a campfire, whistling, and singing along to his portable radio, eager to start the day. He hammered new horseshoes on his horse.

Chikis was lively and entertaining all day. He rode ahead and lay in the shadow of a huge cardon cactus, pretending to sleep with his hat over his face, waiting for me to catch up. He picked desert flowers and decorated the headband of his wide-brimmed cowboy hat, and put it on my small head, covering my eyes. He wore my small cowboy hat on his forehead, galloping through the cirio with his head tipped back to see the trail. He made fat cigars of dead pitahaya fruit buds and puffed noisily, leaving a thin trail of black smoke billowing behind us. He pretended to lasso cholla and barrel cactus, charging toward them on his horse with his rope swinging over-head, looking like a deranged Lone Ranger suffering from dehydration and delusion.

We laughed and the afternoon passed quickly. His past transgressions were forgiven and forgotten. I was grateful for the humor that distracted from the harshness of the desert and agony of the sun.

At sunset Guile was parked in the truck beside a small clearing on the side of the road: a vaquero campground, cleared of rock, but littered with campfire ashes and mule manure. I set up my tent in a gulley that was hidden from trucks passing in the darkness of night on the dirt road. I was nestled in a protective minefield of cholla and spiked agave. Woe unto the serial killer or *narco* or stalking lion who came for me.

I was settling into my tent when I heard a commotion and peeked over the top of the gulley that shielded me from the road.

Two large pickup trucks pulled into our campsite. One was towing a horse trailer occupied by a beautiful horse the color of sunset and a large black *macho* mule. People piled out and left the radio turned up loud. Lively Mexican country music with accordions and guitars energized the static, dry air.

It was Cenovio! He had driven two hours to get here. He had brought his wife, three other couples, a friend, his horse, and a neighbor's mule.

I got out of my tent to say hello and thank him, though I was confused by the party he brought along.

"I have brought you my horse," he said proudly, in Spanish, as he unloaded the red beauty. "He is a magnificent horse, and I love him dearly, but I share with you and the vaqueros! His name is Payaso. He is such a clown, and he looks like one with his white nose and bright red mane." Cenovio caressed Payaso's head and tied him to a small bush.

I lingered, stroking Payaso's back. He did look like a clown, and I christened him Bozo.

A dozen people scurried about unloading bales of hay to sit on and pots and grills for cooking. Guile and Chikis looked tired as they quickly emptied the truck and drove in the desert in search of dead cardon for firewood. Soon, there were two roaring campfires in the clearing, lighting up the night sky and providing a touch of warmth to the freezing night air.

Before long, the grill was hot and five pounds of meat were cooking. No one spoke English, but *no problema*. Cenovio's friends gave me presents: a can of cashews from Costco, a plastic baggie of freshly brined olives, and a chocolate bar. I was touched by the kindness.

Cenovio presented a gallon bottle of tequila to Chikis and Guile. Guile looked at me, unsmiling, and our eyes met. Chikis has *problema*s, and one is drinking. I didn't know what demons Guile might have. The thought of two intoxicated vaqueros in the desert wilderness made me uncomfortable, but that was tomorrow's problem.

Cenovio posed for Facebook photos by the campfire with his cowboy cup of coffee.

"Wait!" He shielded his face behind his outstretched hand. He grabbed the blackened enamel coffeepot off the campfire and pretended to pour coffee into his cowboy cup. "Now," he said, smiling broadly at the camera. Everyone laughed and applauded.

As quickly as they came they left, packing the hay bales and empty coolers back in the truck. They loaded up Chikis's lame horse, and left everything else with us. Cenovio had brought Bozo and a mule, and took only one horse back.

I now had two vaqueros, two horses, a mule, and a truck.

30

In the light of morning, our campground looked like a war zone, with trash and bottles everywhere. Carne asada was still on the campfire from the night before. Cactus had been added to the fire. The meat was charred black and kept cooking; Guile and Chikis wrapped pieces in cold tortillas for breakfast.

Chikis was quiet and his eyes were red. The gallon of tequila was half empty. He leaned against the truck, steadied Bozo with one arm, and lifted his hind leg to check his hoof. I had never seen a vaquero check a horse or mule's hooves, but Chikis did so compulsively.

I was fastening rattlesnake gaiters to my boots when Chikis came over. "I need more medicine for my tooth, and the truck is out of gasoline." He smiled. "Do you have fifteen hundred *pesos* for gasoline?"

I unpacked my pommel bag and took out fifteen hundred *pesos*. Chikis left in the truck.

A chill hung in the early morning air.

Guile rode Bozo and saddled up the *macho* mule for me to ride when it got too rough for walking. The old gray mare was no longer needed. But we had to bring her with us, and she was an unnecessary burden. I didn't understand why Cenovio had left her with us.

Guile wasn't familiar with the area and frequently consulted the map.

There was a large mountain peak hours away, Cerro San Juan de Dios, and we headed directly toward it. I walked until we reached a steep and rocky arroyo.

The *macho* mule was half wild and difficult to control. Guile held the halter forcefully to steady the mule for me to swing up into the saddle. He dropped his head and tried to shake the bit from his mouth, and rubbed his neck and bridle against the ground.

I did okay until the skittish *macho* plunged down the rocky slope and panicked at the bottom when his feet sank deep into sand. This was no mountain mule. He abruptly stopped, kicked his front body into the air, and dropped forward suddenly, whiplashing me almost out of the saddle. One foot flew out of the stirrup, and I was saved by an angel from diving forward off his back. My teeth dug into my tongue and lower lip and my mouth filled with blood. My mouth felt numb, and I was afraid the violent motion had broken a tooth.

Guile raced toward me, jumped off Bozo, threw his arms around my mule's neck and almost pulled us to the ground. I held on to the pommel and tried to stay in the saddle. I was badly shaken; my bloody lip hurt when I breathed.

Afterward, Guile lifted me onto Bozo, and I rode slowly across a vast cactus plain, my neck and jaw throbbing with pain.

For the first time along the old mission trail, gateless barbed wire fences, stretching for miles, blocked our way. I wondered later if they were meant to keep the drug cartels from smuggling drugs through the ranches. If so, they weren't working.

An hour later, we came to another gate and a crude handwritten sign that said Rancho Las Palmas. Guile opened the gate, and we continued down the road to the foot of a small mountain where there was the most beautiful oasis I had seen in the desert.

Large black dogs ran out from under the palms and growled at the mule, and Guile kicked them away with his boot. He called out, but no one answered. "*El vaquero no está aquí. Está con vacas,*" Guile said. The vaquero is not here. He is out with the cows.

There was water, and we rested in the shade while the animals drank.

I felt we were close to San Juan de Dios, and I urged Guile to continue riding through the rancho toward the mountain that loomed ahead.

Guile spoke softly and firmly in Spanish. "No, the old mission is not here. Chikis said it is up the arroyo from the road we were on. Chikis is meeting us on the road. We must find Chikis. We have no food." Guile refused to go further. After filling his water bottle from the clear mountain spring, we headed back in the direction we came.

We backtracked for an hour and reached an intersecting dirt road that appeared to wrap around the base of the mountain. Guile suggested we take it. "It must lead to San Juan de Dios."

The road wound through a large sandy arroyo covered in cactus and brush. It thickened until we couldn't see but a few feet ahead.

Guile smiled and pointed to deep tracks in the sand from a heavy truck. "Chikis!" he said.

We heard something big come crashing through the brush toward us. God willing, it was Chikis.

Instead, we saw a military armored truck with men dressed in camouflage fatigues—two in the back and two in front. The men in the back wore bulletproof vests and carried assault weapons with pistols in holsters at their waist. The truck was camouflaged in shades of brown that blended into the sand. It was eerily quiet, like an electric-powered car.

"Stop!" the driver yelled, as the two men in back reached for their guns; one pulled a neck scarf over his lower face to shield his identity.

This was not good.

Guile quickly explained why we were there. Bozo and I were several yards behind Guile and partially hidden by a low-hanging willow.

"Get out!" the man in front ordered. The men in the back of the truck gestured for us to turn around and leave the arroyo.

Guile asked if they had seen Chikis and our truck in the area.

"No one is here. Go!" They drove into the thick brush and out of sight.

I remained there frozen on Bozo and thanked God that we had just escaped . . . something. What, I didn't know.

Were they the Mexican military or *narcos* smuggling drugs? The drug cartels have been known to impersonate the military, to wear military uniforms and use military equipment. I was just thankful they were gone.

Guile was visibly shaken as he turned the animals around, and we headed back down the arroyo in the opposite direction.

A few minutes later, we heard what sounded like a gunshot.

We didn't turn around to see what it was. Guile whipped his mule, grabbed the rope attached to Bozo's halter, and we plowed through thick brush and out of the arroyo at top speed.

Once we reached the top of the mountain, we looked for our truck. Chikis was nowhere in sight. For the third time that day, we went down the same road and took the fork to Rancho Las Palmas.

It was dark when we got to the rancho. Nobody was there, except the two large black dogs that sniffed the mule and ran back under the palms. Horses that were not there earlier were in a corral.

"The vaquero is out with the cattle tonight," Guile explained.

The sun was down. It was now dark and cold. Guile and I were alone at Rancho Las Palmas in the middle of nowhere.

We had not eaten for ten hours. Chikis had the truck with our food and camping gear, and heaven knew where he was.

Guile found dead cactus and made a fire.

There was a large log to lean against, and I took out my miniature pocket flashlight to check for hibernating scorpions, sleeping giant centipedes, and rattlesnakes. Then I spread saddle blankets on the ground in front. I was shivering uncontrollably from the cold when Guile took his heavy leather chaps and covered my legs. Then he moved the fire closer to me, using his bare hands. I smiled a thank-you. Acts of such incredible sweetness and kindness will stay with me forever.

I sent an emergency SOS with our GPS location to Dale on the satellite phone. A short while later, Dale called. He had Cenovio on the line with us. Guile and I explained the situation.

"I cannot contact Chikis," Cenovio apologized in Spanish. "There is no phone service where you are. I will call a friend who has a rancho an hour from you and see if he can come to you, or if he can find Chikis."

I had paid for emergency medical evacuation insurance with the satellite phone, and Dale asked if he should call for assistance.

"No," I replied without hesitation. "If I am evacuated, the journey will be over, and my dream will end. I'm not ready to do that yet."

Dale understood. Either Chikis would find us, or we would head out at dawn and find him.

I sat in the dark and cold, frustrated that I had agreed to Cenovio's solution. Traveling light with a man and a mule was the only way to follow El Camino Real mission trail through desert Sierras. With a pack mule and a vaquero I could survive for weeks. We ate when we got hungry. We stopped and camped when it got dark. With everything in a truck, I never knew where the truck was, and the driver never knew where I was.

Chikis arrived two hours later, the headlights visible from far away. He was whistling and cheerful as if nothing had happened, as if we hadn't been without food for fourteen hours and left stranded in the dark and cold. He had taken the uncooked carne asada from the night before to a restaurant and had it made into *bistec* soup. Guile heated it on the campfire, while I used the beam from the truck lights to set up my tent.

Guile said hardly a word to Chikis.

———

The next morning, I learned I had been right the day before when I told Guile the road through Rancho Las Palmas led to San Juan de Dios. We could have saved ourselves a lot of pain and suffering, and not put ourselves at risk with drug smugglers in the arroyo, had we continued on this road yesterday.

Mission San Juan de Dios was an hour walk from our campsite. I decided to head out first thing, on foot, and I asked the vaqueros to follow shortly.

When I got to the mission, I was surprised to still be alone. There was nothing for me to do but wait and hope that I hadn't been left behind again.

While I waited, I read through Wenceslao Linck's 1766 diary to the time he discovered and named San Juan de Dios during an expedition from his mission in San Borja to find other mission sites.

Three years later, when Junípero Serra arrived in San Juan de Dios, his infected left leg was covered in sores and so grotesquely swollen that Portolá begged him to return to Velicatá and recuperate. Father Serra refused. "God will give me the strength to reach San Diego as He has given me the strength to come so far. Even though I may die on the way, I shall not turn back. They can bury me where they wish and I shall be happy if it be the will of God," he said.[1]

The pain was so great that he could not stand on his feet. Out of desperation, he asked a muleteer what he would give a lame mule. The muleteer rubbed a mixture of hot tallow and desert herbs on Father Serra's leg and bound it with cloth. The next morning his leg was greatly improved, and Serra continued north to San Diego, and into history.

It was another hour before Guile showed up, riding the mule, with Bozo and the old gray mare in tow.

The sandy arroyo around the mission ruins was filled with footprints. Guile told me to stay near the old rancho while he looked around the arroyo.

He came back thirty minutes later and was visibly troubled. "There were three men here early this morning, and two trucks. They are not vaqueros. They are wearing shoes, not boots. I think they are drug smugglers. We should leave."

I had hoped to walk across the arroyo to the mission ruins and look for the old cemetery, but Guile advised against it. "*Los narcos son hombres malos. Vamos ahora.*" Narcos are very bad men. We should leave now.

We rode quickly back to Rancho Las Palmas. I wanted to take the trail to the northwest toward San Diego, but Guile insisted on riding four hours back to a deserted rancho near the camp where Cenovio had met us two nights before.

I resisted. I had confidence in the map I'd been following for six weeks, and it showed the trail going to the northwest. We had made no progress in two days, and I wanted to continue north and not turn back.

But Guile would not hear of it. "Chikis doesn't know this sierra. I don't either. There are too many *narcos,* and we are not safe." He refused to discuss it further.

A vaquero with serious issues, a second vaquero who didn't know the trails, two horses, a half-wild *macho* mule, and a truck—what a fiasco! I had no choice but to turn back.

Guile was as fed up as I was. The difference was he could do something about it, and I couldn't.

Chikis was at the vacant rancho when we arrived. He had set up camp beside a huge cardon and underneath the shade of a cluster of thin-trunked poplars. He had a grill and skillet on the campfire and was ready to fix dinner.

Guile dismounted and took the saddle off the *macho* mule. "I'm leaving."

I'd seen it coming but was still shocked.

"Whoa, Guile, let's eat. After a good night's sleep, let's see how you feel in the morning," I pleaded. It was getting dark, and we were tired and hungry—again.

But he had made up his mind. He turned to Chikis, "I need a ride back to the highway."

Before I knew it, Chikis and Guile took off in the truck. I looked around the campsite for my gear bags. Chikis had unloaded my tent bag, but my Jetboil, food, and everything else was still in the truck.

How could I be so stupid? I should have checked before letting them leave. But I was so focused on the fact that Guile was abandoning us I wasn't thinking straight.

My feel-sorry-for-Edie voice whimpered, *I am alone at a deserted rancho in an area crawling with narcos. It is cold and windy. I have no food.*

My cowboy voice spoke louder, *Trust all is well, and all will be well.*

I was not alone. I had two horses and a half-wild *macho* mule.

I rummaged around Chikis's campfire and found raw peanuts and a sack of pork rinds. I ate it all.

I had a tent. Thank goodness I had a tent.

I found a secluded place behind the old ranch to set up my tent. I was hidden from view. It was the best I could do. I crawled into my sleeping bag, feeling like a ditched Scarlett O'Hara: *Tomorrow is another day. I'll think about it tomorrow.*

31

The next morning at five o'clock, Chikis was back in camp. I heard him start a fire to boil water for coffee.

It was still dark but I didn't need light to pack my gear and tent. I could do it blindfolded. I'd gotten it down to a science and could pack up in less than half an hour in total darkness. I had a system and knew exactly what to do next, so there was no guessing.

Packing up in the dark was good. I could feel the dirt but not see it.

I was filthy. The filth was part of me.

I didn't care anymore.

In the desert, water is to drink and cook with; it is too precious to waste. We don't clean; we rinse. I ate on a rinsed dirty plate with a rinsed dirty spoon or my rinsed dirty fingers. If food tasted bad, or there was something in it that was odd-shaped, kind of insect-shaped, or wormy-looking, I didn't care. I didn't want to know what it was. If I wanted to eat, I ate what was there.

When I emerged from my tent, a stranger was standing next to Chikis at the campfire.

"*Este es Arnulfo. Él es un amigo.*" This is Arnulfo. He is a friend.

I introduced myself, and we shook hands. Arnulfo sized me up, and I sized him up. He appeared to be the real deal, despite wearing a baseball hat with a blue hoodie. He also wore thick leather chaps and dusty cowboy boots with long silver spurs. I was not sure what he thought of me.

Chikis was speaking. "Arnulfo knows every trail this side of Sierra San Pedro Mártir. He was a vaquero at Rancho Las Palmas, and his cousin is the vaquero there now. His other cousin is the vaquero here at Rancho Cerro Prieto. He can only ride with you today. There will be another vaquero tonight."

I gave Chikis a grateful smile. He had done well and restored some of my faith in him. I was thrilled he had found a local vaquero willing to ride, and there would be no delay.

"I need to pay Guile. How can I get him money?"

Chikis shrugged and shook his head.

"The trail is very bad; it is all cholla," Arnulfo warned.

Chikis insisted I wear his chaps. His thick bullhide leather chaps weighed almost as much as I did, and my waist was so thin Arnulfo had to hold the chaps around me while Chikis helped me on Bozo.

It was the first time I'd worn chaps, and for once I rode straight through cactus like a vaquero. Cholla was everywhere, but I felt invincible. Unfortunately, after a few hours, my legs and hips grew numb from the heavy weight of the thick leather chaps.

Our path was littered with prickly sharp maguey. A few of the maguey were blooming, a canopy of yellow flowers atop six-foot-high cactus spears. After it flowers, the maguey dies and leaves only a tall wood stalk. It is known as the century plant, because it takes many years to flower, flowers only once, and then dies. *At least it flowers before it dies*, I thought, *unlike man, who may live a century and die having never flowered.*

From Father Serra's and other expedition diaries it is difficult to determine their route. Their diaries all mention "roads," but these were mostly old footpaths and animal trails. Linck is the only Jesuit missionary to have traveled north of Velicatá, and here, in the foothills of Sierra San Pedro Mártir, both Crespí's and Serra's expeditions veered northwest from Linck's well-documented route. In this direction, there are few notable landmarks. Serra described the road as "painful and ugly."[1] The land is sterile and dry, no trees, just cardon and cirio and a few scattered desert palms.

Arnulfo and I followed the same arroyos—Rosario and Aliso—as Crespí and Father Serra. Crespí's campsite was near large palms, but there was no running water. He called the campsite Las Palmas, and Father Serra called the area Santiago. We passed what must be that same cluster of palms, since they were the only palms we saw in more than four hours. There was no surface water, just dunes of sand and decayed palm debris, exactly as Crespí described the area two hundred years ago. It was a miserable place to camp, and I was thankful we were not stopping there.

The desert sand was stifling hot. Itty-bitty teensy flies were everywhere and as miserable as the heat. When I walked, they swarmed out of the dust and around my eyes and in my ears; thousands of them, smaller than gnats. They flew in my nose and my mouth. They buzzed in my ears, and stuck to my eyelashes. I pulled my green bandana over my mouth and nose and covered my ears, but the flies went through the cloth.

We finally arrived at Rancho El Pozo, the end of the trail for Arnulfo Murillo.

Cenovio said El Pozo—the well—was where Chikis would stop riding and drive the truck, and Guile would ride with me. Chikis didn't make it past the first day. Within a day, he had taken control of the truck. Heaven knew what Chikis did all day while we trudged through desert sand.

Arnulfo unsaddled the animals, and we waited for Chikis to arrive with the truck. We ate canned tuna and sat outside a vaquero's small hut made of concrete blocks, corrugated metal, and chicken wire.

After two hours sitting in stifling hot heat, we saw a small dust storm and a white truck pulled in front of the rancho. It was Cenovio and gang.

Cenovio had three guys with him, and they all piled out of the truck. José, the vaquero who lived alone on the rancho, was one of them. I wasn't sure who the others were, and why they were here, or why Cenovio was here. Cenovio unloaded more tequila.

I set up my tent in a corner of the old cirio corral far away from the loud revelry.

A short while later, Chikis arrived in our old truck with the new vaquero who would ride with me to El Coyote. He also had Guile in the back of the truck. I walked out to greet them and gave Guile a hug. He was apologetic and embarrassed that he'd left me alone the day before. He said something about El Coyote; I wasn't sure if he was offering to go with me to El Coyote, or if he was telling me he would be at El Coyote next week when I get there. It was times like this that I wished I spoke better Spanish.

I paid Guile double what I owed him. It made him very happy, and me too. I would never forget his kindness when we were stranded at Rancho Las Palmas, and how he moved the fire with his bare hands. I didn't want to leave any unhappiness or ill will behind on the old mission trail.

Cenovio and Chikis introduced the new vaquero, Joaquín Martorell, and his teenage son, Juan, who would be going with us.

I now have two vaqueros, a teenage kid, two horses, a wild mule, and an old truck.

While setting up my tent, I went to put my camera away only to discover that it wasn't in my pocket. I began to panic. Every picture I'd taken since arriving in Loreto was on the camera.

I was sick at the thought of losing it. I tried to think of when I last had it. I remembered that I'd taken some pictures when Cenovio arrived, so it had to be somewhere here. Everyone helped me look. No luck.

Joaquín, my new vaquero, refused to stop looking. He retraced my steps around the well and found it buried in desert sand next to the cirio fence. I embraced him in gratitude. That kind of dedication would serve me well on the trail.

In the morning, Chikis rode with me and Joaquín, and Juan took the truck. As we rode, Chikis became serious. He talked of dreams: a dream to own his own rancho, a dream to provide for his two sons, a dream to own a truck. He wanted to take me all the way to the California border.

"If I take you to Tijuana, will you buy me a truck?" he asked wistfully.

"I may be able to help you get one." I smiled. "Not a new truck but a used one, a farm truck."

I meant it. If Chikis would help me with my dream, I would help with his. I had no faith he would actually go with me to Tijuana, but I encouraged him to dream.

But I had one condition. "Chikis, after El Coyote I want to walk to Tijuana with a pack mule, and no truck."

He nodded his head. "We will ride mules, and carry our supplies on a pack mule."

Joaquín and Juan parked the truck in Rosarito, an old mining ghost town on old San Miguel road, and waited for us. The truck was out of gasoline, and Chikis and Joaquín siphoned a few gallons from the large plastic gasoline container in the back.

Why we are out of gas? I wondered. I had given Chikis fifteen hundred *pesos* for gas three days ago, and Joaquín could have gone for gas today while Chikis and I were riding through the sierra.

Chikis had the truck follow behind us to a small canyon protected on three sides from the blustery north wind. Joaquín parked the truck by the side of the road, and we set up camp in another dust hole.

Chikis was kind and attentive. He put his big tarp underneath my tent, and folded it over, to provide extra warmth. "We need three mules to take us to Tijuana," he said. "My cousin is a vaquero at San José de los Arces and can get the mules. I will ride there tonight and talk to him."

He rode off on the *macho* mule without eating.

I was jolted awake hours later by headlights shining into my tent and a loud truck driving into camp.

It was Chikis.

He shook the outside of my tent. "My cousin drove me in his truck. I left the mule at his rancho. I need a thousand *pesos* to get gasoline for our truck tonight."

I was groggy with sleep and didn't want to get in a discussion about waiting until morning to get gasoline. I gave him a thousand *pesos*.

The truck and Chikis were still gone in the morning when we packed up camp. We were saddled up and ready to go when Chikis drove in, wearing dark sunglasses, and a dirty hoodie pulled up over his head. He was barely able to get out of the truck, and in no condition to drive.

Joaquín took one look at Chikis and decided his son Juan should ride with me, and he would drive the truck.

Juan was a very nice boy, a vaquero-to-be. He liked computers and technology, but not as much as animals and rancho life.

As I walked deeper into Sierra San Pedro de Mártir, the landscape began to change rather abruptly. There was no longer cardon and cirio cactus; now there were trees, cottonwoods and sycamores with beautiful fall foliage. Junípero Serra poetically described the change as "the land began to be more smiling and gladsome."[2] The trees and thick green vegetation provided secrecy from government drones, and the area had become a favorite hideout for drug smugglers.

It was also freezing.

The wind was too cold to breathe, and I put the bandana over my mouth to warm my breath. I had a cough and didn't want to get sick. My chest ached when I breathed, and I hoped and prayed it wasn't another lung tumor.

In midafternoon, Juan and I rode over a steep mountain, and in the middle of the road was our truck.

Joaquín was busy emptying the truck. "*La montaña es mala. No es bueno para un truck,*" he said. The mountain is bad. It is no good for a truck.

It was obvious the truck wasn't going any further. The hood was open, one tire was flat, and the ground was littered with our camping gear and supplies thrown haphazardly all over the road. Chikis was sitting in the passenger seat, his hoodie almost hiding his face, shivering and looking miserable. His eyes were dark and swollen.

Joaquín announced the rocky mountain road was impossible to drive on and he and I would have to go alone with a pack animal and enough food for four days. Juan would go with Chikis in the truck and they would try to meet up with us further north in Sierra San Pedro de Mártir, between Rancho San Antonio de los Caballos and Valladares. If not, we would continue to El Coyote and meet them there.

Joaquín had already saddled up the *macho* mule and was ready to head out. He and Juan quickly loaded a packsaddle on our old gray mare, and two saddlebags with camping gear and food.

"We must hurry," Joaquín warned. "It is going to rain, and it may snow."

We were just about to take off when I felt Joaquín stiffen beside me. I turned to look where he was staring and saw two men carrying assault weapons walking up from the arroyo.

Joaquín quickly motioned for Juan to stand behind him.

It was chilling to encounter men with military-grade weapons in these isolated arroyos where drug cartels smuggle cocaine, heroin, and amphetamines to the rich and famous in Los Angeles and the glassy-eyed homeless in San Francisco. In this land of *narcos*, as in drug-infested neighborhoods, one cannot tell a good guy from a bad guy.

I looked for a place to hide but there was none.

Chikis came alive, jumped out of the truck, and hurried toward the men. Joaquín and Juan stayed on the far side of the truck, listening.

I slipped quietly behind the truck, and crouched down next to the back bumper, partially hidden from view by a red canvas folding lawn chair.

The armed men were engaged in animated conversation with Chikis and appeared to be amused at the sight of our broken-down old truck, and two vaqueros loading pack animals.

They hadn't seen me, and I leaned to the side and tried to hide underneath the raised rear bumper.

The two men were dressed in tan-colored short-sleeve T-shirts, camouflage pants, and lace-up desert boots. One was short and stocky and carried an assault rifle on a band around his neck; the other was taller and more fit-looking, and had his assault rifle hooked over his left shoulder, and his pants tucked into his boots. They both looked unshaven, but clean.

They walked around the truck and glanced at me. They didn't seem to care all that much.

They were laughing. We must have looked like a circus with our old truck and tires and stuff scattered all over the road. I had not had a bath now for about eight days since we left Cataviña, and I smelled and looked homeless. Our animals were tired and worn-out. Chikis looked like death warmed over and could hardly open his eyes in the sunlight.

All of a sudden, two men on dirt bikes came roaring up out of the arroyo. The men with their guns stood in the center of the road, blocking them. The bikes came to a screeching halt. I couldn't hear the conversation.

I was loading my pommel bag on Bozo when a third guy on a motorcycle came over the crest of the hill. He slammed on his brake and skidded to a halt in front of me, with a look of sheer horror on his face. He was terrified, coming upon this scene.

I could only imagine what raced through his head, in the split second he understood his life might be threatened: *Am I at the wrong place at the wrong time? Are they drug smugglers and the military is searching their truck for cocaine? Are they all* narcos? *Are the mules loaded with drugs? Is the dirty American woman carrying drugs to the border? Am I soon to be dead?*

The three men on dirt bikes skidded fast away, slinging rocks behind.

What stories they must have told later of the bizarre encounter, as they tried to make sense of it!

The two men with assault weapons were still standing in the middle of the road, laughing, as Joaquín and I headed out of the arroyo and north into the towering peaks of Sierra San Pedro Mártir.

32

Joaquín rode as fast and hard as Pancho Murillo, and with no mercy. It was dark when we got to the adobe ruins of San Isidoro.

It was pouring rain and sleeting, and the north wind was vicious.

Chikis had packed his large tarp on the packhorse, and Joaquín helped me lay it flat and position my ground cover and tent on top. We folded the heavy tarp over my tent, and Joaquín roped the two ends together. Joaquín put his bedroll nearby under a smaller tarp. I was soaking wet and freezing but managed to boil water in the Jetboil and fix a beef macaroni dinner. It tasted awful, the macaroni half-cooked and hard to chew. But it was hot food, and we were starved and cold and wet.

Icy rain pelted us all night.

I was getting so very tired. *I don't think I'll ever camp again in my entire life after this,* I thought for the hundredth time. I could hardly wait to be at home and take a hot bath. *I don't want to think about it, no, no, no! I'll think about it as I get closer to San Diego.*

We got up later than normal, waiting for the morning sun to rise and warm us. Joaquín had slept on the ground, in the open, with a small tarp wrapped around his bedroll. It kept him dry, but he wore only a light Levi's jacket, no gloves, and a lightweight straw cowboy hat meant for desert sun, not mountain snow.

I awoke on a bed of ice. The large, dirty tarp over my tent was a bad idea. Icy rain had poured in through the top and collected in a puddle on the bottom of my tent. My wet air mattress was frozen into a chunk of ice, and my sleeping bag was saturated with ice crystals resembling snow.

Joaquín managed to find dead cactus in the underbrush. It was wet, but he slowly dried the end with a small butane lighter until it ignited. I tried to fix coffee, but my fingers were frozen and I couldn't open the container. Joaquín opened the coffee easily. His bare hands, like all vaqueros', were weathered like gloves; his were hands that worked and understood how to do things, that never froze, that never grew numb.

A strong sense of gratitude flooded over me. The campfire with wet wood was a testament to his skill.

Joaquín appeared to be in his forties. He worked as a vaquero on the same rancho as Chikis. He proudly showed me pictures of his family. His wife's name was Karla, and they had three boys; Juan was the oldest at eighteen, and there was an eight-year-old and a four-year-old.

He was very kind, a no-nonsense, get-it-done vaquero. He didn't laugh often, but when he did, he had a really nice laugh that sounded like a shy girl instead of the strong vaquero that he was.

How thankful I was to be here in this hard land with him.

Rugged and isolated, Sierra San Pedro Mártir was a seascape of steep mountain peaks covered in granite boulders. Father Serra described the area as "an immense wall of high mountains."[1] Each peak we climbed plummeted downward to an impenetrable dense ravine, Cañada El Alcatraz, that wound like a snake through the mountains. Joaquín and I zigzagged our way up and down at least a dozen peaks, the horses sliding on loose rock. At the base of each peak we had to hack our way across Cañada El Alcatraz, overflowing with trees and brush that snapped in our faces and tore at our clothing.

A branch ripped through the brim of my hat and gouged my right eye. The pain was instant and intense. My eye swelled almost shut.

Something was lodged in my eye, and I couldn't get it out.

Joaquín dripped water from his canteen in my eye to flush it out, but the pain didn't go away. Out of desperation, I squeezed Neosporin in my bottom eyelid, hoping the oily lubrication would help.

I was in pain the three hours it took to reach old Rancho San Antonio de los Caballos.

At the deserted rancho, Joaquín lit a campfire and boiled water. He soaked a dirty piece of cloth in hot water and rubbed it around the outer rim of my eye, wiping it clear of dirt and mucous. He wet the cloth again, forced my eye open, and dripped water on my eyeball.

I closed my eye and lay in the hot sun for an hour. When I opened my eye, the intense pain was gone, but it continued to feel scratchy and irritated. My vision was blurry, but I could see.

We rode hours through steep mountains covered with loose soil and rock. The mule and horses slid more than walked. We rode slowly; our bodies crouched forward in the saddle to brace against the ferocious wind. Large granite boulders blocked our path, and we were often forced to turn around and ride back to the top of the mountain to look for a passable trail. It was cloudy and overcast when we arrived at Valladares.

Chikis and the truck were nowhere in sight.

Valladares was a remote ramshackle rancho, although someone—perhaps a vaquero—had been there recently. On a table outside the shack, food rotted on plates as if someone had eaten and left quickly.

The nearby arroyo was named for Valladares, the stalwart Cochimí captain from San Borja who was handpicked to be Father Juan Crespí's companion and travel assistant and the San Diego expedition interpreter. Valladares had become sick a few days before in San Isidoro, and they couldn't save him; he died in this rocky arroyo overgrown with wild roses. Crespí was deeply saddened by his death: "I left a cross set up over his grave. I felt his death with all my heart because of the good services he had done for me all along the way."[2]

Two months later Junípero Serra arrived and found Valladares's grave in the thicket of wild pink roses where his dear friend Juan Crespí had buried him. The grave had been dug up by animals, but Father Serra reverently reburied him and wrote in his diary, "His bones were scattered; we collected them, and buried them again. Much water was thrown over the grave to harden the rocky soil. May his soul rest in heaven."[3]

Valladares's bones might have turned to dust, but his spirit still breathes. He has not been forgotten.

It soon began to sleet, and frozen raindrops pelted the ground as I struggled to set up my tent. I was shivering so hard I could barely function.

I knew I had to relax, and I started to pray. I told myself, *All is well*. My body was still freezing cold but my prayer had stopped the physical panic, the downward spiral into uncontrollable fear, just as it had so many times in emergency rooms, hospital beds, and oncology clinics.

As the book of Romans teaches, "suffering produces endurance, and endurance produces character, and character produces hope, and hope does not disappoint us."[4]

I was full of hope. Tomorrow I hoped to make it to El Coyote. I hoped they had a washing machine or scrub board and I could do laundry. I hoped they had a bathtub and hot water to soak in. I hoped the room was warm. I hoped the bed was soft.

It was pitch-dark at five o'clock in the afternoon. I couldn't even see my hand in front of my face. The minute the sun goes down, the world darkens and air freezes, something modern man has forgotten.

Chikis arrived an hour later and knocked outside my tent. He had a large gunnysack of raw chicken—was I hungry? I had not seen him for three days. I would have loved hot fried chicken when we arrived, after a day of Sierra hell and a night of freezing hell. But he didn't offer to fry the chicken, and neither Joaquín nor I had the energy to. Chikis left and said he would be back in two hours. Frankly, I didn't care if he came back or not.

Later, in the foggy haze of restless and hungry sleep, I heard a truck and hoped it was Chikis and not the vaquero who lived here or another stranger.

There was loud talking and music playing on a radio. I lay in my tarp-covered tomb, waiting for it to stop. I heard unfamiliar voices and a woman's laughter. I suspected Chikis had brought his wife. At 4:00 a.m. I was awakened again. Chikis was outside his tent, making noise. Maybe he didn't know what time it was. I stayed in my sleeping bag, waiting for the sun to come up or Chikis to build a fire before I left the shelter of my tent in the freezing cold. There were ice crystals on my sleeping bag and frozen water on the bottom of my leaky tent.

I wanted to shoot Chikis and destroy that old truck with my Home Depot pocket hammer hatchet. Chikis had partied for two weeks with Cenovio's truck and my money. I'd paid more for gasoline than I had for mules, horses, or vaqueros. The truck was supposed to be a support vehicle to provide hay and water to the animals. It was unnecessary. Water had been available on the trail, and most ranchos had hay.

I emerged from my tent and, indeed, there were two wives. Juan was gone, but his mother, Joaquín's wife, Karla, was here. Chikis's wife, Arely, was too.

I now had two vaqueros, two vaqueros' wives, two horses, a wild mule, and an old truck.

Joaquín fried the chicken in a bucket of deep fat. I was starved and ate heartily, ignoring the fat dripping from the meat, making a greasy trail down my dirty arm.

While Joaquín fried chicken, Karla used the mirror of the truck to put on lipstick and makeup. She carefully fixed her hair, then sat Chikis's wife in our canvas lawn chair and styled her hair, as if they were in a beauty parlor. Arely was a cute teenager, with a baby and a husband with serious issues. She deserved to be pampered, but I smiled about the fuss over hair out here in grimy Valladares.

Arely put on chaps, ready to get on a horse, but saw that Joaquín was riding with me, not Chikis. She looked sad and disappointed, and I wished she could come along with us, but we didn't have another horse or mule. Karla got on the old gray mare and rode with Joaquín and me.

We left our gear bags on an old car seat next to the ranch house and took only water. Chikis promised to load our things in the truck and meet us at El Coyote by late afternoon.

I needed to walk. The trail was steep and hard-packed, and my feet and legs felt energized. The energy radiated up my spine and to my head, and I felt euphoric in the thin mountain air.

Karla and Joaquín rode slowly ahead of me. Karla turned on her music. Loud. My euphoria was rudely interrupted. I kindly asked her to please turn down the music. She did briefly, and then turned it back up when they started talking. They talked above the loud music, as people often do nowadays.

After two months of not talking, and being in the silent wilderness, I couldn't bear the noise.

This had not been a spiritually transformative experience like the eight-hundred-mile mission walk from San Diego to Sonoma. The Mexican El Camino Real was too stark and too brutal. But it was physically empowering and had taken me to my physical edge.

A physical edge is like a mountain seen in the distance. As I walk toward it and into it, it becomes one steep hill after another, and before I know it, I am at the top of the mountain. Yesterday in the freezing rain with ice in my tent, soaking wet gloves, frozen fingers, and stiff wet boots, I was shivering uncontrollably and felt close to my physical edge. But I couldn't fall to pieces or pass out. It was just a mountain peak, and after that a valley, and then another mountain. It was a reminder to accept what comes and hold tight to faith.

I had talked to Dale on the satellite phone from Valladares. He was worried. "You are going to be twenty-two miles off course at Rancho El Coyote."

I couldn't do anything about it. I told Cenovio I felt El Coyote was too far northeast of Junípero Serra's route; however, it was the best place for Cenovio to pick up the horses, mule, and his truck. Cenovio was hoping Jonathan Meling would ride north with me. If not, El Coyote and Rancho Meling were the best places for me to find a new vaquero and mules.

———

Joaquín, Karla, and I arrived at Rancho El Coyote in late afternoon. We were hungry, tired, and dirty. We shivered in the freezing north wind, and the light drizzle turned to ice, then snow.

It was December 15.

Chikis was not there.

Everything I owned was in the truck. I had no money for food or rooms. I had no clothes. I had no toothbrush. Karla wore only a light sweater and was coughing and sneezing.

Rancho El Coyote Meling was a cattle ranch and also a dude ranch catering to tourists. Twenty-seven-year-old Jonathan Meling ran the ranch. To my surprise, Jonathan did not speak a word of English. I was thankful that he understood my bad Spanish, and we communicated remarkably well.

He was half Scandinavian and half Spanish and strikingly handsome with dark blond hair and blue eyes. He grew up on the ranch and was happy being a vaquero. More than a century ago, his Norwegian ancestors came to Baja and bought an old historic ranch called Rancho San José, now known as Rancho San José Meling. They worked hard, were thrifty, and survived. When other immigrants failed, they bought their land and it became Rancho El Coyote Meling. The estate was divided through several generations and divided again when Mrs. Meling died a few decades ago.

We sat around the kitchen stove to keep warm. Jonathan Meling had the cook fix dinner, and gave me a room key even though I couldn't pay. "You can pay when Chikis gets here," he suggested.

I offered to pay for a room for Joaquín and Karla, but Jonathan invited them to be his guests and stay in his house, not in a tourist room. He had known Joaquín for years and they were friends.

I asked Jonathan if he would be my vaquero to Tijuana.

"No, I am sorry, but I am leaving tomorrow and will be gone four days." He was confident his fifty-five-year-old cousin, Steven Meling, who spoke English, would know vaqueros who could take me. Unfortunately, Steven would not be back in El Coyote for two days.

Christmas was fast approaching, and every day I was stuck here was wasted and expensive.

"I can't wait two days to talk to Steven. I need to leave El Coyote tomorrow. Do you know any vaqueros who can take me?" I asked.

Jonathan promised to call Steven in the morning and talk to Cenovio, but I was feeling desperate.

"Do you think Chikis could do it?" I asked. Chikis had mentioned working several years at Rancho El Coyote, and I was curious if Jonathan thought Chikis was capable of getting me to Tijuana.

Jonathan smiled and rolled his eyes. He called Chikis by his given name. "Marcos is very bright and a good vaquero, but there are problems." He hesitated for a second.

We both laughed. Enough said.

"You should get back on the mission trail closer to the coast. El Coyote is too remote. There aren't many vaqueros here," Jonathan said. He promised to take me twenty-two miles to San Telmo, where Junípero Serra camped on his way to the coast from Sierra San Pedro Mártir.

My room had a cold, bare concrete floor and three twin beds with clean wool blankets. The room was freezing cold, and I piled all the wool blankets on my bed.

I didn't take a shower. I had no clean clothes to put on afterward. I took off my dirty cargo pants that hadn't been washed for two weeks and quickly jumped into bed. I didn't want dirty pants stained with horse and mule sweat in clean white sheets. I left my ragged shirt and sweaty socks on.

Jonathan promised to deliver my gear to the room if Chikis arrived before nine o'clock that evening.

I knew Chikis was not coming.

The next morning, a light cover of snow was on the ground, and icy drizzle continued to fall. I wrapped a wool blanket around me like a poncho and sat next to the woodstove in the kitchen.

Chikis didn't arrive until noon, but his absence meant Jonathan and I had more time to talk. He finally agreed to be my vaquero to Maneadero, south of Ensenada, and we worked out all the details. In Maneadero, Jonathan would pack up his animals and return to El Coyote, and Cenovio would find another local vaquero familiar with the area to take me to the California border.

Two more vaqueros and then I would be home. While there never was a part of me that truly considered quitting this journey, the going was tough, the most physically grueling thing I had ever done. I was ready to rest. But I knew these memories would enrich the rest of my life, however long or short it was.

33

Cenovio and Chikis arrived at the same time, and with a classic story to explain Chikis's absence. At Valladares the truck would not start, and Chikis thought he was out of gasoline. He called Cenovio, and Cenovio drove several hours to bring gas. When Cenovio arrived, he discovered the battery was dead. Chikis had left the truck door open all night, or the key in the ignition, and drained the battery—just another of Chikis's distractions.

But his wife, Arely, looked like there might have been more to the story. When they arrived she was as white as a sheet and looked scared and exhausted.

I was sad to say good-bye to Cenovio, but not his old *cabalgata* vaquero truck. Cenovio promised he would have another vaquero, and mules, lined up in Ensenada to meet Jonathan and me in three days, to get me to Tijuana. *"Por favor, Cenovio,"* I laughed, *"no más trucks"* . . . no more trucks.

He smiled broadly and made no promises.

Joaquín and Chikis loaded the old gray mare and the *macho* mule in the back of the old truck, with their wives squeezed in the middle of the front seat between them. Cenovio took Bozo in his truck. I watched from the road until they were out of sight. I would miss them.

I had never met a nicer man in my life than Cenovio, and I would be eternally grateful for his help and his *cabalgata* vaquero friends.

It was nine days before Christmas. I hoped to be home for Christmas. I didn't know if it was possible.

The next morning, Jonathan loaded two horses and a mule in a horse trailer, and I loaded gear in the back of the truck. He whistled and his dog, a small female border collie that went everywhere with him, came running and jumped in the back. She was the best mule dog I've ever seen.

I now had a new vaquero, two horses, a mule, and a cute dog.

Jonathan and I drove to San Telmo, where Harry Crosby finished his El Camino Real journey and sold his mules to the Meling Ranch before driving to San Diego. I wished we could have walked and ridden horses instead of driving the truck, but I knew Jonathan didn't have the extra day it would take. Plus, I had walked and ridden much further out of our intended path, just to get to El Coyote.

Jonathan left the truck and horse trailer at a rancho with a friend, and we saddled up the horses and rode to Mission San Vicente. Jonathan and I stayed on our horses and looked over a fence at the mission ruins. The mission was built long after Junípero Serra and the Franciscans left to build missions in California, and the ruins held no special meaning to me.

Out on the trail it was beautiful and sunny, and the spectacular fall colors made the day fairy-tale special and profoundly joyful.

Jonathan was a delightful young man. He had dropped out of school because he loved animals and liked being a rancher. He was happiest on a horse, and the rougher the mountain, the better. My horse couldn't keep up with him. I was happy to slowly traverse the mountain at an angle. Jonathan's horse charged straight up and down. He rode past me several times, rather than sit and wait.

Jonathan's little cow dog—I nicknamed her Vaquera Perra—tried to keep up with our horses, running as fast as her short legs would allow. She didn't like the mule, and the feeling was mutual. The mule intentionally tried to kick her, and would have bitten her if its mouth hadn't been roped shut. The only thing worse than a kicking mule is a biting mule, and our mule was a biter. Jonathan used a special strap, designed for such purposes, to wrap around his mouth to hold it shut. The mule did not want to be led by a rope and fought against Jonathan until he let the mule go free without a halter. When the mule tried to escape down the mountain, Jonathan raced after it on his horse. His lasso went flying in the air and landed with bull's-eye precision around the mule's neck. They both seemed to be having a good time, and the day passed quickly.

We arrived at Rancho San Jacinto as the sun was going down. The ranch belonged to Jonathan's father, who lived in Ensenada, and a young man, Rafael, cared for the ranch and farmed the crops. Rafael lived alone except when Jonathan's father visited. He worked six days a week and took Sunday off to go to an evangelical church in San Vicente. He had no television and preferred to spend his time reading the Bible.

As we sat around the kitchen table, I rejoiced at meeting Rafael. He was just a poor laborer, a modest man of God, yearning for a better life, but accepting of the life he had.

There are many Rafaels. My father was one. There are more of them on earth than any other kind of man. I feel blessed each time I meet one.

Jonathan and I left Rancho San Jacinto at dawn and headed north to Mission Santo Tomás.

We followed a deep canyon that meandered for miles, and we crossed through it half a dozen times.

I had to brace myself each time the mule slid down the steep slope of the canyon wall. At the bottom, the mule would leap forward the last step and, fueled with adrenaline, bolt straight up the other side. My jaw would freeze and my teeth clench as I gripped the pommel with both hands to hold on for dear life.

I had sprained my left wrist the night before leaving El Coyote. It was dark and there were no outside lights. I missed the second step on the porch and went flying off and landed on my left hand. It was swollen midway to the elbow.

My sprained wrist screamed in pain every time I gripped the pommel and every time I pulled back on the reins. The swelling increased with each canyon crossing until I could no longer hold the reins or the pommel even loosely with my left hand.

After four hours we finally escaped the canyon but found ourselves surrounded by fenced fields and no entry gates. Fences didn't bother Jonathan. Like all Sierra vaqueros who ride the open range, he was a virtuoso with barbed wire. At each fence he used pliers to disconnect the barbed wire and step the horses over. It required a lot of coaxing to get our horses to step over the barbed wire; it was near impossible to get our stubborn mule over it.

Toward the end of the day, our pack mule refused to step over one more barbed wire fence. The mule and Jonathan fought for ten minutes. "Get back!" he yelled, and both the mule and I knew he had reached the end of his patience. I moved far to the side.

Jonathan walked toward the recalcitrant mule and, in a flash, the mule bolted to where the barbed wire was more than five feet high, jumped straight up and over as gracefully as a deer. That mule, loaded with gear, landed so softly the cargo was undisturbed.

Jonathan and I looked at each other, astonished.

"I've never seen anything like that in my life." Jonathan smiled. I wished I'd had my video camera turned on.

Once the mule jumped over the fence, he kept going. Tracking down and roping the mule was almost as exciting as his leap over five feet of barbed wire.

After Jonathan got the mule back, we were both exhausted and stopped in a rocky arroyo for coffee. Jonathan made a quick campfire to boil water. When I grabbed my cup off the hot coals, it tipped and spilled boiling hot water on my right hand. My hand immediately began to blister. Now both hands hurt too much for gloves.

We rode the remainder of the afternoon through another cold north wind to Santo Tomás. We tethered the horses and pack mule across the street from Hotel Palomar, a Santo Tomás landmark since 1949. Jonathan carried my gear bag across the street, and I checked in to the hotel. I offered to rent a room for Jonathan, but he had to take the animals to a rancho for hay and water, and he was looking forward to spending time with his friend who lived there.

I went straight to the El Palomar restaurant before unpacking. I sat alone in the cavernous restaurant next to a wood fire and ate for two hours. It was cozy and the food was great, but what made it special was the music. An old-fashioned CD player played music from the '70s and '80s, and every song brought a flood of memories.

A song, "Dust in the Wind," played twice. I felt it was a special request from the spirits on the old mission trail: Don't hang on. Walk on. Move on.

There is a time to hold on and a time to move on. I prayed that God would always be my anchor and my compass.

The song played a second time, and as I listened I thought about the impermanence of life, and of Junípero Serra and what was here when he passed through two hundred years ago. Today, all that was left of Mission Santo Tomás were two stubby pieces of adobe and a few tumbleweeds. I wondered what would be here two hundred years from now.

The next morning Jonathan and I paused briefly in front of the mission ruins before heading north. The last remaining bit of adobe stubble was quickly disappearing and would soon be dust in the wind.

———

The route Junípero Serra took to San Diego followed close to the coast, and Jonathan and I passed endless miles of vineyards. Spirit may have fled the adobe ruins of Mission Santo Tomás, but it remained in the soil. The lasting legacies of the missionaries in Santo Tomás are the vineyards that today produce some of the best wine in Mexico.

Rootstock that produced Santo Tomás wines came from the original plantings of Juan Ugarte, the heroic Jesuit missionary who planted the first vineyards at Mission San Javier and Mission San Miguel Comondú three hundred years ago. Ugarte's wines were famous even then: "The excellent wine that was produced served for all the masses that were said in that peninsula, and what was left over was sent as a gift to the benefactors."[1]

After passing through wine country, Jonathan and I found ourselves hemmed between the beach to our left and mountains and canyons to our right. Highway 1, a two-lane death trap, was in the middle. There was no shoulder and no one obeyed the speed limit, if there was one.

I had no choice but to walk in the brush and bramble along Highway 1, while trying to avoid broken glass and potholes. It took all Jonathan's strength to pull on the reins and keep the frightened animals from bolting when a large truck or loud motorcycle roared by.

Whenever possible, Jonathan cut through canyons and got us off the highway. In the canyons, we entered a different world. Cliffs blocked out highway noise, and the trail wound through trees and meadows. We were in a silent wilderness with wildflowers and bees. It was an alternate reality, a serenely peaceful world unknown to those speeding by on the noisy highway.

Vaquera Perra kept cool by running ahead to where there was a tiny bit of shade, sometimes just a scraggly bush. She would lie down for a minute, catching her breath and cooling off, until we caught up to her. She got up, and her little legs ran as fast as they could to keep up with the horses.

Four miles from Maneadero, six men on horseback joined us. Jonathan was expecting them. The men were friends of Cenovio, *cabalgata* riders, who had ridden with him on weeklong trips into the sierras and between the missions on saint's days.

A man with gray hair and a regal bearing rode in front. He formally shook my hand and introduced the others: "We are here to ride with you to the rancho of your new vaquero, Alfonso María Dueñas Rojas of Maneadero."

I wanted to continue walking but was too exhausted. Cumulative hunger, dehydration, and extreme temperatures had taken their toll. The closer I got to San Diego, the weaker I became—it was as much mental as physical. The end was near. I could let go.

Eight of us—Jonathan, me, and the six men—rode together through the streets of Maneadero like a circus parade, with children laughing and running behind, people coming out of houses and waving, construction workers stopping work on top of buildings to see what was causing such a commotion, cars honking, dogs barking, and fenced horses going wild.

It was almost dark when we got to Alfonso Dueñas's rancho on the outskirts of town. It was a two-acre *ranchita*, really, with more animals than I'd seen on any rancho, and most were in cages: rabbits, geese, chickens, roosters, cows, mules, pigs, and dogs.

Families joined us, and we grilled carne asada, then ate it wrapped in tortillas with heaping spoonfuls of guacamole.

Afterward, Alfonso and I sat at the table and negotiated a price for his services. It wasn't really a negotiation. Alfonso told me the price and terms. There would be no pack mule. He and I would ride horses, or I would walk. His wife, Dora, would drive a truck. There would be no camping. We would stay in ranchos or hotels along the trail. It would take four or five days to get to the border.

"*Esta es mi tierra*," he said confidently. This is my land. He said he knew every road and trail to the border.

The men drank beer late into the night. Vaquera Perra stayed on the porch, watching Jonathan through the screen door. Her eyes were always on him. I could see why Jonathan adored her. She was attentive and well-behaved. I never once heard Jonathan tell her no. He whistled or called her name and she intuitively knew what he wanted, whether it was to herd the mule back in line, or follow closely beside his horse, or dart across a dangerous highway. She drank from his water canteen, ate from his burrito, and slept in his bed.

I was going to miss her. I was going to miss Jonathan too.

I was up before dawn, packed and ready to head out. I waited two hours for Jonathan to wake up, and four hours for Alfonso and Dora.

I fixed Jonathan several packets of my oatmeal. We had eaten it every day on the trail and he really liked it.

Jonathan left happy—in a truck with a friend, the two horses, mule, and Vaquera Perra. I was sad to say good-bye to them, even the ill-tempered mule.

The sun was hot by the time the horses were saddled, and Alfonso was ready to go.

My horse was old and looked close to death. I asked Alfonso if she had a name.

"*Sí, su nombre es Valla*," he replied.

I wasn't sure what *Valla* meant. A better name would have been Vieja, which means old. She looked like Jim the Cab-Horse, the emaciated horse from *The Wizard of Oz*.

Alfonso said his horse was named El Palomino. El Palomino had seen better days too.

Alfonso didn't look much healthier. It was a struggle stepping his legs through the heavy leather chaps and notching them at the waist. He labored to get on his horse. It took him three attempts to swing his right leg up and over, but once in the saddle, he rode straight and tall and was delightfully happy and full of energy.

I now had an aging vaquero, a vaquero's wife, two aging horses, and a truck.

Riding a horse and being a cowboy brings out the best in a man. In the saddle, Alfonso looked like a storybook vaquero, with polished spurs and boots, a new dark denim Levi's jacket, red western-style shirt, and white felt hat.

El Palomino must have felt Alfonso's excitement because he looked years younger, too, and held his head erect, and pranced regally on the hardpan road.

Seeing a man dressed head to toe as a vaquero, riding a beautiful spirited horse through the countryside and small villages, aroused curiosity and interest—and Alfonso loved the show. Men pulled over in trucks to talk, and merchants called to him from roadside stands.

We rode northeast, through the beautiful rolling hills of Maneadero. Alfonso stopped several times to visit family members. I got the impression we were as much on a ride to visit family as to follow El Camino Real to the border.

But at this point I was so close to the end I didn't care. I had surrendered to the journey. It wasn't what I had planned, but sometimes we have to let go and enjoy the surprises in life. Who knew what was in store? I could hold tightly to what I thought, or I could let go and enjoy this wild ride.

It was a delightful day until we got to Ensenada. Valla was nervous and skittish and turned in small circles as trucks and cars whizzed by, ambulances with sirens blared, and motorcycles roared past. It was impossible to control her. At intersections, cars were impatient to turn and brushed against Valla. One angry driver used his front bumper to push us out of his way.

We slowly made our way to the beach. Alfonso pranced with El Palomino in and out of the surf, entertaining beach bathers. My old mare had a difficult time in the ankle-deep sand, and the waves scared her. It was not pleasant, but it was better than the boulevard.

After a half-hour ride north up the beach, for some reason Alfonso rode east once again toward Ensenada and back to chaotic traffic.

I became nervous in the heavy traffic, got off Valla, handed the reins to Alfonso, and walked two hours to the edge of town.

I soon learned why Alfonso turned away from the beach and back into town—he needed help. He stopped at a small bungalow, the home of a vaquero who knew the mission trail to El Descanso and to the border. Unfortunately, the vaquero wasn't home.

It was my first inkling that Alfonso might not know the trail.

Alfonso took us northeast out of the foothills. We came to fences and had to turn around. People gave us wrong directions. By the time we were out of Ensenada, it was almost dark.

The sun had completely set when we arrived at Rancho Cuatro Milpas in El Sauzal. Alfonso's wife, Dora, was in the truck waiting for us. We drove ten miles to an overpriced motel on the coast, and I paid for two rooms. The room had no heat, but it did have hot water. I shut the shower door, turned on the hot water, and warmed the room with hot steam.

Dale called. It was amazing to have cellular connections after two months of having none. But he was concerned about my progress. "You only rode fifteen miles today. At that speed you won't be in San Diego before Christmas." He had invited family and friends for Christmas and was worried I wouldn't be home.

He didn't understand the challenges, and I tried to explain. "We rode more than fifteen miles. You can't calculate distance as a straight line between GPS pings. We zigzag up and down mountains and hills, and today we rode along the beach and through Ensenada. We probably rode twenty miles or more."

But Dale was anxious for me to get home. "Well, why can't you tell Alfonso to get to the border as quickly and in as straight a line as possible?"

"I can't tell Alfonso where to go when I don't know where I'm going." I laughed.

I thought about the many times in life we give advice when we shouldn't. *Don't tell someone where to go when you don't know where you're going.*

I would try to remember that.

34

We left Rancho Cuatro Milpas at sunrise the next morning and headed northeast to the mountains.

Alfonso was a *cabalgata* rider and not a Sierra vaquero, and El Palomino was not a Sierra horse. By the end of the day, Alfonso and El Palomino were both struggling for breath.

And Valla? I could hardly get her to move. I worried she might die beneath me at any moment.

There were a few trails on the side of the highway, but often not. Alfonso didn't seem to mind. He rode El Palomino onto the highway, expecting traffic to slow or stop for us.

But Valla was unstable on her feet, and I feared she might slip and fall, or throw me off. I begged Alfonso, "Please, let's not ride on the highway!"

I had fought too hard for life to end up as roadkill.

We had been on horses six hours with hardly a break. The wind was cold, and the sky looked like rain. It was time to find a place to camp or spend the night. We rode across a pasture toward Rancho Santa Rosa. Alfonso knocked on the door of the old vaquero shack. No one answered.

"*No problema*," Alfonso said. "*Los caballos aquí.*" We will leave the horses here.

The rancho was rundown with only a small manure-covered cattle lot, an empty water trough, and a small haystack. I waited on the porch while Alfonso found water for the animals and tethered El Palomino and Valla on a long rope in the dirt yard with a bale of hay. Dora picked us up in the truck, and we spent the night at a small *ranchita* by the highway.

When we arrived the next morning, a vaquero from a rancho across the road came over. He had seen old and tired Valla standing in the front yard. He had horses and mules to rent. Would I like him to saddle one for me? Did I need another vaquero?

"*¡Esta es mi tierra!*" This is my land! Alfonso proclaimed proudly, shaking his head and looking offended. He knew the trails. We did not need another vaquero.

By the end of the day, I regretted not hiring the vaquero.

Alfonso said it would be two hours from Rancho Santa Rosa to Mission San Miguel. We encountered many fences, and Alfonso was not prepared for fences. He did not carry pliers, a knife, or a machete. His hands were no longer as tough as the side of a mule. They bled as he pried open barbed wire gates with his bare hands.

After riding four hours, we appeared to be in the middle of nowhere, but Alfonso was confident. "The missionaries built a road from San Vicente to San Miguel. This is the old road," he reassured me. "*Este es El Camino Real.*"

When we came to an old deserted rancho, he announced proudly, "*Este es Rancho La Misión.*" The ancient rancho of the mission extended for miles. "*Esta es la ruta.*" This is the route.

El Palomino and Valla were exhausted. El Palomino was a younger horse and would recover. Valla was old and did not need this journey over steep rocky mountains and through thickets of thorns.

Alfonso made a small whip for me out of a tree limb, and I reluctantly whipped the dear horse, but she would not go. I tried talking sweetly in a cajoling voice, but she would not go. I pleaded with her, but she would not go.

Out of frustration, Alfonso took a lariat and tied Valla to El Palomino. The younger horse, like a tow truck, pulled Valla every step.

I was reminded that sometimes God doesn't carry us; sometimes he pushes us, and other times he pulls us.

I felt Valla's chest heaving beneath me. She did not want to go up a mountain or through canyons or even a flat road. She wanted to stop. She desired eternal rest.

I was beginning to feel like my old horse.

Instead of two hours, it took six hours of hard riding to get to San Miguel. In San Miguel, no one knew where the old mission was. Alfonso stopped people to ask for directions. They led us astray. A man in a truck told us the old mission was east in the hills, and we rode an hour up a mountain until the road ended. An elderly woman walking on the road gave us directions to a church. We rode another hour. It was an old church but not Mission San Miguel.

We finally found the mission ruins a block off the highway we followed into town. We had wasted two hours riding in circles.

Mission San Miguel was another formless slab of adobe. It was enclosed behind a wire fence and we stood outside looking in. The mission had struggled for survival and moved three times in twenty years. Lost mission records and untold personal stories, like the ever-eroding adobe walls, are dust in the wind.

Alfonso took El Palomino and Valla to a local rancho, and Dora took me to Hotel La Fonda. The hotel had been in San Miguel for over half a century, built by a Jewish couple. Dmitri, from Ukraine, and his wife, Sara, born in Siberia, had both lost family in the Holocaust and eventually emigrated—first to Los Angeles and later to San Miguel, Mexico, where they built a beautiful hotel. The hotel was aging gracefully but it, too, looked tired.

Many older hotels in northern Baja have been converted to cancer clinics, appealing to the dying and desperate. Less than a mile from Hotel La Fonda is where Steve McQueen received apricot pits, better known as laetrile, to cure his lung cancer, a virulent strain of cancer called mesothelioma. Cancer kills even cool guys.

Steve McQueen fought a good fight. He tried chemotherapy, surgery, and apricot pits. We all have our Plan D; *D* is for desperate. I have been there. I know how he felt, and why he was willing to try something as crazy as apricot pits to stay alive.

I knew the next day would potentially be my last day on the mission trail. It was three days before Christmas. It was time to go home. It was time to rest. It was also time to celebrate. Dale had put up the Christmas tree, and Whitney and Stefanie were waiting for me to come home to hang the ornaments.

The decorations held precious memories. There were handmade paper ornaments from elementary school, hand-painted plaster ornaments from summer Bible school, and souvenir ornaments collected during family vacations. And Dale's dad, Palmer, had given us an ornament every year for Christmas until he passed away. The last thing we put on the tree was the silver star tree topper Dale had made from cardboard and aluminum foil the first year we were married.

At night, just the simple act of lighting the tree in the evening helped us capture and hold on to the feeling of the Charles Dickens character that promised, "I will honor Christmas in my heart, and try to keep it all the year."[1]

I shook myself out of pleasant memories and into the present, walked over to the window in my hotel room, and stared up at the moon, hanging like an ornament in the night sky. I was grateful not to be in my tent, freezing along El Camino Real. Here I had a soft bed to rest my tired bones.

Before drifting into sleep I prayed, "Dear heavenly Father, thank you for teaching me about life and suffering, and letting me be with these dear people and know them, for letting me feel cold and hungry, for letting me feel afraid, for letting me feel alone—knowing all is well, for you are with me. Thank you for all the lessons you have taught me on old El Camino Real. I am a better person for it. *Muchas, muchas gracias*. Amen."

I was thirty-eight miles from the California border.

There was no easy way to get there. None of the trails to the border followed Junípero Serra's journey. In 1769, Father Serra walked up the beach to San Diego. Today, an eighteen-foot high, three-hundred-foot-long fence extending into the ocean blocks the trail.

I was up before sunrise, anxious to check out the beach. I was hoping we could continue north, following the beach, as Junípero Serra had done, until we reached the border fence.

Hotel La Fonda was on a rocky bluff high above the beach, with no easy access. The wind was howling, and the tide was crushing against the base of the cliff. Even from a distance, my face glistened from wet ocean spray. Father Serra walked the beach to San Diego in late spring, when tides were lower and surges more predictable. I knew it would be foolhardy to take horses on the beach in swelling winter tides—or attempt to walk the beach to the border.

I had one more mission stop in El Descanso, and Alfonso and I continued north as best we could on side streets and through private property. When a massive flood destroyed Mission San Miguel, it was moved eight miles north to El Descanso, and renamed Mission San Miguel la Nueva. Only a few adobe rocks remained. Alfonso and I walked quietly and solemnly through the sad rubble.

As we prepared to leave the old mission ruins, Alfonso could no longer lift himself into the saddle. He stood on a large boulder in front of the mission to hoist himself atop El Palomino, and struggled even then.

After a few minutes of riding alongside the rocky beach road, Alfonso stopped to rest in the saddle. His chest heaved with each slow breath, much like Valla's. I wasn't sure which one would fall over first.

Alfonso no longer rode tall and straight in the saddle; neither did I, and walking was a struggle.

Alfonso was nervous. "If you want to ride a horse to the border, we should ride to Tecate. The border at Tijuana is no good. There is too much traffic. It is Christmas. There will be thousands of cars lined up at the border," he said slowly and painfully. "Tecate may not be any better."

He paused and lowered his head. With labored breath he whispered, "*No es bueno. Nada.*"

I knew Alfonso was finished riding. I had learned it was useless to argue with a vaquero once his mind is made up. Alfonso was ready to load his horses in the truck and drive to the border. As if on cue, Dora pulled up behind us in the truck.

I considered my options. I could get in the truck and drive to the border or double down and press Alfonso to keep going—although I was reluctant to do so because he didn't look well and he sounded worse.

Or . . . I could walk the thirty-eight miles alone to the border. I was too exhausted to walk much more than thirteen miles a day, so it would take three days. That meant I would get to the border on Christmas Day. All I needed for a three-day walk was in my twenty-two-pocket fishing vest in my gear bag. Alfonso and Dora could meet Dale at the border and give him the rest of my gear.

I could do it!

And then I stopped my wild scramble thoughts.

Some people say that a feeling of completeness is good. But I say a feeling of incompleteness is better. It means there's still something left to do. For if we have done all we dreamed to do already, doesn't that mean we are ready to die?

Did I *really* want my mission walk to be over?

I never did like endings. That's why I fought so hard to live.

I started to smile, and then to laugh. I tingled with anticipation of another adventure.

Alfonso already had the horses loaded. He and Dora were ready to go, with or without me.

I climbed merrily into the truck.

I would save one last walk on El Camino Real mission trail. Save it, and savor it.

When I needed an infusion of grace I would put on my hiking boots and start walking along the beach exactly as St. Junípero Serra did, and I would find my way through the California border to Mission San Diego, where it all started. As I looked out the dust-pocked window, watching the beautiful, harsh, brutal desert whish by, I thought, with a smile, *When I come back, it's going to be the most beautiful walk of my life.*

And that was that. I was ready to go home. I was ready to see my family, and tell them the ridiculous stories of the cactus wounds, the crazy mules (and vaqueros), the *narcos*, the hardworking and loving people, the missions. All of it. I had so much to tell.

I still didn't know how much time I had left. I knew there was another PET scan right around the corner, in ten days. There always was.

And with each scan, I would pray to God to give me strength to face the news with grace and peace. I was no longer terrorized by the thought of cancer coming back.

The mission walk was my transition point, where I moved beyond disease, where I found stillness of mind, where I surrendered to grace, and where, through grace, the fear of death was slowly replaced with peace.

The long walk had taught me that it was within my power to get rid of fear. And now I knew, without a doubt, that when my time came, I would be ready.

But *not yet*.

My mission walk wasn't over. *Not yet!*

I closed my eyes and whispered a prayer that God would allow me to keep on walking, and that he would grant me . . .

A warm bed to rest upon, I care not where.

Food to nourish and replenish, I care not what.

Sun through a window, I care not the dwelling.

Kindness and affection, I care not from whom.

A daily place of worship, I care not if inside or out.

Silence and grace . . . For I care only to know Thee. Amen.

I opened my eyes and smiled, the murmurings of Dora and Alfonso talking excitedly about Christmas with their grandchild a soothing soundtrack to my thoughts. I knew that Dale would be waiting anxiously for the call I would make as we neared the border. That he would meet me there, eagerly embrace my bony frame, and take me home to warmth, comfort, family, and food.

This Mexican trek had been my journey alone, just as my journey in death will be solitary. As in life, I knew Dale would want to finish with me. We would walk the last walk alone, together. I was so thankful that for as long as I had breath in my body, I had that man by my side.

But I knew now, as never before, just how much strength I had on my own.

There were more battles ahead. I knew there would be hardship and suffering. But God would be there to guide us through it.

All is well.

ACKNOWLEDGMENTS

In gratitude and thanksgiving:

THE BOOK. Thank you to my cousin, David Hearne, for countless hours helping with photographs; to Jay Kramer, my friend and manager, for your constant, unwavering encouragement; to Paul de Souza, my agent, whose belief in my story turned this into a book; and especially to Cindy DiTiburio, my developmental editor, who worked with me in the trenches, from writing the book proposal to finished manuscript, and gave me confidence I could actually write a book. Whenever I got stuck, Cindy was always there to get me back on track, with an amazing ability to suggest changes that made a huge difference. I couldn't have written this book without you.

LIFE. For those who walk with me through time immemorial, in sickness and in health, sometimes alone, but always together:

My cherished family: Dale Herman Sundby; our children—Whitney and Stefanie Sundby, and Sarah and Rebekah Littlefield, my brother Edmond's children, graciously loaned when he passed from this earth; sister-in-law, Mary Dorene Sundby Kamerzell; and lifelong friends Janet Gail Boelen Sinn, Mindy Harris Wilner, Jeanie Carlstead, Diana Holm, Linda Browning Bruckner,

Eileen Guttmann, Ron and Fan Graham, Arch and Jeanie McGill, John Pina, and Gini Staude Tidy. What you have given, and what you have done, is beyond love.

———

THE ABYSS. For those who lifted, and keep lifting, me out of *The Abyss*.

The medical team that saved my life: Stanford—Dr. George Albert Fisher, Annie Johnson (physician assistant), Margaretha Fledderus (NP); Dr. Jeffrey Norton, Dr. Joseph Shrager, Dr. Albert Koong, Dr. Billy Lee, Dr. Maximillian Diehn and Gillian McFarlane (NP); Dr. Steven Curley (Houston, MD Anderson Cancer Center); San Diego—Dr. Greg Heestand, Dr. Paul Goldfarb, Dr. Robert Murad, Jane Davidson (physician assistant).

Sisters, family, and friends who are always there with encouragement after every setback, ready to celebrate even the tiniest victories: Leann Littlefield Gunderson, Brian, Gregg, Velvet Sunderland, and Kimberly Faul; Liz Littlefield O'Shaughnessy; Jeanna Littlefield Regier and Donna Tedeton; Linda Littlefield Rondinella, Adrianna Bailey, and Chad; Edmond Littlefield (deceased), Lydia and Samuel Littlefield; Ollie Juanita Littlefield Dickey and Christina Claypool; Dawn Smith Koenning; Ann Littlefield Coleman, Randy Powell, and Mary Jensen.

Bosom buddies, always ready to walk, talk, hang out: Catherine Woods Lazarides, Pat Erzinger, Robyn Delgado, Cheryl Albuquerque, Michele Caudron, Stella Ezeji-Okoye Dyer, Carmel Gouveia, Renate Hecht, Susan Iafe, Jeanne Larson, Virginia Iqbal, Joy Penner, Bonnie Nickel, Carol Broad, Lea Brekke, Liane Kornbluth, and Laura Kramer.

Cancer friends whose strength and courage inspired and empowered: Mary Lourd Smith, Sally Canfield Coupe, Margie Simineo, Marko Glogovac, Barbara Isgur, Joan Johnston, Steven Wang, Beverly Wheat, Paul Baker, Debbie Capati, Julie Breakstone, Kay Richardson, Ryan Hidinger, Hazbi Tierney, Judy Hegarty, Maire Scharpegge, Martha McArtor, Jacques Hautelet, Lenore Levine, Gerald Murphy, Lorna Ritter, Mary Holz, Elizabeth Sozanski, Larry Bock, and Charles Avvampato.

Prayer warrior classmates from Cyril, Oklahoma: Deloris Castillo Henley, Janet Boelen, Latrell Gibson Ramos, Mike and Brenda Short, Diane Cribbs Snider, Ron and Janet Janousek, Len Janousek, Raynelle Teeter, Bobby Rose, Gary Burd, Karla Burd Schumann, Debbie Swagerty Greiner, Becky Ackley Thompson, Dennis Bates, Don Davis, Duffy Cribbs, Janice Cowan Esmon, Jayne Yeager Ivy, Liz Short Monroe, Walter Robertson, Terry Ellis, Ruby Barr Simmons, Donna Spencer Self, Delma Kay Bilyeu Leonhart, and Denise Gilmore.

Pastors and lay ministers: Lawrence Waddy, Randal Gardner, Bob Orphey, and Mark and Laura Hargreaves.

Yoga friends who prepared food when I was sick: Carmel Gouveia, Jeanie Carlstead, Jane Elizabeth McCormick, Vicky Hellman, Danna Cottman and Joe Mayo, and Gerhard and Alex Gessner.

FOLLOW THE BELLS. For those who walked with me along El Camino Real, and love those bells as much as I do: Joyce Blue Summers, Deb Dawley, Ron and Sandy Briery, Ron Graham, Steven Woody, Meg Grant, JoBeth McDaniel, Joy Penner, Cori and Tom Grunow, Ruth West, Marucia Britto, Lin Galea, and Kurt Buckley.

HOLY GROUND. For making my crazy dream of walking El Camino Real from Loreto to San Diego come true: Harry Crosby and his maps; Trudi Angell and her mules; Cenovio Gamboa Lazcano; Nacho Chiapa; and my twenty vaqueros: José "Chema" María Arce Arce of Rancho San Esteban; José "Che" Martinez Castro of Rancho El Pasito; Raymundo Vargas Mayoral of Rancho Paso Hondo; Cesar Villavicencio Aguilar of Rancho San Martin; Carlos Antonio Villavicencio Lopez of Rancho La Presa; Abraham Villavicencio Villavicencio and his son Adrian of Rancho San Sebastian; Agustín Villa Romero of Rancho Santa Cruz; Gertrudis "Chico" Arce Arce of Rancho San

Luis; Patricio A. Ojeda of Santa Marta, INAH; Carlos Aaron Villavicencio of Rancho Santa Cruz; Tomás Murillo of Guerrero Negro; Francisco "Pancho" Murillo Flores; Marcos "Chikis" Medina Arce; Porfirio "Guile" Aviler Aquilar; Arnulfo Murillo Grosso of Rancho Cerro Prieto; Joaquin "Lira" Martorell and his son Juan; Jonathan Presiche Meling of Rancho El Coyote Meling; Alfonso "Pancho" María Dueñas Rojas of Maneadero.

NOTES

CHAPTER 2

1. L. A. G. Ries, et al., eds., "SEER Survival Monograph: Cancer Survival Among Adults: U.S. SEER Program, 1988–2001, Patient and Tumor Characteristics," National Cancer Institute, SEER Program, NIH Pub. No. 07–6215 (2007).

CHAPTER 8

1. Deuteronomy 20:3–4 NIV.
2. Meg Grant, "Against All Odds," *AARP Magazine*, December 2012/January 2013, 68.

CHAPTER 9

1. George Wharton James, *In and Out of the Old Missions of California* (Boston: Little, Brown, 1905).
2. Mrs. A. S. C. Forbes, *California: Missions and Landmarks: El Camino Real*, 3rd ed. (Los Angeles: Official Guide, 1915).

CHAPTER 10

1. Ron Briery, *California Mission Walk: A Hiker's Guide to California's 21 Spanish Missions Along El Camino Real* (Eagle Point, OR: Peregrino Publishing, 2012).
2. Forbes, *California Missions*, 45–47.

3. James, *In and Out of the Old Missions*, 379.

CHAPTER 11

1. Francisco Palóu, *The Expedition into California of the Venerable Padre Fray Junipero Serra in the Year 1769, as Told by Fray Francisco Palou (1787)*, trans. Douglas Watson (San Francisco: Nueva California Press, 1934), 56.
2. Juan Crespí, *A Description of Distant Roads: Original Journals of the First Expedition into California 1769–1770*, trans. and ed. Alan K. Brown (San Diego: San Diego State University Press, 2001), 339.
3. St. Francis de Sales, *Introduction to the Devout Life*, ed. John K. Ryan (1609; repr., New York: Doubleday/Image Books, 1972).

CHAPTER 12

1. "I Need Thee Every Hour," lyrics by Annie S. Hawks and Robert Lowry (1872).

CHAPTER 13

1. James, *In and Out of the Old Missions*, 133.
2. Although these words are often called "The Prayer of Saint Francis," they first appeared in 1912 Paris, in a Catholic magazine called *La Clochette* (The Little Bell). The identity of the author is unknown. See Christian Renoux, "The Origin of the Peace Prayer of St. Francis," The Franciscan Archive, http://www .franciscan-archive.org/franciscana/peace.html.

CHAPTER 14

1. Frances Rand Smith, Mollie Merrick, and F. R. S., "The Burial Place of Father Junípero Serra," *Hispania* 7, no. 5 (November 1924): 285–98.
2. Psalm 46:10 NIV.
3. A paraphrase of Ecclesiastes 11:5.
4. James, *In and Out of the Old Missions*, 381.
5. G. Pascal Zachary and Ken Yamada, "What's Next? Steve Jobs's Vision, So on Target at Apple, Now Is Falling Short," *Wall Street Journal*, May 25, 1993 (republished October 6, 2011).
6. Mona Simpson, "A Sister's Eulogy for Steve Jobs," *New York Times*, October 30, 2011, http://www.nytimes.com/2011/10/30/opinion/mona-simpsons-eulogy-for -steve-jobs.html.

CHAPTER 16

1. Johann Jakob Baegert, *Observations in Lower California*, trans. M. M. Brandenburg and Carl L. Baumann (1771; repr., Berkeley: University of California Press, 1952).

CHAPTER 17

1. Baegert, *Observations in Lower California*, 117.
2. Peter Masten Dunne, *Black Robes in Lower California* (Berkeley: University of California Press, 1968), 62.
3. Garci Rodríguez de Montalvo, *The Labors of the Very Brave Knight Esplandián (Sergas de Esplandián)*, trans. William Thomas Little (1510; repr., Binghamton, New York: State University of New York, 1992), 508–9.

CHAPTER 18

1. Francisco Javier Clavigero, *The History of (Lower) California*, trans. Sara E. Lake and A. A. Gray (1786; repr., Redwood City, CA: Stanford University Press, 1937), 147.

CHAPTER 19

1. Dunne, *Black Robes*, 153.
2. Arthur Walbridge North, *Camp and Camino in Lower California* (New York: Baker & Taylor, 1910), 43.

CHAPTER 20

1. Baegert, *Observations in Lower California*, 41.
2. Ibid.

CHAPTER 21

1. Isaiah 7:24 ESV.
2. Baegert, *Observations in Lower California*, 33.

CHAPTER 22

1. William C. S. Smith, *A Journey to California in 1849* (Fairfield, WA: Ye Galleon Press, 1984), 10.

CHAPTER 23

1. Baegert, *Observations in Lower California*, 125.

2. Dunne, *Black Robes*, 419.

CHAPTER 24
1. Clavigero, *History of (Lower) California*, 30.

CHAPTER 25
1. Smith, *Journey to California*, 8.
2. North, *Camp and Camino*, 138–39.
3. Vladimir Nabokov, *Speak, Memory: A Memoir* (New York: Vintage Books, 1989), 19.

CHAPTER 26
1. North, *Camp and Camino*, 85.
2. Smith, *Journey to California*, 44.
3. Arthur Walbridge North, *The Mother of California* (San Francisco: Paul Elder, 1908), 97.
4. James H. Bull, *Journey of James H. Bull, Baja California 1843*, ed. Doyce E. Nunis Jr. (Los Angeles: Dawson's Book Shop, 1965), 43.

CHAPTER 27
1. Smith, *Journey to California*, 43.
2. Wenceslaus Linck, *Reports and Letters: Report of 1765*, trans. Ernest J. Burrus (Los Angeles: Dawson's Book Shop, 1967), 35.

CHAPTER 28
1. Junípero Serra, *Diary of Fra. Junípero Serra, OFM: Being an Account of His Journey from Loreto to San Diego March 28 to June 30, 1769* (North Providence, RI: The Franciscan Missionaries of Mary, 1936), 19.
2. Smith, *Journey to California*, 46.
3. Matthew 10:28 ESV.
4. Dunne, *Black Robes in Lower California*, 351.
5. Isaiah 35:7 NIV.

CHAPTER 29
1. Erle Stanley Gardner, *The Hidden Heart of Baja* (New York: William Morrow, 1962), 129–40.

2. See Matthew 6:19–20.

3. Smith, *Journey to California*, 46–47.

CHAPTER 30

1. Palóu, *Expedition Into California*, 62.

CHAPTER 31

1. *Diary of Fra. Junípero Serra*, 30

2. Ibid., 32.

CHAPTER 32

1. Junípero Serra, *Writings of Junípero Serra, Vol. I*, trans. Antonine Tibesar (Washington, DC: The American Academy of Franciscan History, 1955), 81.

2. Crespí, *Distant Roads*, 203.

3. Tibesar, *Writings of Junípero Serra*, 85.

4. Romans 5:3–5 NRSV.

CHAPTER 33

1. Clavigero, *History of (Lower) California*, 187.

CHAPTER 34

1. This quote is not from Dickens's *A Christmas Carol* but rather from an adaptation of his work into a play: George M. Baker, "*A Christmas Carol*, Arranged as an Entertainment, from Dickens's Christmas Story," *Our Boys and Girls 1871*, ed. Oliver Optic (Boston: Lee and Shepherd, 1871), 53.

BIBLIOGRAPHY OF
HISTORICAL SOURCES

Homer Aschmann, *The Central Desert of Baja California: Demography and Ecology* (Riverside: Manessier, 1967). Originally published by University of California Press in 1959.

Johann Jakob Baegert, SJ (M. M. Brandenburg and Carl L. Baumann, translators), *Observations in Lower California*, 1771 (Berkeley: University of California Press, 1952).

Herbert Eugene Bolton, *Rim of Christendom* (New York: MacMillan, 1936).

James Hunter Bull, "A Journey Through Lower California 1844," Doyce E. Nunis Jr., ed. (Los Angeles: Dawson's Book Shop, 1965).

Ernest Burrus, SJ, *Jesuit Relations—Baja California* (Los Angeles: Dawson's Book Shop, 1984).

Juan Cavallero Carranco, SJ (W. Michael Mathes, translator), *The Pearl Hunters in the Gulf of California 1668: Summary Report of the Voyage made to California by Captain Francisco de Lucenilla* (Los Angeles: Dawson's Book Shop, 1966).

Francisco Javier Clavigero, SJ (Sara E. Lake and A. A. Gray, translators and editors), *The History of Lower California* (1789; repr., Stanford University Press, 1937).

Juan Crespí (Alan K. Brown, translator), *A Description of Distant Roads: Original Journals of the First Expedition into California, 1769–1770* (San Diego: San Diego State University Press, 2001).

Harry W. Crosby, *The King's Highway in Baja California: An Adventure into the History and Lore of a Forgotten Region* (Salt Lake City: Publishers Press, Copley Books, 1974).

————, *Antigua California: Mission and Colony on the Peninsular Frontier, 1697– 1768* (Albuquerque: University of New Mexico Press, 1994).

————, *Gateway to Alta California: The Expedition to San Diego, 1769* (San Diego: Sunbelt Publications, 2003).

Bernal Diaz (J. M. Cohen, translator), *The Conquest of New Spain (Mexico)*, (London: Clays, 1963). Written in 1581.

Benno Ducrue, SJ (Ernest J. Burrus, SJ, translator), *Expulsion of the Jesuits from Lower California (1767–1769)* (1784; repr., St. Louis: Jesuit Historical Institute, 1967).

Peter Masten Dunne, SJ, *Black Robes in Lower California.* (Berkeley: University of California Press, 1968).

Helen DuShane, *The Baja California Travels of Charles Russell Orcutt from 1882 to 1919* (Los Angeles: Dawson's Book Shop, 1971).

Fr. Zephyrin Engelhardt, OFM, *Missions and Missionaries of California*, vols. 1 and 2, 2nd ed. (San Francisco: James H. Barry, 1913–1914).

Mrs. A .S. C. Forbes, *California Missions and Landmarks: El Camino Real* (Los Angeles: Official Guide, 1915).

Maynard J. Geiger, OFM, *The Life and Times of Fray Juniper Serra, O.F.M.* Two volumes. (Richmond, VA: The William Byrd Press, 1959).

———— *The Serra Trail in Picture and Story* (San Francisco: James H. Barry, 1960).

Peter Gerhard and Howard Bulick, *Lower California Guidebook* (Glendale, CA: Arthur Clark, 1958).

William T. Hornaday, *Camp-Fires on Desert and Lava* (New York: Scribner, 1908).

George Wharton James, *In and Out of the Old Missions of California* (Boston: Little, Brown, 1905).

Fr. Eusebio Francisco Kino, SJ (Ernest J. Burrus, SJ, translator), *Kino's Plan for the Development of Pimeria Alta, Arizona and Upper California: A Report to the Mexican Viceroy in 1703* (Tucson: Arizona Pioneers Historical Society, 1961).

———— (W. Michael Mathes, translator), *First from the Gulf to the Pacific: The Diary of the Kino-Atondo Peninsular Expedition (1684–1685)* (Los Angeles: Dawson's Book Shop, 1969).

Max Kurillo and Erline Tuttle, *California's El Camino Real and Its Historic Bells* (San Diego: Sunbelt Publications, 2000).

Max Kurillo, Erline Tuttle, and David Kier, *The Old Missions of Baja & Alta California 1697–1934* (El Cajon: M&E Books, 2012).

Miguel Leon-Portilla, *El Camino Real y las Misiones de la Peninsula de Baja California* [*The Camino Real and the Missions of the Baja California Peninsula*]

(Mexico City: Fundación Manuel Arango, Instituto Nacional de Anthropologia e Historia, 2008).

Wenceslaus Linck, SJ (Ernest J. Burrus, SJ, translator), *Diary of 1766 Expedition to Northern Baja California* (Los Angeles: Dawson's Book Shop, 1966).

————, *Reports and Letters 1762—1778* (Los Angeles: Dawson's Book Shop, 1967).

José Longinos Martinez (Lesley Byrd Simpson, translator), *California in 1792: The Expedition of José Longinos Martinez* (San Marino: Henry E. Huntington Library, 1938).

W. Michael Mathes, *The Land of Calafia: A Brief History of Peninsular California (1533–1848)* (Tecate, CA: Corredor Historico CAREM, 2009).

Richard A. Minnich and Ernesto Vizcaino, *Land of Chamise and Pines: Historical Accounts and Current Status of Northern Baja California's Vegetation, University of California Publications in Biology*, vol. 80 (Berkeley: University of California Press, 1998).

Garci Rodríguez de Montalvo (William Thomas Little, translator), *The Labors of the Very Brave Knight Esplandián (Sergas de Esplandián)* (1510; repr., State University of New York–Binghamton, NY, 1992).

Vladimir Nabokov, *Speak, Memory: An Autobiography* (New York: Vintage Books, 1989).

Edward W. Nelson, *Lower California and its Natural Resources (Memoirs of the National Academy of Sciences, vol. 16, 1st memoir)* (1922) (Riverside: Manessier Publishing Company, 1966).

Arthur Walbridge North, *Camp and Camino in Lower California* (New York: Baker & Taylor, 1910).

————, *The Mother of California* (San Francisco: Paul Elder, 1908).

Fray Francisco Palóu, OFM, *The Expedition into California of the Venerable Padre Fray Junipero Serra and His Companions in the Year 1769* (San Francisco: Nueva California Press, 1934).

———— (Herbert Eugene Bolton, editor), *Historical Memoirs of New California*, 4 vols. (New York: Russell & Russell, 1966). Originally published in 1926.

Francisco María Piccolo, SJ (George P. Hammond, translator), *Informe on the New Province of California 1702* (Los Angeles: Dawson's Book Shop, 1967).

Sergio Morales Polo, *The Mission of San Javier*, This Is Loreto Collection, vol. 3, *The Mission of San Javier* (Loreto, BCS: Editorial Londo, 1999).

Gaspar de Portolá (Donald Eugene Smith and Frederick J. Taggart, editors), "Diary of Gaspar de Portolá During the California Expedition of 1769–1770," *Publications of the Academy of Pacific Coast History* 1, no. 3 (1909).

Richard F. Pourade, *The Call to California: The Epic Journey of the Portolá-Serra Expedition in 1769* (San Diego: Union-Tribune, 1968).

————, *Time of the Bells* (San Diego: Union-Tribune, 1961).

Felix Riesenberg Jr, *The Golden Road, The Story of California's Spanish Mission Trail* (New York: McGraw Hill, 1962).

Captain Woodes Rogers, *A Cruising Voyage Around the World* (1712; repr., London: Cassell, 1928).

Paul Sanford, *Where The Old West Never Died* (San Antonio: Naylor, 1968).

Junípero Serra, OFM, *Diary of Fray Junípero Serra, O.F.M.: Being an Account of the Journey from Loreto to San Diego March 28 to June 30, 1769: The Documentary Preface to the History of the Missions of California* (North Providence, RI: The Franciscan Missionaries of Mary, 1902).

———— (Antonine Tibesar, translator), *Writings of Junípero Serra*, vol. 1. (Washington, DC: American Academy of Franciscan History, 1955).

William C. S. Smith, *A Journey to California in 1849* (Fairfield: Ye Galleon Press, 1984).

Frances Rand Smith and Mollie Merrick, "The Burial Place of Father Junípero Serra," *Hispania* 7, no. 5 (November 1924).

Miguel Venegas (anonymous translation, 1759), *Great Americana: A Natural and Civil History of California* (Worcester, MA: Readex Microprint Corporation, 1965).

Edward W. Vernon, *The Spanish Missions of Baja California* (Santa Barbara: Viejo Press, 2002).

Vincente Vila (Robert Selden Rose, editor), "Diary of Vincente Villa: The Portolá Expedition of 1769–1770," *Publication of the Academy of Pacific Coast History* 2, no. 1 (1911).

Marie T. Walsh, *The Mission Bells of California* (San Francisco: Harr Wagner, 1934).

Walt Wheelock, *Byroads of Baja* (Glendale: La Siesta Press, 1971).

Francisco Zevallos (Manuel Servin, translator), *The Apostolic Life of Fernando Consag Explorer of Lower California* (Los Angeles: Dawson's Book Shop, 1968).

ABOUT THE AUTHOR

EDIE LITTLEFIELD SUNDBY was born the second youngest of twelve children on an Oklahoma cotton farm without electricity and running water. She went on to graduate from the University of Oklahoma and became one of the first female sales executives at IBM and later a VP for Pacific Telesis. She was diagnosed with stage 4 gallbladder cancer and was given less than three months to live. Despite 0.9 percent odds of survival, one million milligrams of chemo, and four major surgeries, she is the only person to have walked the 1,600-mile California Mission Trail from Loreto, Mexico, to Sonoma, California. Her essays have appeared in the *Wall Street Journal* and the *New York Times*.

FOR MORE ABOUT
EDIE'S JOURNEY,
INCLUDING
COLOR PHOTOGRAPHS
AND
AN INTERACTIVE MAP,

VISIT
WWW.THEMISSIONWALKER.COM